344.73   Torrans, Lee Ann,
Torrans   1952-

          Law and libraries.

LAW AND LIBRARIES

LAW AND LIBRARIES

The Public Library

LEE ANN TORRANS

LIBRARIES
UNLIMITED

A Member of the Greenwood Publishing Group

Westport, Connecticut • London

Library of Congress Cataloging-in-Publication Data

Torrans, Lee Ann, 1952–
   Law and libraries : the public library / Lee Ann Torrans.
     p. cm.
   Includes index.
   ISBN 1–59158–035–8 (alk. paper)
    1. Public libraries—Law and legislation—United States. I. Title.
KF4315.T67   2004
344.73'092—dc22   2003065944

British Library Cataloguing in Publication Data is available.

Library of Congress Catalog Card Number: 2003065944
ISBN: 1–59158–035–8

First published in 2004

Libraries Unlimited, 88 Post Road West, Westport, CT 06881
A Member of the Greenwood Publishing Group, Inc.
www.lu.com

Printed in the United States of America

The paper used in this book complies with the
Permanent Paper Standard issued by the National
Information Standards Organization (Z39.48–1984).

10 9 8 7 6 5 4 3 2 1

To: Coleman Torrans—a fine young man.

To: Millie Henry and the memory of Lewie Henry—two people with enormous hearts and the dedication and energy to follow their hearts.

CONTENTS

1

INTRODUCTION

> But above all, the courthouse: the center, the focus, the hub; sitting
> looming in the center of the county's circumference like a single cloud in
> its ring of horizon, laying its vast shadow to the uttermost rim of hori-
> zon; musing, brooding, symbolic and ponderable, tall as cloud, solid as
> rock, dominating all: protector of the weak, judiciate and curb of the pas-
> sions and lusts, repository and guardian of the aspirations and hopes. . . .
> —William Faulkner, *Requiem for a Nun*

There is a reason courthouses are found on the square in the center of most
small towns that have been designated as their county's seat. They are the
venue of last resort and in them are heard only the most egregious and mis-
erable tales. This is where the laws are enforced—but in theory, it is not
where laws are made. It is because these looming courthouses are there,
because they exist in a place of prominence both literally and figuratively that
a library, also a place of great importance and prominence, must defer to the
law. Members of all large organizations are obliged to understand the law as
it applies to their duties. The greater the scope of the duties the greater the
understanding of the law impacting those duties becomes. The laws governing organizations are often best expressed and communicated to both staff
and patrons through guidelines and policies.

Patience and Fortitude are the names of the two great lions that guard the
New York City Public Library. These are the two greatest qualities any librarian involved in creating library policy that reflects the law must possess.
Patience is required to work and rework the policy so that it reflects the law
of the state in which the library is located and observes the federal statute;

This is done by consulting representatives of those impacted by the policy, those implementing the policy, fellow library administrators, and attorneys who represent the library. Fortitude is required to implement and enforce the policy in many instances, particularly when controversy arises.

No administrative position escapes controversy and few policies do not at some time meet with resistance. When you meet the inevitable controversy, reread these words: "No administrative position escapes controversy; it is how you manage that controversy that will distinguish you as an effective administrator." Your goal when controversy arises should not be to make the problem disappear but to examine your policy and its guidelines. Evaluate your policy and your communication of that policy to all who work in the library in light of the law it is intended to reflect. Laws and their interpretations evolve and the courts play a role in this evolutionary process. Every lawyer looks at the statute governing their case repeatedly. Though they may have read it twenty times, one hundred times, rereading it as it applies to the case at hand gives it new meaning.

Controversies often illuminate weaknesses in your policy, its guidelines, or the training of those enforcing the policies. In reflection upon the policy, it is important to review the law that the policy is intended to enforce. Courts often enforce laws in progressively different manners. This is the nature of the law. Your policy and its supporting guidelines should not be so rigid as to not reflect a society that inevitably changes over time.

Policies are implemented by flexible guidelines. Understanding the distinction between policies and guidelines is crucial in creating effective policy. If there is no flexibility in your guidelines then you are not necessary to the library—you are little more than a robotic bureaucrat. However, bureaucracy has not been the domain of libraries or librarians. Humanity and flexibility in administering policies gives librarians and the library they represent its all-important humanity, its soul—for in the end the librarians are the soul of the library. This intrinsic understanding by librarians of their role in society has elevated libraries from the bureaucratic image many government agencies retain. Libraries and librarians continue to retain an image of trust and honor, and that is no small feat in this world of controversy. However, their image has recently been modified. Judith Platt, a spokeswoman for the Association of American Publishers, noted that librarians can be radical. "They've got their radical factions, like the Ruby Ridge or Waco types," who want to share all content for free.

To create effective policy a library's mission must be clearly examined and articulated. In many ways the mission of our libraries remains identical to that of Benjamin Franklin's original U.S. library, founded in 1731. We remain a nation of immigrants, and for those who have arrived more recently, the library, especially the library-sponsored Internet, is often a crucial link to their former country. Libraries serve virtually every age group, every race, and every profession, and there are very, very few Americans who have never used a library. Serving our broad and diverse society with policies that allow a library to grow with society is the goal of effective policy making.

The World Wide Web and Internet access provided by libraries has created new legal issues not wholly addressed by the laws related to print communications. Libraries must by law address adult access to the Internet differently than a minor's access, while being mindful that what is appropriate for a sixteen-year-old child is not appropriate for a five-year-old child. The laws that govern these duties and the complex case law are neither clear nor consistent. Each library must examine its population and determine the best policies for its physical, financial, and local circumstances. It is often said that all politics are local; the application of that concept to libraries would translate to the notion that all library policies are local. What works in New York City may not be appropriate for Truth or Consequences, New Mexico. The one constant, however, is patience and fortitude.

SCOPE OF THIS BOOK

While this book recognizes that librarians are not lawyers, its very existence addresses the fact that anyone who chooses to administer a public facility as important as a library must understand the law as it applies to them. Libraries are governed by a legal framework as broad as any that covers other endeavors in our society. It includes employment law, cyber law, intellectual property law, civil rights law, laws governing handicap access, privacy laws, and issues of liability.

This book is not intended to give legal advice. Always consult an attorney if there is a legal question. This book is intended to alert the librarian to the existence of legal issues and help, with the advice of their city attorney or private attorney, draft policies that will promote the well-being of the library and serve its broad and diverse public needs, balancing the rights of the individual with the rights of all who access the library.

Not every librarian at every level must be familiar with every element of library management, but the inevitable consequence is that, in management, all problems surface at the top. Often the problems have been percolating and simmering for quite a while and when they do finally surface, only the tip of the iceberg may be evident, initially. Being familiar with the laws that affect libraries and the creation of policies that apply these laws to the library may decrease the impact of the controversy.

The scope of this book is broad. Many libraries' human resource departments address issues pertaining to employment and their reference departments address issues pertaining to public access. However, ultimately, the administrator of the library will be responsible for any conflicts that arise from the implementation of the policies. It is the responsibility of the administrator to train or provide training for all who work or volunteer in the library and be certain that they understand library policy.

DEVELOP POLICIES AND PROCEDURES THAT REFLECT THE LAW

Developing policies and procedures for your library will serve the library well and this book is designed to help you to address legal issues with formal policies and procedures and informal decisions made in the library and to support these formally enunciated polices and procedures with working guidelines. In the act of development of library policies and supporting procedures, the opportunity will be presented to think through new issues and determine precisely what is best for your patrons, community, and administration.

This text is intended to present legal issues that can be addressed by policy and managed by procedure and guidelines. The very act of creating and using policies, procedures, and guidelines that follow the law is an imitation of the law. Clear, specific, and formally enunciated policies, procedures, and guidelines are the only basis from which to enforce these policies. The law itself requires that your policies be specific. They alert all who employ the library facilities to what is and is not acceptable.

While some matters are best dealt with informally, take the opportunity to review your library's policies and procedures. Ask yourself, if I were gone unexpectedly for a year, could a temporary librarian take these policies and procedures and manage the library? Could they modify the procedures as necessary and maintain the purpose of the policies? Do the policies truly reflect the essence of the library? Are the library policies flexible enough to accommodate changes and are the procedures and guidelines specific enough to guide the functioning librarian? Hopefully, this book will guide you to develop policies and procedures that will govern your library both when your library is under direct public assault and when things are running smoothly.

If you as the librarian have been called to the mayor's office or the City Council to face an angry group of patrons, can you say, "I followed library policy, which reflects our library's mission," whether that decision is defending the selection of material, Internet access, or in protecting the privacy of a patron by refusing to turn over a patron's circulation record? Do you provide the records of minors to their parents, or are you obliged by law to protect the privacy of minors? Do you know what the law of your state is regarding patron privacy and minors, and under what circumstances you must turn over those records? There is not always a clear answer. The first step is understanding the law of your state and from there developing a policy.

Thomas Jefferson believed in an educated public with free and unfettered access to information. These are the great principles of our country and of the American Library Association. He drafted the U.S. Constitution and included in it the copyright clause that is litigated to this day. Jokingly, he stated that Benjamin Franklin could not have drafted the Constitution because he would have included too many attempts at humor. His thoughts on access to information, copyright, and education are as relevant today as they were over two hundred years ago.

Admittedly, it is not fair to put the librarian in the position of understanding these many complex legal issues, but if you are reading this, you already understand life is not fair.

HOW TO USE THIS BOOK

Much is of this book is detailed, and that detail is not relevant in the day-to-day management of a library. Simple familiarity with options will enable the librarian to decide whether to address the issues presented by policy or handle the issue on a case-by-case basis. Just as a decision is made to create a specific policy, decisions are made to omit policies on certain issues. Understanding the details of the legal issues may aid the library staff in coming to this conclusion.

A staff member deeply involved in a single issue, such as privacy, would benefit from the detail of that chapter and the issues raised may signal a need for guidelines. Perhaps the most difficult challenge is for the small library with fewer staff, who are accustomed to handling most issues on a case-by-case basis. Many of the problems that are front and center in the urban areas simply do not exist in small rural libraries. The decision then becomes whether or not to adopt policies and guidelines for situations or issues for which there is no historical factual basis. Without the factual reference the details provided here will help librarians to draft guidelines and policies where there has been no history of problems, if in fact the librarian even desires guidelines and policies. However, understanding that there are hot spots of legal contention is important for all librarians.

CHAPTER GUIDE

Chapter Two, Sexual Harassment in the Library

This chapter reviews the important balance that must be addressed between the patron's First Amendment right and access to a broad range of materials through the library and the employee's right to be free from dealing with offensive conduct. These rights are viewed in terms of what they mean in terms of potential financial impact upon the library as a result of litigation.

Chapter Three, Employment Law in Libraries

Interviewing, evaluating, promoting, and discharging employees are all governed by some laws. Public library employees are generally governed by civil service laws as well. Observing and coordinating these limitations and constrictions can become routine, though from time to time the routine should be matched against current developments in the law.

Chapter Four, Patron Privacy in the Library

Privacy of library patrons is an issue at the forefront of most library hot topics. A library patron's privacy is governed in large part, but not exclusively, by law. A library policy on patron privacy is essential. The guidelines that support this policy will depend on the laws of the state in which the library is located and decisions that individual libraries make, such as policies regarding privacy for minors. Perhaps no legal issue that impacts the library requires a greater balance and artistry in its creation and application than that of patron privacy.

Chapter Five, Copyright in the Library

In understanding the importance of the balancing process that takes place between the patron's right of access and the copyright holder's right of control, the history of the law of copyright is essential. Many librarians do not realize that our law of copyright is not simply legislation, but was a subject of important debate at the time of our country's founding. Copyright is addressed in our Constitution, which refers to patents and copyrights and allows them to be granted *"for limited Times."* Article One, Section Eight, of the Constitution granted to Congress the power "To promote the Progress of Science and useful Arts" by securing copyrights and patents "for limited Times."

Chapter Six, Copyright and Electronic Access

The issue of copyright impacts the very existence of the library, and while the law with regard to copyright and print is evolving, it is much more established and predictable than the law that governs electronic access to copyrighted material, which is fast becoming one of the most important services libraries provide. Examining this law is similar to taking a photo of a football game in the first quarter. The final play has yet to be made. This law is evolving and changing daily and does not uniformly adopt the laws of print access to electronic access. Nowhere is a periodic review of a library's policy and guidelines more important than in the fast-changing area of copyright law.

Chapter Seven, The Fair Use of Copyrighted Material

Historically this area of copyright law has presented libraries with the greatest potential for infringement. This is rapidly changing as electronic resources become the research tool of choice. However, the fair use of copyrighted materials is an issue that should be addressed by library policy and staff, and patrons can easily be educated about this topic. The law on the fair use of copyrighted materials is relatively static and easy to understand.

Chapter Eight, Unpublished Materials and Library Use

Many libraries contain diaries of settlers from their area or letters of early residents. These are unpublished materials. It is important to understand both how these unpublished materials can and cannot be used and the court's bias toward the author of unpublished materials.

Chapter Nine, Library Archiving and Internet Service Provider Status

This can be a complex area of the law, but if broken into small segments it can certainly be understood and applied by the library staff. Certainly, policy that supports these issues is one that will require the input of the entire library staff with legal support. This could be an area the library chooses not to address by policy, but it should not be ignored. If the library chooses not to address this issue there should be a clear understanding of the benefits and detriments associated with policies on the issue embracing Internet Service Provider status. Further, this issue should be revisited by the library staff minimally on an annual basis.

Chapter Ten, Regulation of Access to Information in a Library

This issue is probably one of the hottest areas of debate in our country; it should also be seriously debated at the policy and guideline level of every library in this country every year at least. There are federal laws that govern access to information and there are state laws that govern access to information. There is potential civil and criminal liability for denying or providing access; clearly the library is caught in the middle with room for error on either side of the issue.

Chapter Eleven, License Agreements in the Library

Understanding the license agreement is essential and generally speaking is the first step in creating library policy on the use of licensed resources. It is important to attempt to anticipate where liability for infringement upon licensed materials begins and ends with both the library and the patron and where there is a dual liability. The basis of the understanding is often found in the license itself. Some libraries actually condone the knowing breach of this agreement and "assume the risk" of liability. In essence they take a chance on not being sued. If your library chooses this course of action it should not be a choice by default. The library has an obligation to discuss this course of action with the city or county attorney and all should be in agreement.

Chapter Twelve, Library Web Sites and Legal Constrictions

A very popular argument that defense lawyers like to make to a jury is that anyone with a filing fee can file a lawsuit. And they do. Libraries are not immune from suit. Libraries have been sued for linking to Web sites and for refusing to link to others. Having a policy on links to Web sites may seem superfluous, but if your library were sued it would be helpful to your position if you have a well-thought-out, well-debated policy based upon your counseled interpretation of the law, and that the library did the best it could to link to specific Web sites, or alternately, to refuse to do so.

Chapter Thirteen, Trademarks in the Library

This chapter is included because not all libraries have gotten the word. You cannot paint a mural that includes a trademarked character. Most libraries understand this, but there are some that still do not. Having a policy on the proper use of trademarked symbols is simple, straightforward, and can keep the library out of trouble.

Chapter Fourteen, Disabilities and Public Libraries

The importance of an ongoing evaluation of barriers to access is an important function for all library staff. Of equal importance is training for the staff. Barrier-free access is a goal to be accomplished by the inclusion of all staff in recognizing barriers, and consideration of their opinion should be an ongoing process.

Chapter Fifteen, Policies and Procedures—A Difference with Significance

This concluding chapter addresses individual policies that libraries might consider. Clearly, a library in a town of 15,000 residents will operate with fewer policies and guidelines than a library in a large metropolitan area, and more decisions will be made on a case-by-case basis. This is one of the great advantages and beauties of a small library. However, even small libraries might consider policies and guidelines in the event the unexpected occurs. Good policies and procedures can, at the very least, provide the librarian with a sound basis for restrictions, and this could save hard feelings. Good relations are important for libraries, and maintaining them with sound policies is good business.

2

———•••———

SEXUAL HARASSMENT
IN THE LIBRARY

Most public library employees participate in civil service. The law associated with public employment and the inherent principles of discipline and discharge can be viewed through a multifaceted prism that originates with the notion that public employees should serve the public and should at the same time be free of partisan political influence. Their job security should not be jeopardized with each new political administration. This concept forms the basis of public service law and was first addressed in 1883 in the Pendleton Act.[1] Civil service laws have evolved into statutes that require employees to be discharged "for cause" rather than to accommodate political whim.

Public employment law, however, has expanded with public employment and with employment law in general. Many state, city, and county public employees are represented by a union. These evolving entities have brought a mix of laws governing the law of employment impacting the library including administrative, constitutional, civil service, collective bargaining, and wrongful discharge. These varying bodies of law are not all in agreement and there are significant tensions between the laws. There are few absolutes; rather, employment law is an interpretation of the various bodies of law that govern the situation.

The operation and maintenance of libraries and the employment of librarians and other library employees is governed by local law. Some public libraries are entities of the county, while others are entities of the city, while others are hybrid entities of both. Many libraries are managed by a library board, which provides relief to the library from its obligation to adhere to the law. In *Layton v. Swapp*,[2] the library board was determined by law to be subject to Section 1983 of the Civil Rights Act.

Civil service laws are found in most municipal charters and ordinances and state constitutions and state statutes. They are not identical from entity to entity but retain great similarities. Often they must be applied on a case-by-case basis.

SEXUAL HARASSMENT

Librarians have come a long way from the bun-sporting, sweater-wearing, sensible-shoe, historical stereotype. Many librarians are men, many are young, and few wear buns. The library's image as a reclusive environment has been exploded in the Supreme Court where issues of pornography viewed in the library take front and center stage. Today, Times Square is home to Disney shows, not seedy pornographic peep shows. Pornography is now found in the library and on our children's Internet access.

Federal law provides that employees (and this includes librarians) should not be sexually harassed. The issue then becomes what is sexual harassment? Who determines what sexual harassment is? Are librarians protected from sexual harassment by other employees, by their supervisors, from patrons?

NO ONE GETS TO SEXUALLY HARASS THE LIBRARIAN!

The word *sex* is used in Title VII as a prohibition against discrimination. It was added to Title VII during the last minutes of debate on the floor of the House of Representatives to the Civil Rights Act of 1964. The inclusion of sex as a basis for discrimination under Title VII has been found by the courts to strike "at the entire spectrum of disparate treatment of men and women resulting from sex stereotypes."

Title VII prohibits two types of sexual harassment in the workplace:

1. quid pro quo
2. hostile working environment

Quid pro quo sexual harassment occurs when a supervisor conditions job benefits on an employee's participation in sexual activity. This is not often a library issue. However, the concept of a hostile working environment has been the center of litigation and is a growing issue in libraries.

Hostile working environment harassment occurs when an employee's working conditions are altered by the creation of a hostile environment because of the employee's sex. "When a workplace is permeated with discriminatory intimidation, ridicule, and insult that is sufficiently severe or pervasive to alter the conditions of the victim's employment and create an abusive working environment, Title VII is violated."[3]

Equal Employment Opportunity Commission (EEOC) regulations determine that "an employer may also be responsible for the acts of nonemployees, with respect to sexual harassment of employees in the workplace, where the employer (or its agents or supervisory employees) knows or should have known of the conduct and fails to take immediate and appropriate corrective action."[4] See no evil, hear no evil, speak no evil does not work in the workplace environment. Employers must be sensitive to the conditions of their employees and take action should they observe even the hint of harassment or sexual intimidation.

An employer has an affirmative defense to a hostile work environment claim if the employee has suffered no tangible job consequences.[5] Affirmative defenses are used by defendants once they have been sued. After the employer has been sued for the consequences of sexual harassment the employer may defend their conduct by demonstrating, first, that the employer made a reasonable effort to protect employees from harassment, and second, that the employee unreasonably failed to take advantage of these measures.[6]

A hostile work environment was first addressed by the U.S. Supreme Court in 1986.[7] The Court held that a hostile work environment, like quid pro quo harassment, is a form of invidious sex discrimination that violates Title VII. Here the Court borrowed the EEOC Guidelines of Sex Harassment[8] to create a standard defining sexually harassing conduct and expounding upon when this conduct is actionable under Title VII. The Supreme Court noted the conduct must be "sufficiently severe or pervasive 'to alter the conditions of employment and create an abusive working environment.'" *Severe* and *pervasive* are legal words of art and are applied on a case-by-case basis to the issue before the court.

In *Harris v. Forklift Systems, Inc.,* the Supreme Court admitted that it could not provide a "mathematically precise" test to determine when conduct is sufficiently "severe" or "pervasive" to be actionable under Title VII. *Harris* defined who is capable of defining what sexual harassment is—*the reasonable person*. The reasonable person standard is an important standard.

Chief Justice Rehnquist, writing for a unanimous Court in *Meritor Savings Bank v. Vinson,* concluded that "a hostile or offensive environment for members of one sex is every bit the arbitrary barrier to sexual equality at the workplace that racial harassment is to racial equality." Harassing behavior can come from patrons as well as employers or co-workers. The hostile or offensive environment form of harassment is more pervasive than quid pro quo claims of sexual harassment.

The Civil Rights Act of 1991 granted the right to a jury trial that could be implemented to determine whether certain conduct rises to the level of sexual harassment. Damages for sexual harassment include the possibility of compensatory damages for actual losses and the possibility of punitive damage awards to punish the employer. In order to determine whether sexual harassment has occurred the jury will be instructed to observe the totality of the circumstances. This is important because a court cannot pick only those elements that it feels demonstrates that the plaintiff's environment was hostile enough to merit a remedy. Rather, it is required to look at the entire working environment.

MINNEAPOLIS PUBLIC LIBRARY EEOC CLAIM

A reference desk librarian and eleven of her colleagues brought an EEOC complaint against the Minneapolis Public Libraries central branch. This was the first EEOC investigation of pornography Internet access in libraries.[9] The most significant factor in this case is that the librarians complained to their supervisors routinely about pornography that was both on the screens and being printed out. Of the 140 or so library employees, 47 signed a letter saying, in response to a library patron's complaint about other patrons accessing sexually explicit material, that "Every day we, too, are subjected to pornography left (sometimes intentionally) on the screens and in the printers. We do not like it either. We feel harassed and intimidated by having to work in a public environment where we might, at any moment, be exposed to degrading or pornographic pictures."[10]

Further, lewd behavior was observed in the library. After notifications to their employers were met with no response the complaint was filed with the EEOC.[11]

In May 2001, the EEOC's Minneapolis office found the library *may have created* a hostile work environment by exposing the staff to sexually explicit images on unrestricted computer terminals. The EEOC suggested to the library that it pay each of the twelve complaining employees damages and noted that should mediation fail, either the EEOC or the librarians could pursue the case in court.

THE FIRST AMENDMENT COLLIDES WITH SEXUAL HARASSMENT

Can a Title VII sexual harassment case serve to limit the patron's right to exercise their First Amendment right to access legal pornography? Probably. The purpose of Title VII must be kept in the forefront in this analysis. Its purpose is to eliminate workplace discrimination, including sexual harassment.

Sexually explicit pictures and verbal harassment that occur in the workplace are not protected expression because "they act as discriminatory conduct in the form of a hostile work environment."[12] The issue here is whether this conduct should be any more acceptable because it occurs during a patron's access of sexually explicit albeit legal material. Is the act of accessing pornography online in a library different from one employee posting sexually explicit pictures in their work carrel in view of other employees? These issues are yet to be resolved specifically. However, there is an indication that the conduct of patrons in accessing pornographic material may be subjugated to the librarian's right to work in an environment that is free of pornography.

In balancing the patron's First Amendment rights the courts participate in the potential of regulation of discriminatory speech in the workplace. This regulation of the patron's First Amendment access to Internet pornography constitutes a time, place, and manner restriction that is permissible when necessary to protect employees who are members of a "captive audience."[13] Librarians would qualify as a captive audience. Here there must be a balance between the librarian's right to privacy and the patron's right to Internet access. Should the court limit the patron's right to Internet access, the purpose of the limit would be to protect the librarian from sexual harassment, though the effect would be a First Amendment prior restraint on access to material.

The goal of protecting the librarian from sexual harassment must be accomplished in the least restrictive manner. There are five possible options the library may take with regard to expressive behavior:

1. Prior restraint stops the communication before it happens; this is the classic form of censorship.

2. Subsequent punishment includes the revocation of the patron's library or Internet privileges.

3. Time, place, and manner restrictions regulate content-neutral elements of expression; an example would be restricting game-playing on library terminals or the downloading of music from Internet sites.

4. Allowing expression includes not taking any action one way or the other, thus permitting the expression to happen by default.

5. Protecting expression includes actively ensuring that the expression will take place; for example, advising librarians they are not to limit access to the Internet by patrons in any manner.

Library policy that protects the librarian must not act as a "content-based blanket restriction on speech," as was found by the Supreme Court when it struck down the Communications Decency Act. However, expression that is sexually harassing to the library may be restricted. Each library must thoughtfully and deliberately craft a policy that balances both the patron's right of access and the librarian's right to work in an environment free of sexually explicit material.

THE BOTTOM LINE IS OFTEN FINANCIAL

It may be impossible to give both the librarian who desires protection from a hostile work environment and a patron who wants access to legal pornography all the concessions they desire. Courts have historically limited a person's First Amendment rights in favor of Title VII protections. A very practical approach in libraries is often motivated by financial realities and limitations.

Employees, however, have the potential to mount a successful suit against a library through the EEOC and ultimately in court. Their damages could be assessed in the hundreds of thousands of dollars, potentially reaching the millions for larger libraries. Employees have the potential to retain counsel on a contingency basis. The true financial liability a library faces is from a hostile work environment suit. This reality cannot be denied when developing a sexual harassment policy for the library.

SEXUAL HARASSMENT POLICY—ANALOGIES TO EDUCATION LAW

In creating a sexual harassment policy, it can be helpful to observe legal progress that has been made in the area of education. The U.S. Department of Education has developed a publication titled *Sexual Harassment in Higher Education—From Conflict to Community*,[14] that notes:

Among the most important steps that institutional leaders must take to this end are: (1) carefully drafted definitions of what constitutes sexual harassment and clear policies that prohibit such actions; (2) accessible grievance procedures that are communicated to and understood by all members of the academic community; and (3) ongoing efforts to educate the campus community about the nature of sexual harassment and its destructive impact within the community. Taken together, these three steps represent the best practice that institutions have experienced after more than a decade of aggressive response to the problem.

CONCLUSION

Sexual harassment must be "severe, persistent, or pervasive" for claims to succeed in court. However, in the library it should never rise to that point. Policies should be implemented that are designed to identify, report, and address the issues. The goal is not to litigate whether or not the sexual harassment was "severe, persistent, or pervasive."

NOTES

1. 22 Stat. 403 (1883).
2. Layton v. Swapp, 484 F. Supp 958 (D Utah 1979).
3. Harris v. Forklift Sys., Inc., 510 U.S. 17 (1993).
4. 29 C.F.R. § 1604.11(e).
5. Burlington Indus., Inc. v. Ellerth, 542 U.S. 742, 765 (1998).
6. *See id.*
7. Meritor Savings Bank v. Vinson, 477 U.S. 57 (1986).
8. The EEOC considers offensive gender-based conduct as actionable under Title VII:

Although the Guidelines specifically address conduct that is sexual in nature, the Commission notes that sex-based harassment—that is, harassment not involving sexual activity or language—may also give rise to Title VII liability (just as in the case of harassment based on race, national origin or religion) if it is "sufficiently patterned or pervasive" and directed at employees because of their sex. EEOC, Policy Guidance on Current Issues of Sexual Harrassment, Sex Guidelines, 29 C.F.R. section 1604.11(c), (e) (1993).

Congress granted the EEOC power to issue regulations under the Civil Rights Act of 1964. These regulations are nonbinding administrative interpretations of the Civil Rights Act. They "constitute a body of experience and informed judgment to which courts and litigants may properly resort for guidance." Meritor Sav. Bank v. Vinson, 477 U.S. 57, 65 (1986) (quoting General Elec. Co. v. Gilbert, 429 U.S. 125, 141–42 (1976)).

9. *See* Kim Houghton, *Note, Internet Pornography in the Library: Can the Public Library Employer Be Liable for Third-Party Sexual Harassment When a Client Displays Internet Pornography to Staff?*, 65 BROOK. L. Rev. 827 (1999).

Carl S. Kaplan, *Cyber Law Journal: Controversial Ruling on Library Filters*, N.Y. TIMES, June 1, 2001, <http://www.nytimes.com/> (accessed January 17, 2001).

EEOC, *Unfiltered Computers "Harass" Librarians*, <http://overlawyered.com/archives/01/june1.html> (accessed Dec. 28, 2003).

10. *Letters from Readers*, STAR TRIB (Minneapolis), Feb. 12, 2000, at 18A.

11. *See, e.g.*, Ann Donnelly, *Porn Access Unbearable for Some on Library Staff*, THE COLUMBIAN, July 26, 1998, at B13; *see also* David Burt (of the Family Research Council), *Dangerous Access, 2000 Edition: Uncovering Internet Pornography in America's Libraries*, at 17–19 (reporting several such complaints), <http://www.frc.org/> (accessed March 10, 2002). David Burt is a partisan in these debates, but I have no reason to doubt that the people he quotes were genuinely offended by being involuntarily exposed to sexually themed material.

12. Robinson v. Jacksonville Shipyards, Inc., 760 F. Supp. 1486, 1535 (M.D. Fla. 1991).

13. See Nadine Strossen, *Regulating Workplace Sexual Harassment and Upholding the First Amendment—Avoiding a Collision*, 37 VILL. L. Rev. 757, 766–67 (1992).

14. Robert O. Riggs and others, *Sexual Harassment in Higher Education, from Conflict to Community* (1993), <http://www.library.unt.edu/ericscs/vl/harass/digests/highed.htm> (accessed July 22, 2003).

3

EMPLOYMENT LAW IN LIBRARIES

If you wish success in life, make perseverance your bosom friend, experience your wise counselor, caution your elder brother and hope your guardian genius.

—Joseph Addison

It is not uncommon for library employees to be hired, supervised, promoted, and at times dismissed by the head librarian. Rarely do these employees have contracts. Employees who work without contracts are known as "at-will" employees. At-will employees serve at the pleasure of the employer or at the employer's will, and if there are civil service guidelines in place, pursuant to those guidelines.

Because employment is so important to the preservation of the family and of society, and because jobs may be the most valuable asset a family possesses and may be the basis for the survival of the family, there are laws that cover employment. In the relationship between employer and employee, U.S. society has addressed the complex interdependence between individuals and the increasing ability of those in positions of power (employers) to harm the powerless; both federal and state laws have addressed this imbalance. Both at-will and contract employees may be terminated for cause but termination is not always the best solution.

AT-WILL EMPLOYEES

The employment-at-will rule provides that the employment relationship, absent a contract to the contrary, is "at-will," meaning that either the employer or the employee can terminate the relationship at any time, for any reason, or even for no reason, without legal liability attaching.

Federal and state statutes in some instances protect an employee from discharge when they have done nothing wrong. The key here is "in some instances." In many instances, employers are entitled to hire and to retain persons with whom they and their co-workers can work. Federal and state employment discrimination laws limit the ability of employers to discharge employees if that discharge is motivated by the employee's status as a member of a protected class, and if that protected class is defined. Many attempts have been made in the last decade to broaden the scope of these enumerated protected classes, but they have failed.

Our country has cherished the right of employers to run their own businesses and to hire those persons who will best serve their interests. The legal doctrine of at-will employment embodies the concept that the employee serves at the will of the employer. Employers can legally change the terms and conditions of employment at will. Employers can dismiss employees at any time for any or no reason, without notice or severance pay. Most employment in the United States is contingent employment with no legally guaranteed terms or continuity.

If civil service rules govern the library employee, they must be observed. For example, a civil service employee must not be demoted without cause. A transfer of a civil service employee is permissible if the transfer does not involve reduced salary and duties. This would be considered a demotion. Further, testing of civil service employees for advancement must be objective. A candidate for a position may be required to be a resident of the city or county before taking the examination. Experience, licensing, or training may be required of the candidate for specific positions, such as the attainment of an MLS for an institution accredited by the ALA. Attainment of specific academic accomplishments may be required of candidates for designated positions. U.S. citizenship or good character and responsible conduct may be prerequisites for employment.

If a civil service exam is given prior to employment, or as a prerequisite for advancement, it must employ a standard or measure sufficiently objective so as to be capable of being challenged and reviewed by other examiners of equal ability and experience. Complete objectivity is often impossible, but a reasonable evaluation is required.

Narrower protections come from statutes prohibiting discharge, for example, for jury service, filing workers' compensation or OSHA claims, or testifying in court.[1] Common-law limitations on the ability of the employer to fire at will arise from both contract and tort law.[2]

IMPLIED CONTRACT

Statements in employee handbooks and oral promises made during the interview or during the initial period of employment have been found to constitute implied contracts limiting the employer's ability to fire without just cause.[3]

The significance of an implied contract exception to the at-will doctrine has been minimized in recent years, however, because of employers' attempts to state clearly, usually in the contract, if there is one, as well as in a prominent location in the employee handbook, that the employment relationship is an at-will relationship.

WRONGFUL DISCHARGE FOR PUBLIC POLICY REASONS

The courts have infringed upon the employment-at-will doctrine by carving out a niche for public policy. For example, an employee cannot be fired for refusing to give false testimony. This would be "against public policy." To discharge an employee for this reason has been defined to be a wrongful discharge. The terminated employee can recover from the employer if the court determines that the firing violated public policy and was a wrongful discharge.

In one of the earliest reported cases discussing public policy in the employment context, *Petermann v. International Brotherhood of Teamsters Local 396,* the court held the employer liable for firing an at-will employee for refusing to commit perjury. Such a firing was deemed to have violated public policy by an attempt to encourage untruthful testimony. The employment-at-will doctrine developed rapidly after the Petermann decision and has broadened its scope.[4]

Protected Classes

It is unlawful under federal law to discriminate between persons with regard to the hiring of that person, the terms of employment, training, promotion, advancement, firings, or working conditions because of:

- age, for persons over forty years old
- disability
- race or color
- national origin
- religion
- sex
- pregnancy

These limitations do not apply if there is a bona fide occupational qualification that is required for the job.[5] For example, a pregnant employee would not be the proper employee to participate in the heavy lifting of relocating a library from the first floor to the second. Discrimination would be appropriate in this instance. A blind employee would not be able to participate in shelving.

ADA Protections

The Supreme Court has concluded that the protections of the Americans with Disabilities Act (ADA), at least in the employment context, should be reserved for those individuals who "as a group, occupy an inferior status in our society, and are severely disadvantaged socially, vocationally, economically, and educationally."[6] This description does not extend to protect individuals who, no matter how unfortunately, are prevented from holding the particular job they prefer as opposed to being unable to work in any meaningful way.

The purpose of the ADA[7] is to allow individuals who, because of their disabilities, are prevented from or hampered in participating in the mainstream of American life. It was aimed at an "insular minority," not a broad majority. The ADA protects persons who:

- have a physical or mental impairment that substantially limits one or more of the major life activities of such individual
- have a record of such an impairment
- are regarded as having such an impairment

Thus, to understand and apply the Act's provisions to real-life circumstances, one must determine what is meant by:

- "a physical or mental impairment"
- "substantially limits"
- "major life activities of such individual"

The Act provides no definitions of these terms. However, the Equal Employment Opportunity Commission (EEOC) has attempted to address this omission by way of regulation.

The Americans with Disabilities Act of 1990 specifically refers to 43 million disabled Americans with the potential of "160 million under a 'health conditions approach,' which looks at all conditions that impair the health or normal functional abilities of an individual."[8] Likewise, the Supreme Court noted that there were more than 100 million Americans with vision impairments, 28 million with impaired hearing, and 50 million with high blood pressure.[9] It found these numbers far larger than the 43 million specifically articulated by Congress in the Act.[10] Therefore, the Court concluded that any legislative history was irrelevant and the intent of the Act, as written, required consideration of mitigating and corrective measures in determining whether an individual was considered disabled for purposes of the Act.[11]

These numbers are significant. They give us a key to understanding the scope of the disability envisioned by the Congress in its enactment of the ADA.

PROMISSORY ESTOPPEL

An equitable doctrine, promissory estoppel, has been asserted under circumstances similar to those giving rise to tort claims for fraudulent inducement.[12] Promissory estoppel can be applied even though no contract exists if three requirements are met:

- a promise is made upon which the promisee reasonably relies
- the promisor reasonably should have expected the promisee to rely on it
- enforcement of the promise is the only way to avoid injustice[13]

Although the at-will employee cannot assert contractual breaches upon termination because of the nature of the at-will employment relationship, the lack of a contract allows claims for promissory estoppel. Do not promise an employee an inducement to take a job and then fail to honor that promise.

EMPLOYEE EVALUATION

Employee evaluation is important to maintain morale. If someone is not pulling his or her weight, consequences may be manifested in many different areas and it may be difficult to document this deficiency. Documentation is the key to fairness.

Staffing Adequacy

First, in evaluating employees, it could be helpful to determine how your library is staffed as compared to other libraries of the same size. Is your staffing above or below the national average? This might help in a decision regarding the reasonableness of expectations for the staff.

Job Description

Each job should have a written description that enumerates the specific responsibilities of that position. This should be updated annually and should be an honest reflection of all the tasks required for that position. This is an important tool, not only for the employee and for the basis of an employee evaluation, but also because it helps the head librarian manage the library effectively. There are both scientific methods to determine the actual use of an employee's time and anecdotal methods.

Several Web sites can guide you in crafting or updating a job description model. The Washington Library Media Association maintains an excellent and extensive bibliography that outlines many Web sites that will help you create job descriptions for your library (see *http://www.wlma.org/Profes sional/responsibilities.htm*).

Only with this job description can a fair and accurate evaluation be made of the employee's performance on an annual basis. Evaluating an employee's performance on set and communicated criteria is the only fair way to promote, demote, or dismiss an employee.

Certainly some librarians will be better with interpersonal skills, while others will be better with administrative and technical tasks. Using this type of task itemization will serve as a tool for performance evaluation and perhaps as a tool to assign those tasks to the employee who is best suited for that task. The important point here is to have criteria by which employees can be judged on a consistent and uniform scale and to document the results.

JOB INTERVIEW

The law relating to what may and may not be asked during an interview is simple and based in courtesy and common sense. However, it is essential to understand that during a job interview questions may not be asked for the purpose of discriminating on the basis of race, color, religion, sex, national origin, birthplace, age, or physical disability. Any question asked during the selection process must be related to the job.

This rule applies to all questions posed throughout the entire employment process, whether in the application form, during the interview, or in any testing materials administered. You may believe that staffing the library entitles you to know whether an employee is planning on becoming pregnant in the near future, or whether childcare is likely to become a problem. The question cannot be asked in that fashion. Rather it can go only so far as to determine whether the potential employee can work the hours that the job requires. While you cannot ask whether the employee has any disabilities, you may certainly inquire as to whether they can perform all the tasks normally expected in that position.

The qualities of a good library media staff person can be found at the Washington Library Media Association Web Site (see *http://www. wlma.org/ Professional/jobdescriptions.htm*). This is an important departure point for an interview. Interview a prospective employee to illuminate whether they have these qualities.

- Would you describe yourself as a life-long learner? How do you participate in life-long learning?
- Do you consider yourself to have leadership skills? Give me an example of your personal leadership qualities and how they have been used.
- What experience do you have in management? Which would you prefer to manage: people, a program, a collection, or a budget, and why?
- Tell me about your research skills.
- What are your favorite resources in and outside the library?

• What is the most beneficial library trend you have observed in the last three years? What is the most detrimental?

This is not intended to be a sample of a legal interview. Rather, this is an example of a portion of an effective legal interview, and used here to demonstrate that these types of questions will elicit much more than facts; they will elicit attitude and the ability to interact with the world, and provide ways to assess the employee's perspective of his or her role in the world and in the library. Good interview skills can be learned and can elicit all the information needed to form an opinion of the potential contributions that the applicant can make without venturing into areas protected by law.

INTENTIONAL INFLICTION OF EMOTIONAL DISTRESS AND EMPLOYMENT TERMINATION

In some states, a suit can be brought for the intentional infliction of emotional distress that occurs in conjunction with an employment termination. Generally, in these states, to establish a cause of action for intentional infliction of emotional distress in the workplace, an employee must prove some conduct that brings the dispute outside the scope of an ordinary employment dispute and into the realm of extreme and outrageous conduct. Only in the most unusual of employment cases does the conduct move out of the "realm of an ordinary employment dispute" and into the classification of extreme and outrageous.

The mere fact of termination of employment, even if the termination is wrongful, is not legally sufficient evidence that the employer's conduct was extreme and outrageous under the rigorous standards set in most states.[14]

CONSTRUCTIVE TERMINATION OR DISCHARGE

Constructive discharge occurs when an employer makes conditions so intolerable that an employee reasonably feels that resignation is their only option. The courts will find constructive discharge on an objective basis, not a subjective one; that is, the court will evaluate whether a "reasonable person" would have found the working conditions so onerous, so humiliating, that a "reasonable person" would have no alternative but to resign. The court will objectively examine the conditions of the work situation to determine whether a constructive discharge has occurred. The court generally will not take into account the employer's state of mind. Consequently, the employee does not need to prove that an employer subjectively intended to force the employee to resign.

Derogatory comments resulting from disciplinary proceedings do not constitute constructive discharge. Nor do unfavorable work evaluations support a constructive discharge claim. Humiliation or embarrassment stemming from a transfer to a different position within a school district is not significant enough to support a claim for constructive termination.

CONCLUSION

Some employees may have a contractual relationship with the library. However, most library employees will be "at-will" employees. These employees do not have a contract governing the terms of their employment, and may be fired "at will."

NOTES

1. *See* Elletta S. Callahan, *Employment at Will: The Relationship Between Societal Expectations and the Law*, 28 AM. BUS. L.J. 455 (1990).

2. David J. Walsh & Joshua L. Schwarz, *State Common Law Wrongful Discharge Doctrines: Up-Date, Refinement, and Rationales*, 33 AM. BUS. L.J. 645 (1996).

3. *See, e.g.*, Toussaint v. Blue Cross & Blue Shield of Michigan, 292 N.W.2d 880 (Mich. 1980); Small v. Springs Indus., 357 S.E.2d 452 (S.C. 1987). *See also* Stephen F. Befort, *Employee Handbooks and Employment-at-Will Contracts*, 1985 DUKE L.J. 196; Berube v. Fashion Centre Ltd., 771 P.2d 1033 (Utah 1989); Finley v. Aetna Life & Cas. Co., 520 A.2d 208 (Conn. 1987); Eales v. Tanana Valley Medical-Surgical Group, 663 P.2d 958 (Alaska 1983). An express contract specifying a fixed duration for the employment, of course, by definition negates the employment-at-will relationship.

4. 344 P.2d 25 (Cal. 1959). Petermann sued for breach of contract, and not for the tort of wrongful discharge, arguing that public policy should prohibit an employer from firing an at-will employee for truthfully testifying. The court found for Petermann on the contract claim. Nevertheless, the court's discussion of public policy in this case laid the groundwork for the development of the tort of wrongful discharge. *See* Green v. Ralee Eng'g Co., 960 P.2d 1046, 1048 (Cal. 1998).

5. 42 U.S.C. 2000 (e)21.

6. Kessler v. Equity Management, Inc., 572 A.2d 1144 (Md. 1990).

7. *See* 42 U.S.C. §§ 12111–17 (1994). Title I's prohibition against employment discrimination states: "No covered entity shall discriminate against a qualified individual with a disability because of the disability of such individual in regard to job application procedures, the hiring, advancement, or discharge of employees, employee compensation, job training, and other terms, conditions, and privileges of employment." 42 U.S.C. § 12112(a) (1994).

See 42 U.S.C. §§ 12131–65 (1994). Title II states: "Subject to the provisions of this sub-chapter, no qualified individual with a disability shall, by reason of such disability, be excluded from participation in or be denied the benefits of the services, programs, or activities of a public entity, or be subjected to discrimination by any such entity." 42 U.S.C. §12132 (1994).

See 42 U.S.C. §§ 12181–89 (1994). Title III provides: "No individual shall be discriminated against on the basis of disability in the full and equal enjoyment of the goods, services, facilities, privileges, advantages, or accommodations of any place of public accommodation by any person who owns, leases (or leases to), or operates a place of public accommodation." 42 U.S.C. § 12182(a) (1994).

8. *See* Sutton, 119 S. Ct. 2148.

9. *See id.* at 2149.

10. *See id.*

11. While not discussed by the Court, further support for this conclusion is found in the congressional findings incorporated into the Act. For example, 42 U.S.C. § 12101(a) (6) states, "people with disabilities, as a group, occupy an inferior status in our society, and are severely disadvantaged socially, vocationally, economically, and educationally." This description hardly seems applicable to the plaintiffs in Sutton who admittedly, like tens of millions of other Americans, have normal vision with the use of eyeglasses or contact lenses, and who are trained as commercial pilots. Further, § 12101(a) (7) describes individuals with disabilities as "a discreet and insular minority who have been . . . relegated to a position of political powerlessness in our society. . . . " Again, this description hardly fits the plaintiffs in Sutton.

12. *See* Cortlan H. Maddux, *Comment, Employers Beware! The Emerging Use of Promissory Estoppel as an Exception to Employment at Will*, 49 BAYLOR L. Rev. 197 (1997).

13. Restatement (Second) of Contracts § 90 (1981).

14. *See* Publications, Eighth District Court of Appeals, El Paso, Texas, *Texas Eighth District Court of Appeals—Writing on Causes of Action for Wrongful Termination*, <http://www.8thcoa.courts.state.tx.us/> (accessed June 30, 2002).

4

PATRON PRIVACY IN THE LIBRARY

Whatever we do in the future, whatever technologies we employ, whether libraries are physical or virtual, we must continue to provide that safe place.

—Karen Coyle

Privacy of library patrons is an essential element of library service to patrons. It creates a trust between the library and its patrons and is essential for community faith. If a patron conducts him or herself in accord with both the law and valid library restrictions, that patron is not only entitled to the privacy of his or her records but in some instances to the privacy of his or her actions. A library patron's privacy is governed in large part, but not exclusively, by law.

Privacy in the library can be divided into four broad categories: privacy of circulation records, privacy of electronic records, privacy of Internet activity, and privacy of behavior. Both adults and children are entitled to privacy. In some instances, however, parents are entitled to knowledge of their children's activities and access to their records, and in some instances and in some states, they are not. In some states, the age of the child is a factor to be considered in the issues of child privacy, and in some states, age is not a factor. Public libraries and academic libraries that provide services to minors must also address the privacy issues of minors. This chapter will examine both the rights of privacy and the restrictions a library may impose upon its patrons.

Imagine this scenario: The Recording Industry Association of America (RIAA) has served upon your library a subpoena for your records as an Internet service provider (ISP), a status the library has properly claimed pursuant to Section 152 of the Copyright Act, which addresses the rights of libraries to receive the protections accorded Internet service providers. The subpoena seeks to require the library to turn over user information of an individual allegedly engaged in peer-to-peer (P2P) file sharing. What do you do? First, be certain your 152 status is current if you are a Section 152 library. Second, call your attorney. Hopefully, the library has policies and guidelines in place to deal with this issue that require all subpoenas to be forwarded to a designated representative of the library who can address these legal issues with counsel for the library. How is this scenario different if the library has not been designated as a Section 152 library?

This scenario is based on the recent case, *Recording Industry Association of America (RIAA) v. Verizon.*[1] RIAA used a controversial subpoena provision introduced by the 1998 Digital Millennium Copyright Act (DMCA) under section 17 U.S.C.§ 512(h). With this subpoena power RIAA demands that Verizon Internet Services reveal the identity of a Verizon subscriber who allegedly used KaZaA peer-to-peer software to share music online. Verizon refused to divulge the subscriber's identity, claiming that the provision didn't cover alleged copyright-infringing material that resides on individuals' own computers, only material that resides on an ISP's own computer. Verizon was sued in its capacity as an Internet service provider. The court agreed with Verizon's interpretation of the statutory language, holding that both the terms of 512(h) and the overall structure of section 512 lead to the conclusion that a subpoena under this particular section of the statute (512(c)(3)(A)(iii)) may only be issued to an ISP engaged in *storing* infringing material on its servers and does not allow a subpoena to issue where the ISP, as in this case, is *merely acting as a conduit* for data transferred between two Internet users. The court noted that P2P software was "not even a glimmer in anyone's eye when the DMCA was enacted" and that Congress is best equipped to deal with this issue. Libraries have the option of being designated as an Internet service provider.

This case perfectly illustrates the great difficulty libraries have in adhering to the law. First, they must understand what the law is—if courts cannot agree upon that how can librarians interpret the law? A district court judge made his best decision applying the law to the facts and the Court of Appeals reversed the decision. If legal professionals, employing the best counsel available, present the case to a judge whose decision is reversed on appeal, it can easily be understood that librarians have a more difficult task. There may be no absolutely right or wrong decision. Here, the most important issue for the library is a conscientious, deliberate attempt to make the correct decision— an attempt that includes a review of the law and its application to the facts presented to the library. In short, the best a library can do in many instances is make a good faith effort to apply the law to the facts presented to it.

Scenario number two: Two FBI agents come to the library to discuss a person or persons who have been using a specific library terminal. For the past two weeks they have been tracing incoming and outgoing e-mail from this terminal with their *Magic Lantern* software program, and unbeknownst to the library, have operated ongoing surveillance in the library for the past two weeks. This sounds more like a movie plot than your community library, but remember that the September 11 terrorists used public library e-mail facilities. Does the library cooperate in this investigation? Do they protect the conduct of their patrons? Do they protect the records of the patron? Do they openly answer the FBI's questions?

There is no hard and fast answer to these questions. Here, federal and state laws will guide the librarian in their decision. A distinction must be made between the records of a library patron and the conduct and behavior of a library patron. Only in a handful of states are the activities of the library patron protected, although the American Library Association strongly supports library patron confidentiality. These decisions will generally be made on a case-by-case basis. The library may feel comfortable discussing the library patron's conduct and behavior, but request that a warrant be issued for records, particularly if the state law requires a warrant. Federal law does not protect library records, though it does protect records that represent access to videos. Most state laws do not protect library records, and protection may not extend to law enforcement when it does extend to private citizens.

A library's circulation record is a business record as defined by the Foreign Intelligence Surveillance Act (FISA). FISA, in effect since 1968, has its own courts that meet in private, and libraries receiving an order from a court dealing with FISA are instructed to not divulge any information about an investigation. This warrant will require turning over the circulation record. However, the important point here is that a warrant is required and is relatively easy for the law enforcement agency to obtain.

Scenario number three: A page comes to a senior librarian and advises her that she believes persons are participating in illegal activities through the Internet. Each time she walks by the terminal she observes graphic pornography, and she is offended by all the pornography and is concerned that child pornography is being downloaded. She believes that the public interest in disclosure outweighs the individual's interest in privacy. She gives her notice and states that she intended to work in an uplifting environment, and not for a purveyor of smut.

This scenario involves a balancing between the rights of the patrons to access materials of their choice through the Internet and the rights of the librarians to be free from viewing these materials. The library must be comfortable with its policies and guidelines addressing Internet access to pornography. The library should be certain that minors are not viewing pornography, and pornography of minors is not being viewed, both of which violate the law. However, when pornography of minors is involved, several additional issues are at stake. The U.S. Supreme Court has made a decision holding that Congress may not prohibit child pornography created by using adults who look like minors, or by using computer imaging. Justice Anthony

Kennedy's majority opinion described the Child Pornography Prevention Act of 1996 as "proscrib[ing] a significant universe of speech" that fell "within the First Amendment's vast and privileged sphere." Since such speech was not "obscene" under the Court's prior definition, and did not involve real children in its production, the Court found that the government had no constitutionally adequate grounds to suppress it. Virtual child pornography is not "intrinsically related" to the sexual abuse of children. The link between the images and child abuse was too indirect.[2]

Additionally, it can be quite difficult to determine whether the pornographic depiction involves children (whether real children or virtual children). Experts spend days in court testifying as to the age of the depicted child in trials which turn on the age of the person portrayed in the pornography. Librarians, however, are required to determine this based on a brief view of the image.

In these cases it is important to be certain the library has a no-tolerance policy of the viewing of minors in pornography and the viewing of pornography by minors. Other decisions are left to the library's discretion. One option would be to transfer the employee to another department. However, if the library does allow the viewing of pornography by its patrons, and there is an indication that the pornography is being left on the screen to harass the librarians, this should not be tolerated. This can be interpreted as sexual harassment and no one gets to sexually harass the librarian. Patrons who sexually harass a librarian should have their library rights terminated at the very least. A discussion with the district attorney regarding the conduct of the patron should be considered at most.

An Equal Employment Opportunity Commission ruled that unrestricted Internet surfing at the Minneapolis Public Library created a hostile workplace for librarians, violating Title VII of the Civil Rights Act of 1964. However, this case should be strongly distinguished from activities at other libraries. The case was characterized by an indifference by the library administration to issues which could have been addressed and were ignored. The decision has been strongly criticized as "out of step" with the First Amendment. Implementation of recessed monitors and privacy screens, as well as placing restrictions on printers and print release stations and the restriction of library privileges for violators are considered to be solutions more sensitive to the First Amendment. However, the wholesale avoidance of the librarians' issues was not considered to be a proper balancing of patrons' and librarians' rights.

For this scenario, many issues must be addressed and there is not one right or one wrong solution.

Scenario number four: A parent who has signed to be responsible for a child's library card demands to see the child's circulation record for the last twelve months. Does the library have an obligation to protect the child's privacy or to accommodate the parent? Does the fact that the child has overdue books and fines that are payable change the library's responsibility to share this information with the parent? Does the age of the child impact the library's obligation to the parent? Is the responsibility to share the information greater with the parent of a seven-year-old patron than with a parent of a seventeen-year-old? Does the status of the parent making the request have an impact on the obligation of the library, that is, does a non-custodial parent have the same rights to review the child's records as a custodial parent, and how does the library determine whether the parent is a custodial parent or a non-custodial parent?

Here, the state's laws on issues of library privacy come front and center. If the state has laws on privacy of library records for minors, they are paramount in making this decision. A library is best served by having guidelines regarding privacy for minors and applying them. Generally, most libraries respect the privacy of a child's circulation records unless a fine is due. In those instances a parent has a right to review the records regarding the fine. The age of the child also plays an important role for some libraries, which distinguish between the rights of privacy of a child under twelve and a child above twelve. Most libraries share this policy for the application for the library card, which must be signed by the adult.

Typically, simply because parents are divorced, and a child resides with the "other" parent, access should not be denied to the non-custodial parent, unless there is a specific court order limiting access to the child's records, or parental rights have been terminated. However, in some instances parental rights have been limited by the courts.

Ten years ago none of these issues were on a librarian's radar screen. Today they are front and center, and each of them involves the balancing of a library patron's right of privacy with the library's and the community's right of safety. This concept of balance is the basis of all laws, and the difficult questions are not black and white. The difficult questions come in shades of gray. The close calls, the questions that present themselves in shades of gray, are the questions that define the art of the law, and it is in dealing with these issues, with policies and guidelines and by interpreting these guidelines correctly, that the art of librarianship is made most visible.

Each library should have one person designated to be the expert in issues of library patron privacy. More often than not this will be the director. However, there should be some person to which all employees may turn at all times for issues concerning privacy. These limitations change monthly. Recently, a federal judge reversed course and ordered Verizon to identify a person who had been offering downloads from his Web site to the public. However, on December 19, 2003, the U.S. Court of Appeals for the District of Columbia reversed the order of the court and protected the identity of peer-to-peer file sharers.

The court noted that the Digital Millenium Copyright Act did not require the ISP to identify subscribers who infringe upon copyright. The court noted it was the duty of Congress to draft legislation to require an ISP to identify users. The DMCA as enacted did not require this. The court also noted Congress was corrently considering such legislation.

This chapter addresses the legal basis for the patron's right of privacy and why this right is important not only to the patron, but to the continued success of the library and the public's faith in the library as a safe institution.

THE PATRON'S RIGHT OF PRIVACY

There is an ethical responsibility to safeguard information that is disseminated from the library regarding its patrons, and the legal responsibility varies in individual states. To protect a patron's right of privacy it is important to understand the federal and state laws that apply to library patron privacy. Library policies addressing each facet of patron access to library facilities should be carefully drafted, considering at each level the library patron's rights of privacy. This policy should be communicated to all levels of employees within the library, the administration, the staff, and volunteers, at a bare minimum, both yearly and upon the event of new employment. Library policies that are vague and non-specific will be held to be unenforceable and void for vagueness.[3]

In explaining the importance of specific, non-vague policies, the U.S. Supreme Court held that there must be "fair notice and fair enforcement" of laws. In a library there should be fair notice and fair enforcement of policies. In *Village of Hoffman Estates,* the Supreme Court stated:

The degree of vagueness that the Constitution tolerates—as well as the relative importance of fair notice and fair enforcement—depends in part on the nature of the enactment. . . . The court has . . . expressed greater tolerance of enactments with civil rather than criminal penalties because the consequences of imprecision are qualitatively less severe . . . greater tolerance must be accorded civil enactments. An ordinance which prohibited the showing of films "not suitable for young persons" as vague.[4]

PATRON PRIVACY

In drafting a library patron privacy policy, a distinction should be made between the privacy of records and the privacy of activities and communications. These activities are governed by statute and its case-law interpretation. Generally these laws will be state laws, with a few exceptions for federal laws. State laws vary from state to state. Federal laws are consistent throughout the states.

It is important to understand there is no federal law that governs library patron records, with the exception of video records for videos obtained through a library facility. While federal law does not govern print circulation of general public library records, it does govern video circulation library records. There are federal laws that govern student records at educational institutions created through the library whether they represent video recordings or any other records.

In most states there are no laws that govern patrons' non-recorded or non-documented activities within your library. This information and its privacy are determined by the library's policy. However, some states, such as Colorado, do have such statutes that can serve as a model for your state.

Recently, librarians and patrons' records have come under close scrutiny with regard to the actions of the September 11, 2001, terrorists. It is more important than ever to know where the line is drawn with regard to patron privacy. Some states have extensive patron privacy laws, while most have adopted the Model Uniform Open Records Act, which includes a provision that provides for the confidentiality of library records.

Library patron privacy laws all have one thing in common: they protect the records of the patron. Federal and state laws are not the same as professional codes and guidelines. Statutes take precedence over professional codes and guidelines. In some instances, American Library Association (ALA) positions may not conform precisely to the individual state's law. It is important to understand both. It is the librarian's duty to reconcile ALA policy, which strongly favors privacy, with the actual laws of the state in which the library is located.

In determining the patron's right to privacy outside the area of records, librarians are guided by professional codes or guidelines relevant to and promulgated by their own area of expertise. Not all of these guidelines address the issue of a patron's right to access information. However, the ALA Code of Ethics and Bill of Rights does address this issue. It states that, "We protect each library user's right to privacy and confidentiality with respect to information sought or received, sources consulted, borrowed, acquired, or transmitted." When there is a conflict between the ethical guidelines of the American Library Association and the law it is important for the librarian not only to be aware of the conflict, but to observe the law.

Right to Privacy—Constitutional Analysis

To arrive at a library policy that will govern the privacy of the behavior of the library patron, it is important to understand the constitutional basis on which this right is based. The basis for these formal, ethically enunciated protections of privacy is found in the U.S. Constitution and its Amendments. While an inference may be drawn that there is a constitutional right to library patron privacy, no court has addressed the issue of library patron records as constitutionally protected by the right of privacy.

Such an argument might some day be mounted, but there is no indication that it will be successful. The success of the argument will depend on the framework in which the argument is couched. The U.S. Supreme Court has addressed the right of privacy as a right to be free of unwarranted governmental intrusion. This is a constitutionally protected right. The right "to be let alone" has been defined as the "most comprehensive right of individuals, one that should not be penetrable by the government."[5]

The right to privacy is not specifically set forth in the Constitution; it is provided through the penumbras or protective shadows provided by the Bill of Rights and later Amendments. Specifically, the penumbras surrounding the First, Third, Fourth, Fifth, Ninth, and Fourteenth Amendments create zones of privacy recognized by the courts. There is no clear boundary or limit to the right of privacy; the issue for librarians is whether or not patrons' rights should be protected from unjustified governmental intrusion. Neither the U.S. Constitution nor the Bill of Rights specifically protects a citizen's privacy. This protection has been inferred by the courts. It is the position of the courts that the full protection intended by the Constitution and its Bill of Rights cannot be afforded to the citizens without this inference.

As consumers, we are accustomed to waiving our right to privacy. We accept the necessity of waiving the confidentiality of our medical records to our insurance carrier in exchange for health insurance, and this waiver becomes a part of the contractual relationship between our health insurance carrier and those insured. Some employees contractually agree to participate in drug screening tests, and they waive their right to privacy in exchange for their employment. In some states, our driver's license records and information are sold by the state for profit to the state.

However, where the government is concerned, we do not have a contractual relationship governing our rights to privacy. We must rely on statutes and the case law interpreting these statutes to protect our rights of privacy. We intuitively understand that our tax records will be private and this personal information will not be made public, although we may not specifically understand why this information is private. Private schools that receive government funds are governed by these privacy laws. The U.S. Congress has considered the issue of library patron privacy and has rejected the statutory codification of this right.[6]

Right to Privacy—Statutory Analysis

There is no federal library patron privacy statute, nor is there any case interpreting the right to privacy provided by the U.S. Constitution as applied to a library patron. There are but a handful of states with library patron confidentiality or privacy statutes that exceed the Model Uniform Open Records Act.

When the U.S. Congress was asked to create a legal right (a statute) for the purpose of protection of library patron's records, it refused. There is no federal court case protecting library patrons' right to privacy. The constitutional right to privacy has never been tested in terms of a library patron's right to privacy or confidentiality. Congress was specifically requested to provide the same confidentiality rights and protections to libraries that it applies to video rental stores in its creation of the Video Privacy Protection Act of 1983. Congress refused to enact the proposed bill.[7]

In essence, rights to privacy exist in federal legislation regarding every topic imaginable, except library patron privacy. There are privacy rights for video rentals (including library videos), cable records, consumer records, banking records, employment records, health records, and tax records. There are no federal library patron record privacy statutes.

Representatives introduced legislation to protect not only video files, but also library records. Congress considered the inclusion of the protection of library records and refused. The Video Privacy Protection Act would have enabled customers whose video records are disclosed without their consent to sue for damages of up to $4,000. In order to obtain video records under the statute, law enforcement officials must secure a court order by showing that there is "clear and convincing evidence that the subject of the information sought would be material evidence in the case." Further, the law gives an individual an opportunity to challenge the court order before records are disclosed. The "clear and convincing standard," the strongest one regulating law enforcement access to privately held files, is patterned after the confidentiality provisions of the 1984 Cable Communication Policy Act.

This bill was the result of the Senate hearings on the nomination of Robert Bork to the Supreme Court. A reporter for Washington's *City Paper* asked an employee of a video store about Robert Bork's rental practices. The employee provided the reporter with a record of Bork's video selections maintained by the store. The reporter published an article that was represented to be a description of Bork's viewing habits.

State Laws and Patron Privacy—Weak Tea

Forty-eight states have some modicum of a law that pertains to library records.[8] Many states adopt model uniform standard laws promulgated by professional legal associations, the most notable being the Uniform Commercial Code. States choose whether or not to adopt these standards in whole, in part, or with modifications. The Open Records Acts is a model uniform statute that has been adopted by most states. This is more commonly known as the state Freedom of Information Act. The actual Freedom of Information Act is a federal statute.

Patron privacy and confidentiality, in the context of the Uniform Open Records Act adopted by thirty-five states, is protected as an exception to the Open Records Act, in addition to the Family Educational Right to Privacy Act (FERPA) protections.[9] Pursuant to the Uniform Open Records Act, the librarian, in the capacity of the guardian of patron information, must withhold patrons' records from the public. When a privacy provision is an exception to an open records law, the keeper of patron records is not required to divulge the information to an inquiring member of the public, but the librarian retains the option of divulging this information under specific circumstances.

The portion of the Uniform Open Records Act[10] cited below is the standard Library Confidentiality statute found in a majority of states. Essentially this uniform statute excepts or excludes library patron records from being accessed through the state Freedom of Information Act. Put in a different light, library patron records cannot be accessed through the state's Freedom of Information Act. The pertinent section states: "A record of a library or library system that is excepted from required disclosure under this section is confidential."

The federal Freedom of Information Act guarantees *to citizens* the right to access federal government records. The Open Records Act guarantees to citizens the right to access state government records and has generally been interpreted more narrowly than the federal act. That means more records have historically been accessed through state acts than the federal act.

The word "citizens" is italicized because typically government entities are *not* citizens. Members of law enforcement seeking records are not considered legally to be "citizens" requesting access through the Open Records Act or the Freedom of Information Act. The federal Freedom of Information Act[11] and the Open Records Act have been enacted to provide citizen access to federal records. Individual state Freedom of Information Acts guarantee citizen access to state records. Under state Freedom of Information Acts, governments and their agencies are required to provide the fullest possible disclosure of information to the public.[12] The purpose of the Act is to permit *citizens* to know and understand the business of their government.[13] Accessing private patron information does not serve a legitimate purpose of understanding the business of government.

Iowa has a standard Model Open Records Act. In this state, law enforcement's access of records was not protected.[14] The state was permitted to obtain public library circulation records. The library and its patrons claimed a First Amendment protection of the circulation records. They alleged that forced disclosure of the library circulation records would violate the First Amendment because such disclosure would chill the library patrons' claimed First Amendment right to read and acquire information.

The court discarded the privacy claims of the library patrons favoring disclosure pursuant to a criminal investigation on the basis of a "weighing of interests" standard of review. The law enforcement interests far outweighed the patron's claims of privacy.

President Nixon refused to produce his taped conversations, and claimed that the government could not force the production of tape-recorded conversations between the President and his advisers, as well as other various presidential documents, for use in a pending criminal conspiracy trial. A generalized need for confidentiality of high-level communications and the doctrine of separation of powers were the theories advanced in support of the President's claimed privilege. The government argued that its interest in the underlying criminal prosecution outweighed the President's generalized claim of confidentiality. The government's interest in obtaining the tapes and documents, in conjunction with claims that the confidentiality asserted by the President would violate Fifth Amendment due-process protections and Sixth Amendment confrontation rights of the criminal defendants in the conspiracy trial, persuaded the Supreme Court to deny the President's claim of confidentiality.[15]

The Uniform Open Records Act and Library Confidentiality

The Uniform Open Records Act is a model law promulgated by a national committee and recommended for adoption by state legislatures. This is commonly done with many standard laws to provide a model for state legislatures. Generally, various state legislatures will adopt the majority of the uniform law, making specific changes to suit their constituencies. The Uniform Commercial Code is an example of a model law that has been adopted by all states, with minor variations from state to state. This model Uniform Open Records Act is designed to give the public the right to access government records. That is its whole purpose. It is a state law similar to the federal Freedom of Information Act. Library records are in fact government records in many instances. For this reason, the Uniform Open Records Act protects these library records, which are government records, from public access through the Open Records Act. This model law does not otherwise create an expectation of privacy regarding library records. It simply means that a patron's records may not be reached through the Uniform Open Records Act.

The section entitled "Exception: Records of Library or Library System" states as follows:

(a) A record of a library or library system, supported in whole or in part by public funds, that identifies or serves to identify a person who requested, obtained, or used a library material or service is excepted from the requirements of the Open Records Act unless the record is disclosed:
   (1) because the library or library system determines that disclosure is reasonably necessary for the operation of the library or library system and the record is not confidential under other state or federal law;
   (2) under the Uniform Open Records Act; or
   (3) to a law enforcement agency or a prosecutor under a court order or subpoena obtained after a showing to a district court that:
      (A) disclosure of the record is necessary to protect the public safety; or
      (B) the record is evidence of an offense or constitutes evidence that a particular person committed an offense.
(b) A record of a library or library system that is excepted from required disclosure under this section is confidential.

A few states go a step further, and provide the option of civil damages for the disclosure of library user files without the user's consent. Some statutes require a subpoena to be obtained prior to obtaining the records, but most do not. Some courts have interpreted open-records laws to apply only to citizen access to information. Thus, these model laws have no power over government investigations. The more protective statutes are not attached to an open-records law and unequivocally prohibit disclosure of confidential patron information to both government entities and private entities.

Most existing statutes provide for certain exceptions to the rule of patron confidentiality. Confidential information may be disclosed with the consent of the patron in question, for example, to compile statistical data on library use or to collect fines and penalties.

An important feature of this law is that it respects the rights of law enforcement or prosecutors to obtain patron information with a court order or subpoena. It does not deny the right to that information without a court order or subpoena. And notably it does not provide the same right to non-prosecutor members of the bar, criminal defense attorneys of a co-conspirator, or civil attorneys. This law does not intrinsically protect a child's records from parental review.

Subpoenas and Court Orders

Subpoenas can be issued directly by attorneys in some states and in others the attorney must request that the district clerk issue the subpoena. The significant point here is that courts do not issue subpoenas. This power lies solely at the discretion of the requesting attorney. It can be virtually impossible for a librarian to determine whether the attorney has abused his discretion in issuing the subpoena. Because subpoenas do not require a court hearing and are not supported by a court's order no court reviews them prior to their issuance. That review comes only if and when the subpoena is challenged by a motion requesting a court hearing, which may be filed by either the library or the opposing party in the suit from which the subpoena emanates. Subpoenas typically do not require the immediate return of records. The return of the requested information is set at a specific time in the future. This provides the library the opportunity to consult with its attorney and challenge the subpoena if there appears to be a legitimate cause for challenge.

Many times the attorney who has issued the subpoena is not familiar with the special protections afforded to library patron records and activities. This means that the library will be required to retain an attorney to quash the subpoena. In other instances, the library may be required to turn over the records. In states where the parent is entitled to the records of a child in matters governed by the states' family code, the parent may not need a subpoena. The Uniform Open Records Act adopted in most states does not address the obligation to respond affirmatively or negatively to subpoenas issued outside the domain of government investigators or prosecutors.

Court orders, unlike subpoenas, carry with them the direct possibility of contempt of the court for failure of compliance because court orders are just that, orders of the court. These are issued by the court after a hearing requesting specific information. Most states do have a criterion that the judge must apply in determining whether to issue an order for access to records. It is not always clear on the face of the order or the subpoena that these requirements have been observed, thus creating cause for review.

In the case of civil subpoenas, the librarian may be caught in the middle, and may face liability in either direction. A subpoena, issued by an attorney for a husband in a divorce matter, may be for records to which the husband is not entitled. The librarian may face liability to the wife for providing this information. Each and every employee of the library should be familiar with a library policy to contact the attorney for the library *any time* a subpoena or court order is delivered, so that the attorney may review the legality of the subpoena.

The American Library Association has published specific and detailed guidelines for the handling of a subpoena. Libraries should review these guidelines and adopt those that are most suitable for that particular library.[16]

What Are Patron Records?

It is important to know specifically what the library is required by law to protect or to produce by court order or subpoena. To that end, the definition of library records must be examined.

Registration records are records used to initiate an account with a library. These are clearly library patron records of a permanent nature. Circulation records are another clear category of library patron records, whether they are kept in a wooden box or on computer disk. As long as the identity of the patron has not been purged, the patron has circulation records. The issue here becomes how long is it necessary to retain the identity of the patron to support internal library statistical information. Can this information not be just as usable for the library without the patron's identity as with the patron's identity? Software exists to purge a patron's identity on a timely basis.

If the library is able to identify the user of each computer terminal, then the issue becomes whether or not the cache history of that user is a record. Is the cache history backed up on the library's hard drive? This back-up copy of the user's cached history could be a computer record retained by the library. Backed-up library records are also library records.

Example of Effective State Patron Privacy Laws

The three best examples of patron privacy laws are found in Colorado, New York, and Arkansas.

Perhaps no state has a more effective patron privacy and confidentiality law than the State of Arkansas, enacted in 1989.[17] The Arkansas law applies to libraries that receive public funds, of any nature. The irony here is that while Arkansas may have the strongest library patron laws, it ranks among the lowest in pay to librarians and has the lowest librarian-patron ratio in the country.

In this statute, library records that contain names or other personally identifying details regarding the patrons of public, school, academic, and special libraries and library systems supported in whole or in part by public funds are prohibited from disclosure except as specifically permitted by the statute. A library may disclose personally identifiable information concerning any patron only to the following people under these specific circumstances:

- to the patron
- to any person with the informed, written consent of the patron, given at the time that the disclosure is sought
- to a law enforcement agency or civil court, pursuant to a search warrant

As a form of deterrence for information gained in violation of this statute, the law also requires that personally identifiable information obtained in any manner other than this is not receivable as evidence in any trial, hearing, arbitration, or other proceeding before any court, grand jury, department, officer, agency, regulatory body, legislative committee, or other authority of the state or political subdivision of the state. This Act also makes such disclosures of this information a crime, subjecting the person disclosing such information to a $200.00 fine and not more than thirty days in jail. This would clearly deter a person from disclosing this information. This Act notes that it does not create a case of civil liability for a disclosure; it does not, however, prohibit one either. The proponent of such a case would be required to prove a duty, a breach of duty, and damages.

Colorado has the broadest patron-privacy law. Patron privacy is protected by Colorado Statute 24–90–119, entitled "Privacy of user records." What is significant about this statute is that it protects the interaction between librarian and patron in addition to the records. This statute provides that:

a publicly supported library or library system shall not disclose any record or other information which identifies a person as having requested or obtained specific materials or service or as otherwise having used the library. Records may be disclosed in the following instances:

(a) When necessary for the reasonable operation of the library;

(b) Upon written consent of the user;

(c) Pursuant to subpoena, upon court order, or where otherwise required by law.

Most librarians intuitively understand the first two items in this list. However, when addressing the "reasonable operation of a library," a library should consider whether the identity of the user is necessary for the library functions. This is an issue addressed now by software that tracks user information; the retention of the user's identity is an important consideration in determining precisely how much information is needed for the reasonable operation of the library.

The last item leaves work for librarians. In essence it reads: Libraries may disclose records where otherwise required by law. The determination of "where otherwise required by law" can be a difficult one and one that will require the advice of counsel from state to state.

The State of New York defines library records in detail and with specificity as records related to the circulation of library materials, computer database searches, interlibrary loan transactions, reference queries, requests for photocopies of library materials, title reserve requests, or the use of audio-visual materials, films, or records, and it further notes that the definition is not limited to these stated items.[18] A Wisconsin printing company found that its computers were being hacked into via a computer terminal located at the New York Public Library, and requested the identity of the computer user pursuant to the state's Freedom of Information Act.[19] The New York court found that these records should be protected:

> Were this application to be granted, the door would be open to other similar requests made, for example, by a parent who wishes to learn what a child is reading or viewing on the "Internet" . . . or by a spouse to learn what type of information his or her mate is reviewing at the public library.[20]

This case is significant for what it does state and for what it does not state. It is important to note that the requesting party was not associated with law enforcement. There is no indication as to how the request would have been received had a law enforcement agency requested the records. Further, the request might well have been upheld had a subpoena been issued rather than a Freedom of Information request. This interpretation is significant for states that have a library patron privacy act grounded in their Freedom of Information Act. For libraries located in these states, close attention must be paid to whether the request is made by law enforcement, because often the Freedom of Information Act will not apply to law enforcement, and to whether the request is made by subpoena or court order that are not directly impacted by the state's Freedom of Information Act.

FERPA EXPLAINED

The Family Educational Right to Privacy Act (FERPA) governs educational records. For public libraries that are joined with community college libraries, FERPA will apply to the records of students; it will not govern the records of community library patrons. The only group given actual rights by the Family Educational Right to Privacy Act (Buckley Amendment) are parents and adult students.[21] FERPA rights do not apply to public libraries.

"Access"—Definition

Parents and adult students have the right, upon request, to access their own or their child's records within a "reasonable" time, and no later than forty-five days after the request. "Access" generally refers to in-person inspection of the original records, but in most cases does not entitle parents to obtain photocopies of the records.[22]

"Records"—Definition

The definition of "records" is of significance to librarians. In one extreme, we all know that grades are protected records. In the other extreme, school directory information is not protected. Where in this continuum do library records fall? On one extreme, FERPA has an emergency exception. Schools may release records to "appropriate persons" in a health or safety emergency, as necessary to protect the health or safety of the student or others.

Disclosures in connection with litigation and law enforcement are permitted. Schools may release records in response to subpoenas.

General data that does not personally identify the student can be released. However, the release of information without reference to a particular student's name may violate FERPA if the information is "easily traceable" to a student.

Information may be shared with other educators on a reasonable basis. It is the school's responsibility to set out a written standard for determining when there is a legitimate educational reason for inspecting student records.

Schools have obligations to keep a log of many of these disclosures, and persons who receive records have obligations not to redisclose them except as permitted by FERPA. Here again, the library needs a policy.

FERPA Definition of Records

FERPA defines records as "those records, files, documents and other materials which: contain information directly related to a student; and are maintained by an educational agency or institution or by a person acting for such agency or institution."[23]

FERPA records are not limited to documents in the official "student file"—the material may be in a teacher's desk, nurse's office, or principal's file, among other places.

Regulations note that student information may be recorded in a variety of ways, "including, but not limited to, handwriting, print, computer media, video or audio tape, film, microfilm, and microfiche."

Regulations define "personally identifiable information" as not only that which includes a student's name, but also as records that include the student's parent's name, the family's address, an ID number, such as a Social Security number, or information that makes the student's identity "easily traceable."

IMPACT OF USA PATRIOT ACT

The USA PATRIOT Act (USAPA), created as a result of the terrorist acts of September 11, 2001, also applies to libraries. The bill is 342 pages long and makes changes, some large and some small, to over fifteen different statutes. Terrorists come in all forms, shapes, and sizes, as we observed at Columbine High School. Within fifteen days of September 11, 2001, the USA PATRIOT Act became law. The acronym stands for "The Uniting and Strengthening America by Providing Appropriate Tools Required to Intercept and Obstruct Terrorism." The Act recognized the advances in technology for law enforcement surveillance. Historically, wiretap orders designated a particular technological device, such as a telephone or specific computer. The USA PATRIOT Act permits law enforcement to apply to the judicial system for "roving wiretaps" that are "technology neutral" and that cover a person located anywhere in the United States rather than a particular technological device. E-mail headers and URLs visited by the designated person are also available for surveillance. The guidance for obtaining a roving wiretap order from a court, as directed to federal agents by the Department of Justice, is available online.[24]

Specifically, the USA PATRIOT Act permits law enforcement agencies to apply to the court in a closed hearing for an order for the "production of any tangible things (including books, records, papers, documents and other items) for an investigation to protect against international terrorism or clandestine intelligence activities, provided that such investigation of a United States person is not conducted solely upon the basis of activities protected by the first amendment . . . "[25] If the court determines that a reasonable basis for the issue of a search warrant has been made by the law enforcement agency, the magistrate or the judge hearing the matter will sign a court order. This means a search warrant has the authority of a court's order and failure to comply with this order will result in contempt. No one knows the extent to which this law will be applied by the courts, and since the hearing required to obtain the search warrant is closed, it will be difficult to evaluate the standards used until these hearings are challenged through litigation. The USA PATRIOT Act extends to libraries.

For a library, this means that patrons using your computers may be tracked by law enforcement. The library, or even the city, may not know that the computers are being tracked. Library computers may now be tracked without any physical intrusion to the computer system.

The existence of the *Magic Lantern* software program has been confirmed by the FBI. *Magic Lantern* is reported to be a powerful version of a hacking tool, known as a key-logging program. Such a program, when installed, monitors and stores copies of what is typed by the user; this could include a password that starts an encryption program.

Experts believe *Magic Lantern* may be able to secretly install itself on an unsuspecting user's computer in the same manner as a computer virus. The program could be disguised as a harmless computer file similar to a Trojan horse program, and sent as an attachment to a benign computer e-mail. The FBI states that *Magic Lantern* will only be used "pursuant to the appropriate legal process," which means as a result of, and limited by, a court-approved search warrant. However, lawyers in the field of privacy worry that the program could violate citizens' civil rights to be free from unreasonable searches and seizures.

The USAPA expands all four traditional tools of surveillance—wiretaps, search warrants, pen/trap orders, and subpoenas. The government may now observe Americans' Web surfing, including terms entered into search engines, by merely presenting to a judge anywhere in the United States that the observation of the Web surfing could lead to information that is "relevant" to an ongoing criminal investigation. The person being observed does not have to be the target of the investigation. If granted, this application to the court for observation does not obligate the surveillance team to report their actions to the court.

Nationwide Roving Wiretaps

The FBI and CIA can now go from phone to phone, computer to computer, without demonstrating that either is being used by a suspect or target of an order. The government may now serve a single wiretap, a Foreign Intelligence Surveillance Act (FISA) wiretap, or a pen/trap order, which allows law enforcement to capture phone numbers for incoming and outgoing phone calls, on any person or entity nationwide, regardless of whether that person or entity is named in the order. The government need not make a showing to a court that the particular information or communication to be acquired is relevant to a criminal investigation. Pursuant to FISA, surfing though search engines is surveillable even when the person being watched is not the subject of an investigation. In the pen/trap or FISA situations, they do not have to report where they served the order or what information they received. For pen/trap orders, Internet service providers or others who are not named in the order do have authority under the law to request certification from the Attorney General's office that the order applies to them, but they do not have the authority to request such confirmation from a court.

Defense Advanced Research Projects Agency

The Defense Advanced Research Projects Agency (DARPA) is the central research and development organization for the U.S. Department of Defense. It manages and directs selected basic and applied research and development projects for the Department of Defense and pursues research and technology. DARPA holds a Systems and Technology Symposium approximately every eighteen months to communicate their priorities for future programs.

It began awarding contracts for the design and implementation of a Total Information Awareness (TIA) system used to detect terrorists' information signatures. It is a task, the Information Awareness Office (IAO) says, that is beyond "our current intelligence infrastructure and other government agencies." TIA program directors seeks to develop data mining that exceeds current technology for the purpose of "development of collaboration, automation and cognitive aids technologies that allow humans and machines to think together about complicated and complex problems." TIA has been renamed DARPA Terrorism, Defense Advanced Research Project Agency, a research and development program of the Department of Defense (*www.darpa.mil/body/tia/tia_report_page.htm*).

According to the IAO's blueprint, TIA's five-year goal is the "total reinvention of technologies for storing and accessing information . . . although database size will no longer be measured in the traditional sense, the amounts of data that will need to be stored and accessed will be unprecedented, measured in petabytes."

The Total Information Awareness program is perceived to have the potential ability to provide persistent storage of everything from credit card, employment, medical, and Internet service provider records, and it is from this information that a terrorist profile will be drawn. There is potential to join this program with *Magic Lantern* and mine a patron's library access data.

Internet Service Providers (ISPs)

The USA PATRIOT Act makes two changes to increase the quantity of information the government may obtain about users from their ISPs or others who handle or store their online communications. First, Section 212 of the law allows ISPs to voluntarily hand over all "non-content" information to law enforcement with no need for any court order or subpoena. Second, Sections 210 and 211 expand the records that the government may seek with a simple subpoena to include records of session times and durations, temporarily assigned network (I.P.) addresses, and means and source of payments, including credit card or bank account numbers. The significance here is that subpoenas may be issued without prior judicial review.

The government's scope of surveillance has increased significantly with the USA PATRIOT Act. Government surveillance for suspected computer trespassers is now allowed without a specific court order for access to the library's records. Wiretaps to facilitate this surveillance are now allowed for suspected violations of the Computer Fraud and Abuse Act. This includes anyone suspected of "exceeding the authority" of a computer used in interstate commerce, causing over $5,000 worth of combined damage.

The Computer Fraud and Abuse Act has increased the penalties to include:

1. raising the maximum penalty for violations to ten years (from five) for a first offense and twenty years (from ten) for a second offense

2. ensuring that violators only need to intend to cause damage generally, not intend to cause damage or other specified harm over the $5,000 statutory damage threshold

3. allowing aggregation of damages to different computers over a year to reach the $5,000 threshold

4. enhancing punishment for violations involving any (not just $5,000) damage to a government computer involved in criminal justice or the military

5. including damage to foreign computers involved in U.S. interstate commerce

6. including state law offenses as priors for sentencing

7. expanding the definition of loss to expressly include time spent investigating, responding, for damage assessment, and for restoration

The USA PATRIOT Act allows Americans to be more easily surveilled by U.S. Foreign Intelligence Agencies. Just as the domestic law enforcement surveillance powers have expanded, the corollary powers under the Foreign Intelligence Surveillance Act have also been greatly expanded, including a general expansion of FISA authority. FISA authority for surveillance on Americans or foreign persons in the United States (and those who communicate with them) has increased from situations where the suspicion that the person is the agent of a foreign government is "the" purpose of the surveillance to anytime that this is "a significant purpose" of the surveillance. Law enforcement may observe Web surfing, including terms entered into a search engine, without a warrant and without designating the person watched as the target of an investigation. The FBI and the CIA may go from phone to phone and computer to computer without demonstrating that each is being used by a suspect or target of the order. All ISPs may hand over all "non-content" information to law enforcement without a need for court order or subpoena.[26]

The Act provides for increased information-sharing between domestic law enforcement and intelligence. This is a partial repeal of the wall put up in the 1970s after the discovery that the FBI and CIA had been conducting investigations on over half a million Americans during the McCarthy era and afterward. The Act allows wiretap results, grand jury information, and other information collected in a criminal case to be disclosed to the intelligence agencies when the information constitutes foreign intelligence or foreign intelligence information, the latter being a broad new category created by this law.

The USA PATRIOT Act was specifically designed for the legal and court-ordered acquisition of Internet service provider records of user billing information. An amendment to the Act, which proposed, for the purpose of a clarification, that the Act would not preempt existing federal and state privacy laws by maintaining existing criteria for records, such as library records, failed.[27]

It is also interesting to note that constitutional protections apply only in our country. The FBI can access matters abroad by means that exceed our Constitution. A good case in point would be the arrest of reputed Russian mobster Alimzhan Tokhtakhounov, arrested in Italy on a U.S. criminal complaint accusing him of fixing the results of the pairs and ice dancing competitions at the Salt Lake City Winter Olympic Games. The complaint, filed in Manhattan federal court, was based on wiretaps made by the Italian government, which had been tapping his telephone as part of an organized-crime investigation. Poring through transcripts, FBI agents said they discovered conversations in which Tokhtakhounov appeared to be arranging a vote swap so a French judge would support the Russian pairs team while the Russians would make sure the French team won in ice dancing.

POLICY FOR COMPUTER ACCESS IN THE LIBRARY

It is important for a library to have clear policies and guidelines with regard to computer terminal use and to follow them. Law enforcement will have the authority to review all records relating to computer terminal use. Some libraries do not require patrons to register for computer use, while others, for reasons of accountability, do require registration for computer access. This accountability may include logging in and out and identification can be made in that fashion.

A library's policy should determine whether Internet use records will be afforded the same privacy protections as other patron records and how long they should be kept. Software to support the library's position is available.

ALA POLICY CONFIDENTIALITY OF RECORDS

The Council of the American Library Association strongly recommends that the responsible officers of each library, cooperative system, and consortium in the United States take the following precautions:

- Formally adopt a policy which specifically recognizes its circulation records and other records identifying the name of library users to be confidential in nature.
- Advise all librarians and library employees that such records shall not be made available to any agency of state, federal, or local government, except pursuant to such process, order, or subpoena as may be authorized under the authority of, and pursuant to, federal, state, or local law relating to civil, criminal, or administrative discovery procedures or legislative investigative power.
- Resist the issuance or enforcement of any such process, order, or subpoena until such time as a proper showing of good cause has been made in a court of competent jurisdiction.[28]

The ALA Code of Ethics states: "We protect each library user's right to privacy and confidentiality with respect to information sought or received, and materials consulted, borrowed, acquired or transmitted."[29]

Upon receipt of process, order, or subpoena, the library's officers should be required in all instances to consult with their legal counsel to determine if such process, order, or subpoena is in proper form and if there is a showing of good cause for its issuance; if the process, order, or subpoena is not in proper form or if good cause has not been shown, they will insist that such defects be cured.[30]

Samples of Internet use polices are located on the Office for Intellectual Freedom's Web page, "Internet Use Policies," at *www.ala.org/alaorg/oif/ internetusepolicies.html.*

CHILDREN'S RIGHTS OF PRIVACY IN A LIBRARY

The library serves both adults and children, and both on a public policy level and a personal level, libraries, and the librarians who manage them, recognize the obligations parents have to supervise and manage the upbringing of their children. With this recognition comes yet again another act of balance and art that a librarian is called upon to implement. The question here is one of degree: the degree to which a library must balance the child's rights to confidentiality and privacy and the parent's right to manage and control the upbringing of that child.

Libraries support a patron's right of privacy. Children are clearly library patrons, albeit library patrons whose parents agree on their registration forms to be responsible for their obligations incurred as duly registered patrons of the library. As minors, children cannot by law enter into contracts. Only adults can enter into contractual agreements on behalf of their children. Children are patrons for whom another has agreed to be responsible. Most states do not have statutes that create separate rights of privacy for children. Society and the law recognize the duties and responsibilities of parents to manage and control the conduct and activities of their children. These rights are also recognized by libraries.

In examining the First Amendment rights that courts have historically afforded to children, a 1969 Supreme Court case plays an important role. In this case it was determined that high school students do have First Amendment rights that they are entitled to exercise, if these rights do not infringe upon the organization's right to self manage, in this case the high school. The Court stated:

First Amendment rights, applied in light of the special characteristics of the school environment, are available to teachers and students. It can hardly be argued that either students or teachers shed their constitutional rights to freedom of speech or expression at the schoolhouse gate. This has been the unmistakable holding of this Court for almost 50 years.[31]

Their rights appear to be even stronger at the public library.

As has been previously addressed, most states have laws that protect the confidentiality of library patrons' records and limit disclosure of this information to the following instances:

1. the proper operation of the library
2. a user request
3. pursuant to a valid subpoena issued by a court or court order

However, some states have statutes that give parents access to the records of their minor children. This includes educational, medical, insurance, and psychological records. These statutes are typically found in a state's Family Code. Access to these records is provided regardless of whether the child resides with the parent. This access is universal, unless in the context of family court adjudication, access to these records is limited by a court order, which is a public record. The issue immediately becomes how a librarian is to know whether this access has been limited. No statute specifically includes access to library records. However, most statutes give a broad access to a child's records and indicate that the enumerated list is not comprehensive. Further, it could be argued that library records are educational records.

AMERICAN LIBRARY ASSOCIATION POLICY AND CHILDREN'S RIGHTS TO PRIVACY

The ALA's Library Bill of Rights states that "a person's right to use a library should not be denied or abridged because of origin, age, background or views." It is a stretch to infer that the sharing of a child's library records is an abridgment of this right, but this stretch can be made, based on the inclusion of the word age. If the sharing of a person's library records is an abridgement of a library right, and this sharing is based on the age (or lack thereof), then the sharing of a minor's library records is a violation of the Library Bill of Rights. It would be preferable for the American Library Association to specifically adopt and enunciate a right of a child to privacy in their records rather than having to negotiate and infer this conclusion. Further, to reduce the inference that the ALA believes that children have rights of privacy to their circulation records, the ALA in its interpretation of its bill of rights states that "parents and legal guardians have the right and responsibility to restrict their children's—and only their own children's—access to any electronic resource."[32] There are inherent conflicts in these two positions and it is the individual library that must decide on the policy best suited for its community.

The law has specifically held that minors are entitled to First Amendment protections. In arriving at conclusions on a case-by-case basis, the courts have always employed an analysis that includes potential harm to minors as balanced with the right sought to be protected. In *Erznoznik v. City of Jacksonville*,[33] the court stated: "Minors are entitled to a significant measure of First Amendment protection, and only in relatively narrow and well defined circumstances may government bar public dissemination of protected materials to them."

Neither the ALA nor the law has given children unrestricted First Amendment rights, and both recognize the necessity of parental involvement in the rights of privacy of minors. This involves the recognition of the fundamental relationship of accountability by a parent for the acts of a minor, and for the responsibility of molding and shaping that minor to participate in society as a responsible adult. The individual library is left to fashion its own policy regarding minors' access to materials.

The courts have recognized the fundamental responsibility of parents to govern the upbringing of their children, but at the same time, they have noted that children require protection that exceeds that of adults. In *Prince v. Massachusetts*,[34] the court recognized that children must be managed by different standards than adults. It stated:

The state's authority over children's activities is broader than over like actions of adults. This is peculiarly true of public activities and in matters of employment. A democratic society rests, for its continuance, upon the healthy, well-rounded growth of young people into full maturity as citizens, with all that implies. It may secure this against impeding restraints and dangers, within a broad range of selection. Among evils most appropriate for such action are the crippling effects of child employment, more especially in public places, and the possible harms arising from other activities subject to all the diverse influences of the street. It is too late now to doubt . . . It is true children have rights, in common with older people, [such as] the primary use of highways. But even in such use streets afford dangers for them not affecting adults. And in other uses, whether in work or in other things, this difference may be magnified. This is so not only when children are unaccompanied but certainly to some extent when they are with their parents. What may be wholly permissible for adults therefore may not be so for children, either with or without their parents' presence.

Parents have historically been responsible for decisions regarding the education of their children and the form this education will take. In *Pierce v. Society of Sisters*,[35] the court recognized parents' rights to direct the upbringing and education of children, and in *Meyer v. Nebraska*,[36] the court recognized parents' right to procure education for children as a protected liberty interest under the Fourteenth Amendment.

If a library is to be guided by the courts in protecting the First Amendment rights of children, it must address the same issues recognized by the courts, that is, that children cannot universally have rights identical to those of parents and must in some instances be afforded greater protection than adults. This protection inherently impinges upon the First Amendment rights of children. Libraries are required to formulate a difficult policy that recognizes their duty both to protect children from harmful materials and to protect their First Amendment right to access materials. Inevitably, a great deal of individual discretion will be required in applying library policies addressing issues of privacy for children as applied on a case-by-case basis.

COMPELLING INTEREST STANDARD TO PROTECT CHILDREN

A standard by which the government measures its duty to protect children is the "compelling interest" standard. This standard makes the protection of children from harmful material more important than the protection of their First Amendment rights. Courts have long recognized that children are not intellectually or emotionally prepared to handle matters that adults may handle. This includes psychologically and intellectually inappropriate material. In *FCC v. Pacifica*[37] and *Ginsberg*,[38] both courts enunciated this position by stating: "There is a compelling interest in protecting the physical and psychological well being of minors. This interest extends to shielding minors from the influence of literature that is not obscene by adult standards." In *New York v. Ferber*, the court held that libraries have a duty to the public for the way they deal with children. As the U.S. Supreme Court has stated: "It is evident beyond the need for elaboration that a State's interest in safeguarding the physical and psychological well-being of a minor is compelling . . . the legislative judgment, as well as the judgment found in relevant literature, is that the use of children as subjects of pornographic materials is harmful to the physiological, emotional, and mental health of the child. The judgment, we think, easily passes muster under the First Amendment."[39]

In *ACLU v. Johnson*,[40] the court found that in New Jersey that which is obscene for a minor may not necessarily be obscene by adult standards.

OLDER CHILDREN ARE ENTITLED TO GREATER ACCESS THAN YOUNGER CHILDREN

Historically courts have recognized that older children are entitled to greater access to reading materials than younger children, and that the reverse is also true, that they should not be restricted to the same access as younger children. The library cannot be responsible for the reading habits of a child. Many families have instituted a parent-child reading program in which the parent reads the book along with the child so that they may discuss the reading material. Some libraries have also encouraged such a program. Libraries cannot act as substitute parents and ultimately it is the parents who must supervise their child's reading selections. The questions with which libraries must grapple is what access the parents will have to the child's reading records so that they can supervise the reading materials. Libraries are once again called upon to perform a balancing act worthy of a circus tightrope walker. On one side of the issue, libraries want to protect the confidentiality of the child's records, but on the other, they want the parents to be responsible for the material to which the child chooses to have access. These difficult policy issues are left to the individual libraries to negotiate with proper guidance from their local counsel as to the state's statutes regarding library patron privacy, parental rights to access children's records, and any specific statutes on children's library records that the state may have adopted.

Kreimer v. Morristown[41] is an important case for librarians on many levels. In this case a homeless man challenged the constitutionality of city library rules regarding the use of the library and rules that governed a visitor's behavior in the library. One of the many holdings in this case centered on the right to access of information. The court, in quoting from another case, reiterated: "[i]t is the right of the public to receive suitable access to social, political, esthetic, moral, and other ideas and experiences which is crucial here."[42] Children were not an issue in this case but certainly their right to access of information must be a factor in any library policy and its application to the concept of the confidentiality of the library records of a child.

Courts have historically recognized that older adolescents have a right to access information that is appropriate for their age group and made a distinction between appropriate material for younger children and appropriate material for adolescents.

In *Commonwealth v. American Booksellers Ass'n,*[43] the court refused to limit access to this work for some minors when other minors could benefit from the access to this work. The court noted that when material is "found to have a serious literary, artistic, political or scientific value for a legitimate minority of *older adolescents,* then it cannot be said to lack such value for the entire class of juveniles taken as a whole."

Other cases have upheld the right of access for older minors by not restricting them to the access of younger minors.

In *American Booksellers Ass'n v. Virginia,*[44] the federal court in Georgia held that a "harmful to minors" restriction could not constitutionally be applied to material in which "any reasonable minor, including a 17-year-old, would find serious value."

In *American Booksellers v. Webb,*[45] the court found that older minors have First Amendment rights and struck a state law that would have restricted their access to the Internet.

Each library must engage in careful deliberation of the risks and rewards of protecting the confidentiality of its minor patrons. This protection may begin at a specific age such as fourteen. If the library decides this is a right that should be protected, it should adopt a formal policy that children of a specific age shall have the privilege of confidentiality of their records. The library should further decide whether this confidentiality should be maintained if the parent is held responsible for fines the child may have incurred. The parent should be requested to sign a statement upon the registration of their children for their own library cards indicating that the parents accept the policy or refuse the policy.

CONCLUSION

There is a federal statute that protects library patron records. Some states have statutes protecting patron library patron records. There is a federal statute that protects the records of library patrons with regard to video tapes but no federal statute protects the privacy and confidentiality of patrons' library records. It is important to know the laws of your state. It is also important to have and to communicate an explicit library policy on every facet of the library's facilities and to educate all employees of the library on patron privacy. Each employee should be instructed to contact the designated library authority upon the presentation of a subpoena, court order of search warrant, and if such authority is absent, to contact the attorney for the library.

Clear library policy on patron privacy in every accessible facet of the library is more important than ever, as is the application of that policy to patron use of library facilities.

APPENDICES ONLINE

The American Library Association's (ALA) Code of Ethics

American Library Association Bill of Rights

Association of College and Research Librarians Standards and Guidelines

United States Freedom of Information Act

ALA Policy on Confidentiality of Library Records, *http://www.ala.org/alaorg/policy manual/libserve.html*

American Library Association OIF/Privacy, *http://www.ala.org/alaorg/oif/privacy. html*

Privacy Rights Clearinghouse, *http://www.privacyrights.org*

Confidentiality of Personally Identifiable Information, *http://www.ala.org/Template. cfm?Section=Interpretations&Template=/ContentManagement/ContentDisplay. cfm&ContentID=31883*

About Library Users, *www.ala.org/alaorg/oif/pol_user.html*

Privacy: An Interpretation of the Library Bill of Rights Policy on Confidentiality of Library Records, *www.ala.org/alaorg/oif/pol_conf.html*

Suggested Procedures for Implementing Policy on the Confidentiality of Library Records, *www.ala.org/alaorg/oif/sigpolcn.html*

Freedom to Read Statement, *www.ala.org/alaorg/oif/freeread.html*

Libraries: An American Value, *www.ala.org/alaorg/oif/lib_val.html*

State confidentiality statute, *www.ala.org/alaorg/oif/privacy.html*

Newly revised Library Principles for a Networked World, *www.ala.org/oitp/prin itro.html*

ALA Guidelines Coping with Law Enforcement Inquiry, *http://www.ala.org/ Content/NavigationMenu/Our_Association/Offices/Intellectual_Freedom3/Intelec tual_Freedom_Issues/Confidentiality_and_Coping_with_Law_Enforcement_Inqui ries.htm*

STATE LAWS ONLINE

The ALA link to individual state laws regarding confidentiality of library records is at *http://www.ala.org/alaorg/oif/pol_conf.html.*

While the right to patron library privacy must be inferred from the Constitution, some states have specific statutes protecting this right. Each library must consult its own state's laws to determine its legal responsibility with regard to patron's privacy and confidentiality of library records.

NOTES

1. No. 03-7015 consolidated with 03-7053 U.S. Court of Appeals for the District of Columbia (decided Dec. 19, 2003).

2. Ashcroft v. Free Speech Coalition, 535 U.S. 234 (2002), 198 F.3d 1083, affirmed.

3. The "void-for-vagueness" doctrine was originally constructed to invalidate penal statutes that do not "define the criminal offense with sufficient definiteness that ordinary people can understand what conduct is prohibited," Kolender v. Lawson, 461 U.S. 352, 357, 103 S.Ct. 1855, 1858, 75 L.Ed.2d 903 (1983). A vagueness challenge will succeed when a party does not have actual notice of what activity the statute prohibits. Yet the vagueness doctrine, unlike the overbreadth doctrine, additionally seeks to ensure fair and non-discriminatory application of the laws, thus reflecting its roots in the due process clause. If a court finds repulsive laws that endow officials with undue discretion to determine whether a given activity contravenes the law's mandates, it will be held to be "void for vagueness." *See* Fallon, Making Sense of Overbreadth, 100 YALE L.J. 853 (1991). *See generally* P. Bator, D. Meltzer, P. Mishkin, & D. Shapiro, Hart & Wechsler, THE FEDERAL COURTS AND THE FEDERAL SYSTEM, 184–88 (3d Ed. 1988).

4. Village of Hoffman Estates, 455 U.S. 489, 498 (1982).

5. *See* Olmstead v. United States, 277 U.S. 430 (1928), which addresses the issue of privacy and wiretapping of phone conversations. "The makers of our Constitution . . . sought to protect Americans in their beliefs, their thoughts, their emotions and their sensations. They conferred, as against the government, the right to be let alone."

6. 277 U.S. 438 (1928), 48 S. Ct 465.

7. Video and Library Privacy Protection Act of 1988, Senate 2361, 100th Cong., 2d Sess., not passed.

8. American Library Association, *State Privacy Laws Regarding Library Records*, <http://www.ala.org/alaorg/oif/stateprivacylaws.html> (accessed May 25, 2002).

9. FERPA, 20 U.S.C § 1232, 34 C.F.R. part 99.

10. Uniform laws are merely proposals made to states for standard laws. The state legislature has the option to adopt them, reject them, or adopt part, reject part, or modify parts of them.

11. Freedom of Information Act, 5 U.S.C. § 552.

12. H.R. Rep. 100–199, Committee on Government Operations, 100th Cong., 1st Sess.

13. Freedom of Information Act, 5 U.S.C. § 552, as amended by Public Law No. 104-231, 110 Stat. 3048. H.R. Rep. 100–199, Committee on Government Operations, No. 93–876, 100th Cong., 1st Sess. 3 (1974). [To accompany H.R. 12471.]

14. Brown v. Johnston, 28 N.W.2d 510 (Iowa Sup. 1983).

15. 418 U.S. 683 (1974).

16. Attempts to gain access to patron records may come from many different sources—from a parent wanting to know what his/her child is reading to a faculty member trying to find out whether a student has checked out a book she or he is suspected of plagiarizing. These inquiries can be easily handled by the librarian who has a confidentiality policy or statement to show and explain to the individual. The more troublesome ones usually come from law enforcement officers. The American Library Association Intellectual Freedom Committee has developed "Guidelines for Coping With Law Enforcement Visits" [8] <www.ala.org/Content/Navigation Menu/Our_Association/Offices/Intellectual_Freedom3/Intellectual_Freedom_Issues/confiden tiality_and_coping_with_Law_Enforcement_Inquiries.htm>, which include the following recommended steps to take when law enforcement agents visit:

- If a library staff person is approached by a law enforcement agent requesting information on a library user, he/she should immediately ask for identification and refer the agent to the library administrator or responsible officer of the institution.

- The library administrator should explain the library's policy or, if lacking an internal one, ALA's confidentiality policy, and the state confidentiality law. Most important, the library administrator should state that personally identifiable information about library users is not available under any circumstances, except when a proper court order has been presented.

- In response to appeals to patriotism (e.g., "A good American wants to help us."), explain that as patriotic, good citizens, library administrators and library staff value First Amendment freedoms and the corresponding privacy rights of library users.

- Compliance with FBI requests made without a warrant or court order is strictly voluntary. **The library administrator must stress to agents that maintaining professional ethics and complying with state law are principles which are not "voluntarily" surrendered.**

- It is illegal to lie to a federal law enforcement officer. Without a court order, however, the FBI or other law enforcement body has no independent authority to compel cooperation with an investigation or to require answers to questions (other than name and address of the person to whom the agent is speaking). The best thing to say to an agent who has asked for confidential information is, "I'm sorry, but my professional ethics (and state law where applicable) prohibit me from responding to your request."

- Notify the American Library Association's Office for Intellectual Freedom (312–944–6780 or 1–800–545–2433) 50 East Huron Street, Chicago, IL 60611. [9]

The library administrator should follow these procedures:

- Meet with the law enforcement agent and a library colleague in the library.

- Be cordial. Explain that libraries support the work of law enforcement agencies, and their ethical standards are not intended to be obstructionist; rather, affirm the importance of confidentiality of personally identifiable information in the context of First Amendment rights. Should an agent be persistent, state again that information is disclosed only subject to a proper court order and that the library's governing body firmly supports this policy, and terminate the interview.

- Report any threats or coercion to legal counsel. Repeated visits by law enforcement agents who have been informed that records will be released only upon receipt of a proper court order may constitute harassment or other grounds for legal action. Seek the advice of legal counsel on whether relief from such action should be requested from the appropriate court.

- Immediately refer any subpoena received to the appropriate legal officer for review. (See sample subpoena in Appendix A.) If there is any defect in the subpoena, including its form, the manner in which it was served upon the library, the breadth of its request for documents, or insufficient evidence that a showing of good cause has been made to a court, legal counsel will advise on the proper manner to resist the subpoena. [A]

- Repeat the entire process, should the party requesting the information be required to submit a new subpoena.

- Through legal counsel, insist that any defects in the subpoena be cured before records are released. Insist that the subpoena be limited strictly to require release of only specifically identified records or documents.

- Together with the library's legal counsel, review any information which may be produced in response to such a subpoena prior to the release of the information. Construe the subpoena strictly and exclude any information which is arguably not covered by a proper subpoena.

- Ask the court, if disclosure is required, for an order that any information produced be kept strictly confidential and that it be used only for the limited purpose of the particular case at hand. Ask that access to it be restricted to the agents working on the case. Sometimes these terms may be agreed to informally by the party seeking the information, but even if such an agreement is reached, ALA strongly recommends that this agreement be entered as a formal order of the court. If there is such a formal order, anyone breaking the terms of the protective order might be subject to a sanction for contempt of court. [B]

- Keep in mind that a polite but firm response is the best way to deflect attempts at persuasion, coercion or misguided appeals to patriotism. When a law enforcement officer realizes that he/she simply will not succeed by such methods, most likely he/she will abandon the effort and take the appropriate course of action by proving to the proper court that he/she has good cause to receive access to such confidential information.

- Be prepared to communicate with local news media. Develop a public information statement which may be distributed to interested members of the public and law enforcement officers detailing the principles behind confidentiality. Such a statement should include an explanation of the chilling effect on First Amendment rights which public access to personally identifiable information about library users would cause. Emphasize that the First Amendment protections of free speech and a free press guarantee the corresponding freedom to read what is written, hear what is spoken, and view other forms of expression. The protection of privacy preserves these rights. An individual's reading habits cannot be equated with his or her character or beliefs. The First Amendment does not apply only to pre-approved or popular beliefs. The First Amendment guarantees the right to hold and espouse unpopular beliefs and ideas. The First Amendment protects dissent. The First Amendment protects against the imposition of a state or community-approved orthodoxy as well as an enforced conformity of expression and belief. The First Amendment protects all Americans' rights to read and view information and decide for themselves their points of view and opinions.

The freedom to read and to consider all types of information without fear of government or community reprisal or ostracism is crucial to the preservation of a free democratic society. The freedom to read fosters and encourages responsible citizenship and open debate in the marketplace of ideas.

The library is a central resource where information and differing points of view are available. Library users must be free to use the library, its resources and services without government interference. [10]

[A] Usually, a motion for a protective order, or to suppress or quash the subpoena, is the vehicle used to resist. A showing of good cause is normally made in a hearing on such a motion, and the court hearing will decide whether good cause exists for the subpoena or if it is defective, and will then decide whether or not the library must comply. Be aware that some states require the unsuccessful party on a motion for a protective order or to quash a subpoena to pay the costs for responding to and hearing such a motion. Check with legal counsel on this issue as well.

[B] Legal counsel should draft the particular protective language, and the library administrator should review it to be sure it adequately protects the information to be produced.

[8] "Confidentiality and Coping with Law Enforcement Inquiries; Guidelines for the Library Administrator," (Chicago: Intellectual Freedom Committee, American Library Association, July 1, 1989) in Judith F. Krug and Anne E. Levinson. Memorandum on Developments Regarding the FBI's Library Awareness Program Since the 1989 Midwinter Meeting, 15 August 1989.

[9] Ibid., 2–3.

[10] Ibid., 3–5.

17. Confidentiality of Patrons' Records, Ark. Code 13–2-701 et seq.

18. NY CLS CPLR § 4509 (2001).

Library records, which contain names or other personally identifying details regarding the users of public, free association, school, college and university libraries and library systems of this state, including but not limited to records related to the circulation of library materials, computer database searches, interlibrary loan transactions, reference queries, requests for photocopies of library materials, title reserve requests, or the use of audio-visual materials, films or records, shall be confidential and shall not be disclosed except that such records may be disclosed to the extent necessary for the proper operation of such library and shall be disclosed upon request or consent of the user or pursuant to subpoena, court order or where otherwise required by statute.

Add, L 1982, ch. 14, § 1, *eff.* Mar 10, 1982; *amd.*, L 1988, ch 112, § 1, *eff.* June 13, 1988. The 1988 Act deleted "Records related to the circulation of library materials." Section heading, *amd.*, L 1988, ch. 112, § 1, *eff.* June 13, 1988. The 1988 Act deleted at fig. 1 "circulation."

19. NYCP CPLR § 4509; In the Matter of Quad/Graphics v. Southern Adirondack Library System, 664 N.Y.S.2d 225, 228 (Sup. 1997).

20. Quad/Graphics v. Southern Adirondack Library System, 174 Misc. 2d 291, 664 N.Y.S.2d 225 (1997).

21. 20 U.S.C. § 1232g.

22. *Id.*

23. 20 U.S.C. § 1232g(a)(4)(i) and (ii).

24. *See* United States Department of Justice, Computer Crime and Intellectual Property Section, *Field Guidance on New Authorities that Relate to Computer Crime and Electronic Evidence Enacted in the USA Patriot Act of 2001*, <http://www.usdoj.gov/criminal/cybercrime/PatriotAct.htm> (accessed March 3, 2002).

25. U.S.A. PATRIOT Act, Title 15, Chapter 41, Subchapter III, Section 1681u, Title 18, Part I, Chapter 121, Section 2709.

26. U.S.A. PATRIOT Act, § 212.

27. U.S.A. PATRIOT Act, H.R. 3162, Title II, Section 215, amending the Foreign Intelligence Surveillance Act (FISA), Title V, § 501(a)(1), <http://leahy.senate.gov/press/200110/USA.pdf> (accessed March 3, 2002).

28. ALA Policy on Confidentiality of Records, February 22, 2004, <www.ala.org>.

29. Adopted by the ALA Council, June 28, 1998, <www.ala/oif/ethics.html>.

30. ALA Policy Manual, 54.15, Code of Ethics, Point Number 3. Adopted by the ALA Intellectual Freedom Committee, January 9, 1983, revised January 11, 1988.

31. Tinker v. Des Moines Sch. Dist., 393 U.S. 503, 506 (1969).

32. ALA Library Bill of Rights, <www.ala/oif/pol_conf.html>.

33. 422 U.S. 211, 212–13 (1975).

34. 321 U.S. 158, 166 (1944).

35. 268 U.S. 510 (1925).

36. 262 U.S. 390 (1923).

37. 438 U.S. 726, 749 (1978).

38. 390 U.S. 629, (1968).

39. 458 U.S. 747, 756-58 (1982) (citations and internal quotation marks omitted).

40. 4 F. Supp. 2d 1029, 1031 (D.N.M. 1998), *aff'd* by the 10th Circuit, No. 98–2199, November 2, 1999.

41. 958 F.2d 1242, 1251 (3d Cir. 1992).

42. Kreimer v. Morristown, *citing* Red Lion Broadcasting Co. v. Federal Communications Commission, 395 U.S 367, 390, 89 S. Ct. 1794, 1806, 23 S.Ed. 2d 371 (1969).

43. 372 S.E.2d 618, 624 (Va. 1988), *cert. denied,* 494 U.S. 1056 (1990).

44. 882 F.2d 125, 127 (4th Cir. 1989).

45. 919 F.2d 1493, 1504–05 & n.20 (11th Cir. 1990), *cert. denied* 500 U.S. 942 (1991).

5

COPYRIGHT IN THE LIBRARY

The primary objective of copyright is not to reward the labor of authors,
but to promote the Progress of Science and useful Arts.
—The United States Supreme Court

The mission of libraries is to ensure access. . . . The nature of copyright
is to restrict access. There's a real tension there.
—Miriam Nesbitt, legislative counsel, ALA,
office of government relations.

The law of copyright and the purpose of libraries are intertwined and govern
one of the most important functions of society—the transmission of knowledge. Copyright law attempts to balance the rights of society with the rights of
the creator of the material, and the library must be aware of the role of copyright as it shares in the important function of the transmission of knowledge.

Because copyright decisions are made on a case-by-case basis, the job of
librarians is made more difficult. There are no strict lines of law delineating
copyright issues. The law of copyright must be understood and applied to
individual situations by the librarian, the attorney, the courts, and by publishers. In the application of the law of copyright by the public library the best
you can do is simply the best you can do. You must be aware of the law and
its historical precedence in application to libraries, and you must be vigilant
about modifications to the law and to its interpretation, because the law of
copyright grows and changes.

The vast majority of laws impact society with their stated limitations. In
rare instances, what is not stated in the law defines the law's effect. Having
one designated copyright officer in a library serves the library's best interests
because copyright can be difficult to apply in all instances.

Section 106 of the Copyright Act is entitled and refers to "Exclusive rights in copyrighted works." This list of exclusive rights does *not* prohibit the loaning and sharing of the copyrighted material. The owner of this material may loan it and may share it, unless such loaning and sharing is initially restricted by an agreement entered into between the purchaser of the materials, such as a licensing agreement. Libraries are able to loan materials based upon the unstated rights of the author or the copyright owner.

Copyright is generally viewed as the right of the author. It is important to understand that most copyrights are not owned by the author, but by the publisher who contracted with the author to publish the material or by the employer who hired the creator of the material for the purpose of creating the material.

For each of the following issues, determining an original work of authorship, a tangible medium of expression, the author or co-author, the employee or who has created a work for hire, the rights the copyright holder has, and what can be copyrighted, there are statutes that govern their interpretation and case law that attempts to define the statute. It is common in copyright law to find cases that reach opposite conclusions. Often this is because the law of copyright has changed through the years; matters that the courts once refused to provide the benefit of copyright protection are now protected.

In a broad sense, all that is necessary to obtain a copyright is the creation of original material that has been reduced to a tangible medium of expression. The protection of a copyright, however, is not as simple; it can involve litigation that is both vexatious and costly. The federal copyright statute is found in Title 17 of the United States Code. These statutes are brief, direct, and straightforward. It is in their interpretation and application to specific factual circumstances that courts and judges often disagree.

FIRST SALE DOCTRINE—PHYSICAL PROPERTY ONLY

The first sale doctrine enables the existence of libraries, used book stores, and video rental stores. The history of the first sale doctrine is the history of copyright itself and developed as case law prior to statutory codification. Formalized by legislation in 1976 as Section 109 and supported by Section 102 of the Copyright Act, the doctrine is framed as a limitation on the copyright owner's exclusive right to distribute works; it entitles the owner of *a particular copy* of a work to "sell or otherwise dispose of" that particular copy *without the permission of the copyright holder.* The first sale doctrine does not restrict the copyright owner's exclusive right to *make* copies or to authorize the making of copies. The first sale doctrine applies exclusively to lawfully made or authorized copies and exclusively to the "owner" of such copies.

Obviously, copyrighted material is purchased every day, and the majority of library collections consist of copyrighted material. It is fundamental that the purchase of a book that is protected by copyright does not give to the purchaser the right to reproduce that book and claim that it is their creation, and in that claim, to apply for the protection of copyright. The purchaser may read and share the book with their family, friends, or worst enemies. The purchaser may place it in a bookstore window or hang it on the wall as a decoration. The purchaser may tear out the pages and frame them. The purchaser may not, however, copy the content. The copyright owner retains those rights. If the copyright has expired, however, the material may be used freely. No one must remit fees to perform a Shakespearean play or to reproduce Emily Dickinson's poems. This can be done freely and without concern of claims of copyright infringement.

WHY IS THE LAW OF COPYRIGHT IMPORTANT TO PUBLIC LIBRARIES?

It is difficult to imagine a world in which a book could be read only by its owner; it could not be shared. This limitation would be impossible to enforce. Copyright laws are not so restrictive as to deny the owner of the book the right to share that book with another. It is obvious, and sometimes the obvious should be stated, that a book may be purchased and read by as many people as choose to pick up the book and read it. It may be given to a friend, who in turn gives it to a friend, who in turn leaves it on an airplane, where it in turn is read again, where it is taken home and delivered and sold to a used book store, where it again is sold, and read again. This is all accomplished within the bounds of the law of copyright. It is this same concept that allows libraries to purchase a book and lend it again and again to patrons. This is something that is simply taken for granted by the public and by librarians. There is no federal statute that allows this to happen. What is also important to understand is that there is no federal statute that prohibits this from happening.

The federal law of copyright imposes restrictions. It does not create possibilities. It does not impose a restriction upon the sharing of material. It does, however, impose a restriction on the copying of material. This is a simple but important concept. While the federal law of copyright does not impose this restriction, the purveyor of the material, the publisher, may impose further restrictions that are greater than the law of copyright. This is typically done with digitized material; this restriction is known as a license. Licenses are covered in a separate chapter.

Libraries must observe copyright laws in the administrative duties of the library, in its collection, and to a limited extent, in the use its patrons make of its collection. It would be unconscionable to hold a library responsible for the extended violations of copyright law of its patrons, and there are simple steps a library may take to protect itself.

WHAT CAN BE COPYRIGHTED

Section 102 of the Copyright Act defines what can be copyrighted. This is a simple and straightforward list. The statute is short and is included below:

(a) Copyright protection subsists, in accordance with this title, in original works of authorship fixed in any tangible medium of expression, now known or later developed, from which they can be perceived, reproduced, or otherwise communicated, either directly or with the aid of a machine or device. Works of authorship include the following categories:
(1) literary works;

(2) musical works, including any accompanying words;

(3) dramatic works, including any accompanying music;

(4) pantomimes and choreographic works;

(5) pictorial, graphic, and sculptural works;

(6) motion pictures and other audiovisual works;

(7) sound recordings; and

(8) architectural works.

(b) In no case does copyright protection for an original work of authorship extend to any idea, procedure, process, system, method of operation, concept, principle, or discovery, regardless of the form in which it is described, explained, illustrated, or embodied in such work.[1]

Most materials can be copyrighted. The notable exceptions are slogans,[2] titles, facts, and factual tables such as weight tables or weight calculators. Matters in the public domain (on which the protection of copyright has expired), slogans, what is known as "hot news," and unrecorded extemporaneous performances cannot be copyrighted.

This seems straightforward. However, there are still very real issues as to what can and cannot be copyrighted. For example, FatWallet, a comparison-shopping Web site that compared prices at the four leading retailers, WalMart, Target, Best Buy, and Staples, was served with a notice letter pursuant to the Digital Millennium Copyright Act advising them that these prices were the subject of copyright and requesting that they cease from publishing these prices. Wal-Mart issued a subpoena to FatWallet pursuant to the DMCA, claiming that its sales prices were protected information. The U.S. Supreme Court has ruled that facts cannot be copyrighted. WalMart withdrew its subpoena requesting information regarding the identity of the poster of the WalMart sales prices.

What materials can be the subject of a copyright? Justice Oliver Wendell Holmes, defining what could be subject to copyright, said, "Personality always contains something unique. It expresses its singularity even in handwriting, and a very modest grade of art has in it something irreducible, which is one man's alone. That something he may copyright unless there is a restriction in the words of the act."[3]

Consequently, the fact that a work is copyrighted does not import merit or value to that work. The legal protection of copyright does not invoke a symbol of quality or merit. Congress explicitly stated that its standard for copyright protection did not include any requirement of "aesthetic merit." It also specified that the "term 'literary works' does not connote any criterion of literary merit or qualitative value."[4]

While it has not always been the case, original works are protected by copyright law as soon as they are created in a tangible medium.

GENEALOGY AND COPYRIGHT

Libraries are often used for genealogy research. Whether genealogy compilations can be copyrighted is an issue patrons raise. Facts cannot be copyrighted, nor can "lists or tables taken from public documents or other common sources."

The compilation of these dates and places of birth, marriage, and death listed and published cannot be copyrighted. These facts are in the public domain and the straightforward listing of these facts is not protected. The source of these facts is in the public domain. There is no creativity in assembling these facts.

However, if the creator has inserted detailed histories, personal information on the parties, or descriptions of the lives of the parties, or edited the facts in some fashion, this modified information is protected by copyright. The U.S. National Genealogical Society has lobbied Congress for protection of genealogical compilations that include such material.

Some genealogical data can be protected by the use of the concept of "originality in selecting" records included in a genealogical database. The originality in selecting the records indicates that the resource does not include every available record. The provider has exercised discretion in the selection of records. This provides protection to the provider, notwithstanding the fact that the original data is in the public domain.

Further, the use of the producer's electronic search capabilities places restrictions on the use to which the patron may make of the database output. This limitation falls into the category of licensing, rather than copyright, and is dealt with in a later chapter.

IMMORAL WORKS AND COPYRIGHT

Courts have noted that material that may not appear to have merit to the court or the community at large may have value and merit to some segment of our society. After a history of refusing to protect "immoral" works by the right of copy, all original works reduced to a tangible medium of expression without regard for their aesthetic merit or value are eligible for protection. Protection is no longer awarded based on the morality of a work. Courts have removed themselves from the business of judging what is moral from what is immoral. They must now evaluate obscenity, which is defined differently than morality.

The issue of morality has influenced copyright decisions in the area of dance. Historically, dance was an artistic medium that was not afforded the right of copy unless it was a part of a drama or dramatical musical production, or told a story. It was not until 1976 that abstract dance became eligible for protection by copyright.

In 1866, a French ballet troupe found itself stranded in New York with no work and no money for passage home. At the same time a theater owner found himself with a cancelled production for his theater. The first blockbuster musical extravaganza was born, *Black Crook*. This production, a combination of ballet with its daring and skimpy costumes and a gothic melodrama, which allegedly had little plot, was filled with one production number after another, and it ran for four years.

Black Crook was presented 204 performances in London, toured into the 1930s, and was revived on Broadway 15 times. During this time, its spectacular and stunning success generated an imitator, *Black Rook*. Admitting the two productions' similarities, a court found in 1867 that *Black Rook* copied *Black Crook* and was found to be "a mere colorable imitation" of *Black Crook*. The court found that only "slight alterations in the dialogues and incidents" were made, and despite minor technical differences, "the result is so nearly the same as to produce the impression that they are identical." In spite of the fact that copyright infringement was found, no damages were awarded because the court believed the spectacle was immoral and it was not the intent of Congress to protect immorality under the copyright laws.

This position was presented again as late as 1963. Copyright protection to a military striptease audition number for a stage version of *Gypsy*[5] was denied. The *Dane* court stated that an audition number did not tend to promote the progress of science or the useful arts because it contained nothing of a literary, dramatic, or musical character. The *Dane* court suggested that to qualify for protection, the number would have to elevate, cultivate, inform, or improve the moral or intellectual natures of the audience.

Early courts did not view works of choreography as sufficiently moral to warrant copyright protection. The widely held view that dance was immoral was one reason why choreography did not share the elevated artistic status of other fine arts that lawmakers deemed worthy of copyright protection.

Although the 1909 Copyright Act provided copyright protection for abstract musical works and paintings, it excluded the abstract works of choreographers. It is important to note that *Playboy Magazine* was copyrighted at this time.

George Balanchine is considered to be the father of American ballet. In 1976, after a heart attack, he consulted with his attorney to draft his will. In discussions with his lawyer, he expressed the view that his ballets could not be copyrighted and could not be bequeathed. His attorney responded that in fact the laws had just changed to be effective in 1978. George Balanchine copyrighted his ballets and bequeathed individual ballets to his friends, former wives, and lovers. Upon his death, the George Balanchine Trust was established to administer the performance of his ballets with the goal of maintaining their quality. It had taken 200 years, but ballet was finally accorded the same protection of copyright as other arts.

MORAL RIGHTS AND THE VISUAL ARTISTS RIGHTS ACT

The Visual Artists Rights Act (VARA), adopted in 1990 in the United States, granted two rights to authors of visual works: the right of attribution and the right of integrity. The right of attribution allows an author to prevent misattribution of a work and to require that the authorship of the work not be disclosed if the author desires to remain anonymous. The right of integrity bars intentional distortion, mutilation, or other modification of a work, if that distortion is likely to harm the author's reputation. It also prevents the destruction of any work of recognized stature.[6]

The standard of the courts in judging works worthy of copyright based upon their morality is long since past. However, this standard should not be confused with moral rights. This term is used in the law of copyright internationally where these rights existed before they were adopted in the United States. Copyright is an economic right. Moral rights are a personal right given statutory standing to creators of visual works. Generally, these may not be assigned by the creator to a third party, although there are some exceptions to infringement under the Act.

Rights of attribution may impact library cataloging practices. Entries should acknowledge all authors in works of multiple authorship; this includes illustrators and photographers who contributed to a work. Their contribution is also entitled to acknowledgment. Where photographs and artworks are used in library promotional material or publications, the photographer or artist must be acknowledged. The permission to reproduce a work must include their contribution.

The right of integrity protects works from being treated in a way that is prejudicial to the author's reputation by materially altering, distorting, or mutilating the work. Some examples of infringement from overseas jurisdictions include altering the size of drawings and changing the color of artworks in publications, morphing images and adapting graphs for Web sites, altering a building without the permission of the architect, and moving a work of art from the place where it was specifically designed to hang, without the artist's consent.

Creators may consent to acts which would otherwise infringe their rights. There is a defense that the infringing act is reasonable in all the circumstances. Remedies range from a public apology to injunctions and damages.

VARA preempts state laws that are more restrictive than the federal law. However some states have granted broader rights than VARA, creating greater limitation and duties than those enunciated in VARA. States that have adopted these laws are California and New York, which have created model laws followed by other states. Those following the California model are Connecticut, Massachusetts, Pennsylvania, and Rhode Island. Louisiana, Maine, and New Jersey follow the New York model. Nevada, South Dakota, and Utah grant limited rights.

THE IDEA AND THE EXPRESSION OF THE IDEA

The expression of an idea is protected by copyright law. The idea itself is not protected by copyright law. For example, Einstein's theory of relativity, $E = MC^2$, is not protected by copyright law. This idea is free for society to adopt and use. Einstein's book, *The Special and General Theory of Relativity*, in which he described theses theories, was subject to copyright protection. To protect his theories would inhibit society's progress. Society must be free to use and build upon his theories of relativity. However, his choice of words, composition, and the organization of the theories in his book are protected by copyright.

In the clothing industry, a dress is the idea and that idea is not subject to copyright protection. That is why within days of the Academy Awards, copies of appealing dresses worn by nominees, presenters, and winners can be found in clothing stores. A drawing that a fashion designer might make for a potential customer would be protected by copyright law while the actual dress would not be protected.

The very act of publishing a book on science of the useful arts is to communicate to the world the useful knowledge that it contains. To copyright the knowledge itself would serve to frustrate knowledge, and would impede the development of society.

RESOURCES FOR THE BLIND AND LEARNING IMPAIRED

An exception is made to the copyright law to allow services to be provided to the blind and learning impaired. Recorded books may be provided to the blind from service organizations. These recordings do not violate copyright law. Reading and Radio Resource *(www.readingresource.org)* serves children and adults who are either visually or physically disabled or learning differenced. Listeners may choose from over 2,500 catalog titles listed in their catalog or can request that materials be recorded. Recordings are currently provided on either a standard two-track cassette or CD-ROM (MP3 format), which the listener may keep. Any child, in grades one through twelve, who qualifies for Special Education services, in either public, private, or home-school setting, may receive state-adopted textbooks, as well as any of their supplementary classroom and outside reading, in an audio format. This also applies to students using English as a second language who are otherwise print impaired. Teachers may order books to be shipped directly to them. Reading and Radio Resource grants permission for these books to be duplicated for other students who are print impaired.

FACTS

Facts cannot be copyrighted. While the medium in which the facts exist, such as a biography, may be copyrighted, the facts themselves are not protected. Determining what is and is not a fact has not always been a simple matter. Generally speaking, classifications of facts are copyrighted. Using facts that appear in print is not a violation. Short news articles that merely report facts and do not represent an author's creativity may be reprinted, with attribution. The ingredients of a recipe are facts and these are not subject to copyright. However, the mechanics of combining the ingredients is a creative endeavor and this is copyrightable. Cookbooks are copyrightable.

The facts documenting any event may not be copyrighted, although the material in which the facts are found are copyrighted. Biographies are filled with facts and these facts may be reused. It is the manner in which the facts are combined, and the facts chosen to be included in the work by the author and the facts chosen to be excluded, the editing of facts, that makes a work copyrightable.

Collections of Facts

In order for a collection of facts to be protected, there must be some editorialization of those facts. There must be a process by which some facts are identified for the project. A telephone directory (white pages, *i.e.* subscriber information) is not protected by copyright. A telephone directory contains no editorialization—no subjectivity as to which names to include and which names not to include. A telephone directory is compiled without any of the creativity required for copyright protection as enunciated in the landmark decision *Feist Publications, Inc. v. Rural Telephone Service Co.*[7] Factual information, such as stock quotes, or scores, or other statistics for games, are not protected by copyright. That is not to say the factual information does not have value. There is important value to time-sensitive current factual information. Up-to-date information, such as athletic-event scores or stock prices, may require a large amount of time and effort to collect. This time-sensitive value is protected by the theory known as "hot news."

Because facts and news are not subject to copyright protection, some public libraries have assembled a collection of news.

Hot News or Hot Facts

While Hot News or Hot Facts are not protected by the law of copyright, state laws may serve to protect these facts. It is true that state copyright laws have been preempted by the federal copyright law. However, the theory of preemption does not prohibit states from enacting copyright laws that exceed the federal law of copyright. In other words, states may have protection that exceeds federal law. Hot News or Hot Facts laws are an example of this concept. To protect time-sensitive information, state laws regarding misappropriation can be used. This is known as the "hot news" doctrine. Under this doctrine, the collector of such time-sensitive information can stop competitors from copying his or her "hot news."

The "hot news" doctrine was first applied in *International News Service v. Associated Press.*[8] Here, the court found a misappropriation of "hot news" or news that was acquired first at an obvious cost.

To determine whether some collection of information was protected under this doctrine, the Court gave the following criteria:

1. the plaintiff generates or collects information at some cost or expense, or;

2. the value of the information is highly time-sensitive;

3. the defendant's use of the information constitutes free-riding on the plaintiff's costly efforts to generate or collect it;

4. the defendant's use of the information is in direct competition with a product or service offered by the plaintiff; and

5. the ability of the other parties to free-ride on the efforts of the plaintiff would so reduce the incentive to produce the product or service that its existence or quality would be substantially threatened.

This concept of "hot news" was extended to sporting events in the case of *NBA v. Motorola.*[9] In the NBA case, the Court ruled that the NBA had not shown any direct competitive effect by Motorola's use, nor had it shown that Motorola was having a "free ride" from the NBA's efforts. Motorola was able to continue transmitting sports statistics to pagers. Here, under federal copyright law, the *facts* of a professional sporting event may be appropriated by a commercial pager company and a commercial online service without infringing upon any rights of the professional sports league or the teams participating in the contest. States may not legislate to protect facts which are exempt from federal copyright protection unless those facts fall within a very limited "hot news" exception which might implicate a state law misappropriation claim with some very specific limitation.

Motorola transmitted live statistics on basketball games to pagers while the game was in progress. The NBA claimed that this violated the NBA's copyright to the game scores and other statistics, as well as their property rights on the games and their exclusive rights to broadcast the games. The 2nd Circuit Court ruled that basketball games, and similar athletic events, are not "original works of authorship" under copyright law, and so scores for basketball games are not protected by copyright.

CLASSIFICATIONS AND TAXONOMIES

While classifications and taxonomies seem archaic and abstract as represented by the cases that define them, they become very real in many small-town libraries where genealogy research is the hot topic. Stealing someone's genealogy research can cause feuds as grand as the Hatfield's and McCoy's. Understanding the roots of the law of classification can arm the librarian with the insight necessary to advise these feuding genealogists of works that are and are not protected.

The act of classification has been found to be a creative endeavor. The classifying of butterflies could be based on many categories. They could be grouped by their color, the shape of their wings, their feeding or breeding habits, their habitats, the attributes of their caterpillars, or by the sequence of their DNA; each scheme of classification could be expressed in multiple ways.

The act of classification of dental procedures has also been found to be a creative endeavor based on the possibilities for classification. Dental procedures could be classified by complexity, by the tools necessary to perform them, by the parts of the mouth involved, by the anesthesia employed, or any of a dozen different ways. It was found by the court that the descriptions of the dental procedures did not "merge with the facts" any more than a scientific description of butterfly attributes is part of a butterfly.[10]

The possibility for variations in classifications exist to an almost infinite degree. The final creation is made by the inclusion of facts chosen, the method of classification, and by the exclusion of facts. Taxonomy has been determined to be a "creation," not a "discovery." The world is not organized, but the taxonomist organizes it in various ways. For example, URLs could be classified as business, personal, or governmental. The decision to include specific URLs, while excluding others, belongs to the taxonomist and is governed by the creativity and originality of the taxonomist. The taxonomy is based in fact, and the taxonomist retains ample freedom to organize and describe the world in individual and creative ways.

PHOTOGRAPHS

While it is hard to think of photographs as hot, new technology, at one point they were on the cutting edge. This new form of technology was ultimately addressed by the law of copyright in both statutory form and case-law interpretation of copyright law. The categories of works protected by copyright have evolved through the years. Although the first photograph, "View from the Window at Gras," was taken by Joseph Nicéphore Niépce in Italy in 1826, it was not until 1865 that photos were added to the protected copyright category. In 1888, the hand-held box camera for portable use, the Kodak camera, was introduced to the world from Rochester, New York. The camera was pre-loaded with a film capable of one hundred exposures and, after shooting, the photographer returned the whole camera to the manufacturer for development and a reload.

Burrow-Giles v. Sarony was one of the first cases involving photography. Burrow-Giles sold 85,000 copies of a photo of Oscar Wilde taken by Sarony on Wilde's United States speaking tour. Burrow-Giles claimed that there was no creativity, no artistry involved in the photo and it was not entitled to copyright protection. The Supreme Court disagreed, and noted the posing, the clothing, and the expression of Oscar Wilde as evidence of originality.[11] Photos were from that time forward entitled to the protection of copyright.

EXTEMPORANEOUS WORKS

Because a prerequisite to the protection of federal copyright law is the requirement that works be fixed in a tangible medium of expression, extemporaneous works are not subject to protection by the federal law of copyright. Street-corner dancers who perform from the heart may not protect their choreography pursuant to federal copyright law if it is not recorded. Comics who perform extemporaneously may not protect their work by federal copyright law. Much choreography that is not reduced to a fixed form of expression is not protected by federal copyright law. Before the United States entered the Uruguay Round Treaty Agreements in 1994, live musical performances were not protected by the federal law of copyright. An unrecorded extemporaneous speech is also not protected by federal copyright law. Extemporaneous performances at libraries that are not recorded are not protected by copyright. However, should interviews or performances be recorded in any fashion, they are protected.

In recognition of this limitation, the state of California has enacted a statute that protects live unrecorded performances. These performances are not preempted by federal statute because they are not covered by federal statute. Here, where performance and performers have a home, California has stepped in to protect live performances, something not protected by federal statute.

California's statute clearly grants common-law copyright protection to improvisational performers. The statute provides that "the author of any original work of authorship that is not fixed in any tangible medium of expression shall receive exclusive ownership in the representation or expression thereof."[12]

ORAL LECTURES

Libraries are often the locus for oral lectures. While a faculty member's written lecture, if original, becomes protected by copyright when written down, the faculty member's oral delivery is not automatically protected from the infringement of copyright. The bar to protect oral lectures is quite high, and only occurs when the faculty member has taperecorded the extemporaneous lecture or the lecture is in some way fixed in a tangible medium of expression.

Regardless of any copyright protection a lecturer may have, a student is entitled automatically to copy the ideas, facts, and concepts in the lecture. Further, there exists in the student-teacher relationship an implied license that the student may take notes on the professor's lecture. If, however, lecture notes are distributed from a professor's lecture, the issue becomes slightly more complex. The issues are whether the student has created a derivative work or created a completely new work to which the student is entitled a right of copy.

A faculty member might also expressly license the use of the lecture by communicating oral and written instructions on the uses or restrictions applicable to the lecture. The faculty member should communicate those instructions prior to the start of the course.

FICTIONAL CHARACTERS

Characters are an extremely important and valuable intellectual property. While characters can be protected by copyright law, nowhere is it more important to recognize the dual protection afforded characters by both copyright law and trademark law. Characters that can be recognized number in the thousands. Superman, Spiderman, Barbie, Barney, Kermit, Miss Piggy, Bert, Ernie, Cookie Monster, Harry Potter, Winnie the Pooh, Tweety Bird, Charlie Brown, Lucy, Snoopy, even Captain Crunch, are all trademarked characters, and in many instances, they are copyrighted characters. If you purchase a poster of one of these characters, you may display it in your library. You may not, however, paint these characters on your wall. You may not interpret them by creating a pink Cookie Monster. Cookie Monster must remain blue unless his copyright owner decides to change his color. Millions of dollars have been spent creating and maintaining these characters. A pregnant Lucy, a tattooed Mickey Mouse, or a devilish Harry Potter would diminish the character that has been so professionally and expensively created and maintained.

Not all characters protected by trademark law are protected by copyright law and not all characters protected by copyright law are protected by trademark law. While it has not been conclusively decided at what point fictional characters should qualify for copyright protection, and there is an area of gray for some characters, for the visually depicted, well-known characters, the protection is much more clear. Fictional characters that are not depicted in a cartoon-like image are more difficult to protect because, although they appear in part of a copyrighted work, they survive independently of that work in other contexts. A movie character found in a novel, such as James Bond, can appear in a movie or a play in a completely different setting, plot, or style, or as a completely different actor.

In 1930, Judge Learned Hand determined in *Nichols* that fictional characters should receive copyright protection under a well-developed character test. Hand concluded that "the less developed the characters, the less they can be copyrighted."[13] In 1955, the Ninth Circuit Court challenged the well-developed character test in *Warner Bros. Pictures v. Columbia Broadcasting System*,[14] known as the "Sam Spade Case." The court held that most characters will not be afforded copyright protection. The rare character will qualify only if "the character really constitutes the story being told." If the character only serves as a "chessman in the game of telling the story," copyright protection will not be secured.

These two cases represent extremes in rulings defining fictional characters that are subject to the protection of copyright. Courts still struggle between Hand's more flexible, but overly broad, standard and the narrow definition of a fictional character found in the "Sam Spade" definition.

Although the tests may differ, the Central District of California has held that James Bond is a copyrightable character. In *Metro-Goldwyn-Mayer, Inc. v. American Honda Motor Co., Inc.*,[15] the court found that Honda infringed MGM's copyright in the James Bond character when it released a commercial featuring a Bond-like character called "James Bob" driving a Honda del Sol. The judge issued an injunction forcing Honda to give up its ad campaign and stated that "there is sufficient authority for the proposition that a plaintiff who holds copyrights in a film series acquires copyright protection as well for the expression of any significant characters portrayed therein. . . . Accordingly, Plaintiffs will likely satisfy the 'ownership' prong of the test." The owner of James Bond, therefore, has a valuable interest to protect.

Harry Potter is an example of a copyrighted character that could not be copied. Harry Potter, in addition to being a copyrighted character, is a trademarked character and these rights are licensed to two different companies in the United States. A review of the registry at the United States Patent and Trademark Office,[16] which can be accessed online, and a review of the Copyright Office,[17] which can also be accessed online, indicate the ownership of these rights.

WHAT IS THE PUBLIC DOMAIN?

Copyright protection does not last forever. That's why copyright is often called a "limited monopoly." When copyrights grow old and die, the works they protect fall into the public domain. The public domain, therefore, refers to works that are not protected by copyright. Subject to certain exceptions, public domain works may be freely copied or used in the creation of derivative works without permission or authorization of the former copyright owners.

Besides "expired" copyrights, the following categories of works are not eligible for copyright protection in the United States:

- U.S. government works (there are exceptions)
- state judicial opinions
- legislative enactments and other official documents
- unadorned ideas
- blank forms
- short phrases
- titles
- extemporaneous speeches
- unrecorded conversations

When you rely on the public-domain status of a work, it is important to make sure that the particular version you want to use is actually in the public domain. Later versions or adaptations (such as translations, revisions, or illustrated editions) of public-domain works may be protected by a separate copyright. Copyright in that later version relates to the fresh layer of creative material added by the second author. For example, the movie *The Wizard of Oz* with Judy Garland is protected by copyright, while the original version by Frank Baum is in the public domain. It is prudent to use only an original public-domain version, not a later copyrighted version, without permission or authorization. Because of state and federal unfair competition laws, appropriate disclaimers may also be necessary.

Although a work may be in the public domain for copyright purposes, other forms of protection may be present. For example, book titles and characters can serve as valid trademarks. Likewise, identifiable people may have the right to control the manner in which their name or likeness is used. Similarly, works such as databases may be protected under trade secret or contract law.

HOW TO DETERMINE IF A WORK IS IN THE PUBLIC DOMAIN

Knowing when a copyright expires allows you to take advantage of the abundance of material found in the public domain. Bear in mind, however, that different rules apply to works created before January 1, 1978, and to those created after this date. Pre-1978 works are governed by the 1909 Copyright Act, and may be protected for up to ninety-five years, provided that certain renewal formalities were followed. Works created after January 1, 1978, are protected under the 1976 Copyright Act for the life of the author plus seventy years.

To determine when a U.S. copyright will expire, you must know the answer to four questions:

- When was the work created?
- Who created the work? (An individual? Two or more individuals? An employee?)
- Is the author alive? If not, when did he or she die?
- When was the work registered or published?

If the work is a pre-1978 work, it may be necessary to determine whether the copyright owner filed a renewal copyright.

In 1999, the president signed into law the Sonny Bono Copyright Term Extension Act. Under the new law—which adds twenty years to most copyright terms—no new works will enter the public domain until 2019. Enacted to ensure adequate protection for U.S. works abroad, the new act restricts access to works published after 1922.

For works created on or after January 1, 1978, which were previously protected for the life of the author plus fifty years, the newly amended copyright term is now the life of the author plus seventy years. If two or more authors prepare a work as a joint work, the copyright will now expire seventy years after the death of the last surviving author. Copyright in works for hire, anonymous works, and works by pseudonym now last for 95 years from first publication, or 120 years from the date of creation, whichever expires earlier.

Works created before January 1, 1978, were previously protected for a total of seventy-five years, provided certain copyright renewal formalities were followed. The new law amends the Copyright Act to extend the term of protection for works currently in their renewal term from seventy-five years to ninety-five years. Under the new law, any work published—or registered—in 1922, went into the public domain on January 1, 1998. Works published in 1923, which would have otherwise fallen into the public domain on January 1, 1999, now remain protected until January 1, 2019. Therefore, any work published prior to 1923 is now in the public domain.

Period of Copyright

Works published prior to 1923 are in the public domain and, unless the work is a work for hire, the U.S. copyright has expired. Most works published after 1963 are protected by copyright. The gray area in determining whether a work is protected by copyright falls between 1923 and 1963. Because the law of perfecting a copyright by registration was different than it is now, and because specific notices and renewals were required for this perfection, materials published during this period may not always be protected by copyright. If they are not protected by copyright, they are in the public domain, and their use may be extensive and subject to the discretion of the user. For example, the movie *It's a Wonderful Life* is not protected by copyright because a renewal was not filed in time.

How to Trace Copyright Between 1923 and 1963

The U.S. Copyright Office is a division of the Library of Congress. This is where copyright is both registered and researched. Copyright may be traced from the following Web site: *www.copyright.gov*. However, tracing a copyright is not an exact science and the results may not be conclusive. The Web site offers online records of registrations and ownership documents since 1978. Copyright Office staff will search its records at the statutory rate of $75 for each hour or fraction of an hour. Search reports can be certified by the Library of Congress on request for a fee of $80 per hour. A definitive search of copyright is not an inexpensive undertaking.

Tracing a copyright for the years of 1923 to 1963 is a difficult procedure without access to the Library of Congress. Libraries throughout the United States maintain copies of the *Catalog of Copyright Entries* (CCE) published by the Copyright Office. This catalog was published in printed format from 1891 through 1978. From 1979 through 1982, the CCE was issued in microfiche format. The catalog is divided into parts according to the classes of works registered. Each CCE segment covers all registrations made during a particular period of time. Renewal registrations made from 1979 through 1982 are found in Section 8 of the catalog. Renewals prior to that time are generally listed at the end of the volume containing the class of work to which they pertain.

Where a copyright has been transferred from one publisher to another there are no entries recording this transfer in the catalog. This information can be obtained only from the current owner of the copyright. This could involve some sleuthing, particularly where one publishing house has been sold to another. Most modern contracts allow for reversion of ownership of the material to the author when a book is determined to be "out of print."

The information a librarian should understand and be able to share is that often it is a simple matter to determine whether material is subject to copyright. It is difficult and expensive to ascertain in some instances whether material is in the public domain. For some patrons, it may be important that they retain an attorney and conduct an exhaustive search. For others, conveying the understanding that some materials may not have a definitive copyright is the best conclusion that can be drawn. When material falls into this gray area and a decision regarding whether or not it is protected by copyrighted cannot be definitively ascertained, the material should be treated as though it were protected by copyright.

Out of Print Is Not Out of Copyright

A work that is out of print does not necessarily mean that it is no longer protected by copyright.[18] The Library of Congress *(http://www.loc.gov/*

copyright/index.html) can help you trace the copyright holder, as can the Copyright Clearance Center *(www.copyright.com)*.

The simplest method for searching the owner of a copyright, which is often not the author, is through the Library of Congress Copyright Search Web site. They have recently implemented a new and easier search system for copyright information. By selecting one of the databases, Books, Music, Serials, or Documents, you can start a search. Each of these databases contains records of registrations and ownership documents since 1978. The information in the databases is searchable by author, claimant, title, and registration number. Patrons, students, and faculty are generally disappointed that searching copyright by subject is not available at this time.

COPYRIGHT RENEWAL, UNPUBLISHED WORKS, AND COPYRIGHT NOTICES

Before January 1978, the duration of all copyrights was split into two consecutive terms. Under the 1909 Copyright Act, copyright only lasted twenty-eight years from the date the copyright was originally secured. However, the copyright was eligible for renewal during the last (twenty-eighth) year of the initial term. If renewed, the copyright was extended an additional forty-seven years, for a maximum of seventy-five years. If the renewal requirement was not complied with, the work fell into the public domain. For example, copyright protection for Frank Capra's classic film, *It's a Wonderful Life* (1946), was lost in 1974 because the owner inadvertently failed to file a copyright renewal application with the Copyright Office during the twenty-eighth year after the film's release or publication.

In 1992, Congress amended the laws to make copyright renewal automatic. Today, any copyright secured after January 1, 1964, is renewed automatically. For copyrights secured before January 1, 1964, but not renewed, copyright protection expires at the end of their twenty-eighth calendar year, despite passage of the automatic copyright renewal law in 1992.

Works created before January 1978 (including very old works), but neither published nor copyrighted, are subject to special rules. These works include unpublished diaries and manuscripts.

Copyright in these works lasts for the life of the author plus 70 years (copyright in works for hire, anonymous works, and works by pseudonym last 95 years from first publication or 120 years from creation, whichever expires earlier), but in no case will their copyrights expire before December 31, 2002. As an incentive to get these unpublished works published, if they are published before December 31, 2002, they are guaranteed at least forty-five years of protection (until December 31, 2047). Before passage of the Copyright Term Extension Act, the bonus term only ran until December 31, 2027.

Mark Twain's manuscript for *A Murder, A Mystery, and a Marriage*, held by the Harry Ransom Center of the University of Texas, was written between the completion of *The Adventures of Tom Sawyer* and the commencement of work on *The Adventures of Huckleberry Finn* in 1876. It went unpublished until 2001. It will be guaranteed protection until December 31, 2047. While the University of Texas owns the manuscript, the copyright and the royalties are the property of the Twain Foundation and the Mark Twain Project at the University of California at Berkeley, which owns the publishing rights to Twain's works.

TERMINATION OF PUBLISHING AGREEMENTS

The Copyright Act grants owners and their families a second chance to make a better deal with publishers. Under the Copyright Act, an author, or his or her heirs, has a chance to renegotiate the terms of the sale or licensing of their copyrighted works. This, however, does not include works made for hire.

Under the two-term system of the 1909 Copyright Act, at the end of fifty-six years from the date of publication, authors may terminate their publishing agreements by serving advance written notice upon their publisher at least two years but not more than ten years prior to the effective date of the termination.

Eugene O'Neill wrote *Long Day's Journey into Night* about his father, one of the great stage actors of his day, James O'Neill. The manuscript was sealed in a safe, along with a document signed by O'Neill that prohibited Random House from publishing the play until twenty-five years after his death. When, two years after O'Neill's death, Carlotta, his wife, asked Random House to publish the play, Bennet Cerf refused, believing himself honor-bound to O'Neill's document. Carlotta, who possessed the legal right to O'Neill's literary estate, withdrew the manuscript from Random House, and presented it to the Yale University Press, which published the play in February 1956. It was an instant success. O'Neill also wrote *The Iceman Cometh* (1939) and *A Moon for the Misbegotten* (1943). When Eugene O'Neill's daughter Oona married Charlie Chaplin, who was over thirty-six years her senior, Eugene O'Neill disinherited her. However, because of the renewal clause of the 1909 Copyright Act, Oona was able to renew the copyright to her own and her five children's benefit. This would not have been possible under the 1976 Copyright Act.

VIOLATION OF COPYRIGHT RESULTS IN AN INFRINGEMENT

If one of the enumerated protections of the law of copyright is violated or infringed upon, there can be both civil and criminal consequences. Under U.S copyright law today, copyright protection attaches to every creative work as soon as the work is created and "fixed in any tangible medium of expression."[19] Copyright infringement occurs when someone with access to a copyrighted work creates a substantially similar work, and uses it in a way that violates one or more of the copyright owner's five exclusive rights—the rights of reproduction, distribution, adaptation, performance, or public display.[20] An individual who has been afforded a certain degree of copyright protection in the United States is not guaranteed protection against copyright infringements that may occur abroad; even though the copyright holder and the copyright infringer may be U.S. citizens. These rights are governed by treaties.

In addition to the person who directly infringes someone's copyright, others who assist in the infringement may face derivative liability; under two theories:

- One who induces, causes, or materially assists in the infringement may be guilty of contributory infringement.[21] Courts generally require that the plaintiff prove that the contributory infringer knew or had reason to know of the direct infringer's infringement and materially contributed to it.[22]

- The doctrine of vicarious liability; derived from the doctrine of *respondeat superior,* or responsibility by the master, may create liability when one has the right and the ability to supervise the infringing activity and derives financial interest from those activities.[23]

For this reason it is important for a library to have a policy that prohibits copyright infringement. This policy should be communicated to both library staff and library patrons. Some copying may be permissible for personal use. This use is significantly different from a commercial use of copyrighted material. Copying is also permissible for "transformative" uses, such as parody and commentary. The television show *Saturday Night Live* is probably the most familiar source of parody.

Finally, copyright protection has a limited term, and works for which the copyright term has expired, or which never had copyright protection, are in the public domain and are free for anyone to reproduce or imitate. U.S. Government publications are an example of public-domain works, although some few government documents are subject to copyright.[24]

CURRENT COPYRIGHT LAW

The Copyright Revision Act of 1976 is the main legal text that governs copyright policy.

In 1978, guidelines for the application of the Act were developed by the National Commission on New Technological Uses of Copyright Works (CONTU), which dealt with issues raised by photocopiers and computers. Expectations were that the document would be reviewed and updated periodically. These guidelines, however, have never been revised. They are available online at *http://www.cni.org/docs/info.policies/CONTU.html.*

The Conference on Fair Use (CONFU), convened by the Working Group, brought together copyright owner and user interests to discuss fair use issues and to develop guidelines for fair uses of copyrighted works by librarians and educators. After four years of meetings, between 1994 and 1998, a final report was issued, but it does not include guidelines for fair-use copying. It contends that widely supported guidelines will be complicated by the competing interests of the copyright owner and user communities.

The Digital Millennium Copyright Act (DMCA) was passed in October 1998 to address the law's five titles. It amended copyright law as found in Chapter 17 of the United States Code. The DMCA:

(1) implement the World Intellectual Property Organization (WIPO) Internet Treaties; (2) establish safe harbors for online service providers; (3) permit temporary copies of programs during the performance of computer maintenance; (4) make miscellaneous amendments to the Copyright Act, including amendments which facilitate Internet broadcasting, and (5) create sui generis protection for boat hull designs.

Of particular interest to libraries was a controversial title establishing database protection that was omitted by the House-Senate Conference. Fair use was not addressed by this Act.

The U.S. Code is not difficult to access. It is a relatively easy matter to consult Title 17, the Copyright Act, regarding questions about copyright coverage of a particular work. The Library of Congress also maintains records of copyright applications.

SONNY BONO COPYRIGHT TERM EXTENSION ACT

In 1995, a bill regarding copyright was introduced in the House and the Senate, and both chambers held hearings. The bill never exited the committee because restaurant and bar owners lobbied Congress for a broader exemption on paying royalties for music broadcasts in their establishments. It took three years for the restaurateurs to be successful with their lobbying and win an exemption from the proposed copyright act. In March 1998, the bill passed in the House of Representatives but stalled in the Senate. In October of 1998, a similar version of the bill reached the Senate floor and passed by unanimous consent. The bill quickly passed in the House with a voice vote, so that members who voted yea or nay could not be identified. There was no debate on the bill as the country was focused on the impeachment proceedings against a president. The Sonny Bono Copyright Term Extension Act (CTEA) is the law as affirmed by the U.S. Supreme Court, and works that were expected to become part of the public domain are frozen under continued copyright for another twenty years.

PUBLIC DOMAIN WORKS DERAILED BY CTEA

Porgy and Bess was published by George and Ira Gershwin in 1935. Prior to the Copyright Term Extension Act, it was set to become public-domain material in 2015. Now, it will be public domain material in 2035. Because it is protected by copyright, permission must be obtained from the Estate of George and Ira Gershwin to perform this play. Representatives of the Estate have stated:

> The monetary part is important, but if works of art are in the public domain, you can take them and do whatever you want with them. For instance, we've always licensed "Porgy and Bess" for the stage performance only with a black cast and chorus. That could be debased. Or someone could turn "Porgy and Bess" into rap music.

Critics of copyright extension respond that is just the point. It is time to do something new and original with *Porgy and Bess*. They believe the lengthy copyright terms stifle artistic innovation and the creation of new works based on the old. A rap version of *Porgy and Bess* would breathe new life into this classic, and with it would come a new audience. It is argued that whole new generations would become familiar with *Porgy and Bess* if it were made a part of the public domain, and society would benefit from this mainstreaming of an American classic tale in music.

Showboat, written by Hammerstein, Kern, and Ferber, was published in 1927. Prior to the Copyright Term Extension Act, it was set to become public domain material in 2007. Now, it will enter the public domain in 2027. It, too, could become embraced by the mainstream if it could be interpreted in a modern fashion. This could only occur if it were made a part of the public domain.

SCOPE OF COPYRIGHT LAW AS DEFINED BY THE U.S. SUPREME COURT

Neither the U.S Constitution nor the U.S. Supreme Court hold that the primary purpose of copyright protection is to provide reimbursement to the creator, although publicly this is conceived to be its primary purpose. The Supreme Court repeatedly reminds lower courts that "[t]he primary objective of copyright is not to reward the labor of authors, but '[t]o promote the Progress of Science and useful Arts.'"[25]

INTERNATIONAL COPYRIGHT LAW

The 1980 World Intellectual Property Organization (WIPO) and the 1984 Paris Convention for the Protection of Industrial Property serve to protect the copyright laws of each nation that signed the various treaties. With headquarters in Geneva, Switzerland, WIPO is one of the sixteen specialized agencies of the United Nations system of organizations. It administers twenty-three international treaties dealing with different aspects of intellectual property protection.

A fake Harry Potter book was released in China in June of 2002. This book had a distinctive Chinese flavor and was titled *Harry Potter and Leopard Walk Up to Dragon*. This version included Chinese ghosts, magic, and kung-fu. Harry turns into a grotesque dwarf after a sweet and sour rain and encounters many of the typical Harry Potter challenges and adventures.

The Agreement on Trade Relations between the United States of America and the People's Republic of China of 1979 ("1979 Agreement") marked the beginning of Western intellectual property protection in China. This agreement has been largely ignored. However, with the Chinese themselves having a monetary stake in the protection of intellectual property these agreements have become more significant. Zhang Deguang of the People's Literature Publishing House has the Harry Potter publishing rights in China and believes the fake has made a negative impact on his book sales. This Chinese company is quickly promoting the rights of ownership of Harry Potter.

Unfortunately, not all countries have copyright treaties with the United States and not all intellectual property that is stolen has an agent in that country with a vested interest in protecting the rights of copy. Copyright simply cannot be the subject of universal protection.

WORKS OF FACULTY OR WORKS FOR HIRE

Typically, faculty and staff members who create works in the course of their employment have created works for hire. It is not uncommon to find contractual exceptions to this concept. Libraries that do not have that exception may be open to creating it.

In a work-made-for-hire situation, the "author" of the work is no longer the individual who created the work. Instead, the author is considered to be the entity that hired the actual creators of the work (such as a corporation for whom the creator works as an employee). Why are works for hire so important? Faculty members like to retain ownership of their works and often do. The question then becomes whether this is a work for hire. This is particularly relevant to the ownership of Web sites created by librarians. Unless you agree with the school that these are subject to joint ownership, you can't take them with you.

In addition, works that were made for hire or by an employee have a ninety-five-year copyright protection term for the owner of the copyright. Karey Mullis, the recipient of the 1993 Chemistry Nobel prize for inventing polymerase chain reaction (PCR), invented a way to replicate large amounts of DNA from infinitesimal amounts of DNA. Since 1986, PCR has literally changed the world—making DNA fingerprinting and even cloning possible. The lab that employed Mullis gave him a $10,000 bonus for discovery and later sold the patent for a reported half billion dollars.

The Copyright Act limits the work-made-for-hire doctrine to the following specific situations:[26]

1. work prepared by an employee within the scope of his or her employment
2. work specially ordered or commissioned for use
3. work contribution to a collective work
4. part of a motion picture or other audiovisual work
5. translations
6. supplementary work
7. compilations
8. instructional text
9. tests
10. answer material for a test
11. atlases

Generally, and always it is recommended that the parties agree to this in writing, any work created for a library is a work made for hire. If the work is to be considered to be created by the creator for the library, this agreement should be in writing. If the employee may take the work with them to new employment, this should be clearly stated contractually between the library and the employee.

When the work's creator is an employee and not an independent contractor, a work is deemed to have been made "for hire." The determination of whether an individual is an employee for the purposes of the work-made-for-hire doctrine is determined under "the common law of agency." What this means is that courts will look at various factors to determine whether the individual is an employee, such as:

- the control exerted by the employer over the employee (that is, the employee's schedule and the hiring of the employee's assistants)
- the control exerted by the employer over how and where the work is done
- the supplying of equipment for the employee's use
- the payment of benefits and the withholding of taxes

Although these factors are not exhaustive and can be difficult to analyze in close situations, it is clear that a work created within the scope of a regular, salaried employee's job is a work made for hire. Typical examples of works made for hire would include the creation of a new Disney character for a Disney movie or an article written for a newspaper by a staff reporter. A poster prepared for a library festival by a library employee would be the property of the library, not the creator, unless there was an agreement to the contrary. A bibliography Web site on science projects for middle-school students developed for the library would be the property of the library, not the employee who created it.

WORKS BY INDEPENDENT CONTRACTORS

If a work is created by an independent contractor, that is, someone who is not an employee, the work may still be a work for hire, but the definition is much harder to meet. In order for the work of an independent contractor to be a work made for hire, one of the following facts must exist:

- The work must be specially ordered or commissioned.
- The work must come within one of the eleven categories of works listed in the definition above.
- There must be a written agreement between the parties specifying that the work is a work made for hire.

If the library contracted with an artist who is not an employee of the library to create a poster for a festival, that artist would be an independent contractor. If the library contracted with a Web site developer to create a site for science projects for middle school students, that creator could be an independent contractor.

WORKS FOR HIRE AND IMPLIED LICENSE

Some educators have invoked the theory of "implied license" in their attempt to "own" the work they created while employed by a school district. Generally, the owner of a work for hire is not the legal author. The author is legally considered to be the hiring party. The hiring party's ability to use the work depends either on the specific terms of the agreement with the author or upon the concept of an implied license to use the work. If forced to rely on an implied license, the hiring party may find that it has only limited rights to alter, update, or transform the work for which it paid.

An implied copyright license is a license created by law in the absence of an actual agreement between the parties. Implied licenses arise when the conduct of the parties indicates that some license is to be extended between the copyright owner and the licensee, but the parties themselves did not bother to create a license and never agreed on the specific terms of the license. The purpose of an implied license is to allow the licensee (the party who licenses the work from the copyright owner) some right to use the copyrighted work, but only to the extent that the copyright owner would have allowed had the parties negotiated an agreement.

The custom and practice of the community are generally used to determine the scope of the implied license. Implied licenses have been used to grant licenses in situations where a copyrighted work was created by one party at the request of another.

CONCLUSION

Copyright is a legal creature, technical and artificial in its creation, with a ferocious bark and a bite that can be no more than a nip or as deadly as a shark attack. Mark Twain was correct in his analysis that there are but a "bathtub-full" of books worthy of the extensive life that copyright provides: "In a century we have produced two hundred and twenty thousand books; not a bathtub-full of them are still alive and marketable."[27] In reality, few works merit the extended protection given to them by Congress. There are precious few truly great works. However, all works are protected equally. Many, many works have meaning to a small segment of our society. There is no financial incentive in reproducing these works, notwithstanding the fact that they could benefit society as a foundation for new works.

SELECTED LINKS

The U.S. Copyright Office Web site, at *www.copyright.gov*, contains an explanation of American copyright basics and a list of frequently asked questions, as well as the complete text of the U.S. Copyright Act of 1976. Topics include copyright ownership and transfer, copyright notice, and copyright infringement and remedies. The site is maintained by the U.S. Library of Congress.

Nolo Press Patent, Copyright, and Trademark Information, at *www.nolo.com*, a section of *Nolo's Legal Encyclopedia* focusing on intellectual property laws, is a collection of articles on legal issues regarding copyright, patents, trademarks, service marks, business names and software development. The articles are prepared and site maintained by Nolo Press, a Berkeley, California, publisher of self-help law books and software.

The Copyright Clearance Center at *www.ccc.com* is an online resource operated by the Copyright Clearance Center Inc. (CCC), which was formed in 1978 as a not-for-profit organization to induce compliance with the U.S. copyright law. CCC, based in Danvers, Massachusetts, provides licensing systems for reproduction and distribution of copyrighted materials throughout the world.

Circular 66 from the U.S. Copyright Office *(www.copyright.gov/circs/circ66.pdf)* explains copyright registration for online works.

NOTES

1. 17 U.S.C. § 102.
2. While slogans may not be subject to copyright, they may be subject to trademark protection if registered with the United States Patent and Trademark Office.
3. Bleistein v. Donaldson Lithographing Co., 188 U.S. 239, 250 (1903).
4. The legislative history of 17 U.S.C § 101 et seq. is found in S. Rep. No. 475, 94th Cong., 1st Sess. (1975); H. Rep. No. 1476, 94th Cong., 2d Sess. (1976); H. Rep. No. 1733, 94th Cong., 2d Sess. (1976).
5. Dane v. M & H Co., 136 U.S.P.Q. (BNA) 426 (N.Y. Sup. Ct. 1963).
6. 17 U.S.C. § 106(a).
7. 499 U.S. 340 (1991).

8. 248 U.S. 215 (1918).

9. NBA v. Motorola, Inc., 105 F.3d 841 (2d Cir. 1997).

10. American Dent. Assn. v. Delta Den. Plans Assn., 126 F.3d 977 (7th Cir., 1997).

11. 111 U.S. 53 (1884).

12. *See* Cal. Civ. Code 980(a)(1) (West. Supp. 1997).

13. Nichols v. Universal Pictures, 45 F.2d 119 (2d Cir 1930) *cert denied* 282 U.S. 902 (1931).

14. 216 F.2d 945 (9th Cir. 1954) *cert denied* 348 U.S. 5971.

15. 900 F. Supp. 1287 (C.D. Cal. 1995).

16. *See* United States Patent and Trademark Office, at <www.uspto.gov.>

17. *See* United States Copyright Office, at <www.copyright.gov.>

18. Thre are two differing court views. One allows copying favoring the use, while one indicates in out-of-print works the only source of income would be income from the use and copy and does not favor copying of an out-of-print use. In *Kinko's Graphics Corp.*, 758 F. Supp. 1522, 1534 (S.D.N.Y. 1991), the court found infringement occurred where "in almost every case, defendant copied at least an entire chapter of plaintiff's book" for the student class pack. There the court noted "out-of-print" materials were particularly sensitive to copyright infringment because this use may be the copyright holder's oly source of income for this work.

But in *Maxtone-Graham v. Burtchaell*, 803 F.2d 1253, 1264 (2nd Cir. 1986), the court placed the focus not on the copyright holder but on the user: "If the work is 'out-of-print' and unavailable for purchase through normal channels, the user may have more justification for reproducing it than in the ordinary case."

19. 17 U.S.C. § 102 (1994). Copyrightable works are broadly construed to include not only books, paintings, and sculptures, but also movies, plays, musical compositions, recordings, photographs, computer software code, architectural designs, and even routine business writings.

20. 17 U.S.C. § 501 (Supp. V 1999); *see also* Nichols v. Universal Pictures Co., 45 F.2d 119 (2d Cir. 1930) (stating test for infringement); 17 U.S.C. § 106 (Supp. V 1999).

21. The doctrine of contributory copyright infringement originated with Justice Oliver Wendell Holmes's decision in Kalem Co. v. Harper Bros., 222 U.S. 55 (1911).

22. Gershwin Publ'g Corp. v. Columbia Artists Mgmt., Inc., 443 F.2d 1159, 1162 (2d Cir. 1971).

23. *See* Polygram Int'l Publ'g, Inc. v. Nevada/TIG, Inc., 855 F. Supp. 1314, 1325–26 (D. Mass. 1994).

24. 17 U.S.C. § 105 (1994) (stating that federal government works are never subject to copyright).

25. Feist Publications, Inc. v. Rural Telephone Service Co., 499 U.S. 340, 349 (1991). *See* Fogerty v. Fantasy, Inc., 510 U.S. 517, 526–27 (1994); Sony Corp. of America v. Universal City Studios, Inc., 464 U.S. 417, 428–29, 431–32 (1984); Twentieth Century Music Corp. v. Aiken, 422 U.S. 151, 156 (1975); Accord Harper & Row v. Nation Enterprises, 471 U.S. 539, 546 (1985).

26. 17 U.S.C. 101.

27. Mark Twain, ERUPTION (Bernard DeVoto, ed., Harper, 1940) (1922) Note that this book is in the public domain.

6

COPYRIGHT AND ELECTRONIC
ACCESS

I'll never darken the door to that post office again if I live to be a hundred.

—Eudora Welty, *Why I Live at the P.O.*[1]

Copyright and electronic access is governed for the most part by license agreements rather than the nuances of the law of copyright. License agreements are agreements in the nature of a contractual agreement between two parties. Most contracts, however, are negotiated by the parties. Most license agreements are not negotiated; they are offered by the purveyor of the material and accepted by the purchaser, in this case, the library.

Generally speaking, society is better served when the courts follow the trends of society rather than attempt to lead them, and generally speaking, that is what courts do. In the area of copyright law, the courts initially attempted to apply print copyright law to technological and electronic issues of copyright. This was not always successful and led to some rulings that were ultimately modified by statute or case law or both. Studying copyright law can be confusing. There are early cases that addressed electronic access to materials that fluttered and foundered, and were ultimately overruled. Reading an old case can leave a misimpression as to the current status of copyright law. The law, and in particular, cyberlaw, changes almost daily.

In reviewing some of the early decisions, it is obvious that the judiciary was unfamiliar with and did not understand the manner in which a computer operates. To a great extent some of the early court decisions have been modified by federal statutory law. The Digital Millennium Copyright Act (DMCA) addressed a court decision that had attempted to apply print copyright law literally to computer applications. *MAI Systems Corporations v. Peak*

Computer, Inc.[2] is an example of an attempt by the courts to apply print law to law that governs electronic access to materials. Peak Computer was a computer software maintenance company engaged to maintain the software of a company that purchased an MAI Systems program. The court found that when Peak performed maintenance on the software, a copy of the software was made in the computer's random access memory (RAM). Since making a copy of the software was contrary to copyright law, Peak was found to have violated the right of copy, despite the fact that the court acknowledged that RAM access is of a "transitory duration." This position of the court was ultimately modified by statute that stated that making a copy on a computer is not an infringement when done solely for the purpose of providing maintenance. This seems like a fundamental and obvious decision, but this case serves to illustrate the difficulty courts have in grappling with a new technology they do not fully understand.

In Texas, some courts and judges have embraced technology. Some federal courtrooms are wired to adopt most computer advances and are managed and overseen by the technology-savvy judges. This is a long leap from the judge who ruled in the *MAI Systems* case.

The law of copyright is filled with opinions that have been abandoned. This cautionary note is sounded to alert the librarian to the fact that not every case published or cited continues to be the law. Many opinions have been modified, and the first efforts of courts to fashion electronic and technological applications based entirely upon the precedent established by print have not always been successful. While the same legal reasoning has been applied, different applications have been fashioned in the electronic and cyber world of copyright.

Some of the laws that have emerged to adapt copyright to the cyber and electronic world are outlined below as federal statutes, or are proposed and pending bills that may ultimately become law. These laws follow a pattern of protecting electronic and cyber materials for the benefit of the copyright holder. While the issue of downloading music with Napster has been resolved, peer-to-peer sharing (P2P) of software programs and music has continued. Librarians' concerns are invoked when extensive efforts to prohibit the right to share information might be applied to libraries and impede the library's ability to share its materials. The VCR and the MP3 have successfully withstood legal challenges. In 1984, the Supreme Court ruled that home video recorders (in this instance, Betamax) did not violate the right of copy as alleged by the movie industry. In 1998, a Recording Industry Association of America challenge to ban sales of the Rio MP3 player, fearing the device might lead to rampant illegal music copying, failed. The court found that consumers have a right to make copies of their music for personal use.[3]

Vigilance is required to navigate the electronic waters of copyright protection as it is applied to the library. Random House sued e-publisher Rosetta-

Books, alleging that the company violated Random House copyrights by selling electronic versions of its books. RosettaBooks had contractually acquired and paid for the electronic-publishing rights to nearly one hundred titles, including several works by William Styron, Kurt Vonnegut, and Robert Parker. On March 8, 2002, the court rendered a unanimous decision in favor of RosettaBooks, affirming that authors retain the electronic rights to their books.[4] In making this decision, the court handed RosettaBooks its second victory in this landmark litigation that proves that authors control electronic rights to their works.

While some of these laws and bills do not directly impact libraries currently, their inroads into the sharing of copyrighted information may ultimately affect libraries. It is important to understand the legal direction the holders of electronic copyrights are taking to understand the potential impact this may have on libraries.

DATABASE PROTECTION

Libraries offer their patrons access to many databases. Database copyright protection is more extensive in Europe than it is in the United States, and this is of great significance in the library community. In the United States, databases can only be protected by copyright as compilations. Section 101 of Title 17 of the U.S. Code defines a compilation as "a collection and assembling of preexisting materials or of data that are selected in such a way that the resulting work as a whole constitutes an original work of authorship." The selection must involve some creative expression. It is through this protection that genealogical databases find protection. While this is not an impossible task to meet, it can be difficult.

Most databases purchased by libraries are copyright-protected, in addition to the license agreement entered into between the database copyright owner and the library. When a creator shows some level of creativity in the decision to include or exclude information in a database, the minimum amount of creativity has been invoked to afford copyright protection. Because most library databases are protected not only by copyright, but more importantly and more extensively by license agreements, the license agreement creates the significant relationship between the parties.

OVERVIEW OF SOFTWARE COPYRIGHT PROTECTION

Software consists of both the computer code and its screen appearance. Various software programs interface with the user in different formats. With software, the actual underlying systems, processes, and algorithms that are embodied in a program are not eligible for copyright protection, even though they may be independently protected as trade secrets, or even qualify for patent protection. Software is no different from any other work eligible for copyright protection. It must be an original form of expression fixed in a tangible medium.

Software programs, like works of fiction, can be built upon the work of another. The work of another does not become the work of the person who built upon it. For example Disney's version of *Beauty and the Beast* builds upon an ancient fairy tale. This does not render the original tale to be the protectable work of Disney. Rather, it is the new features of the tale, the images, and the music that are protected by copyright. Disney has often taken fairy tales and built upon them to create new forms of expression. It is Disney's interpretation of *Beauty and the Beast* that is afforded copyright protection. The image of Belle would be a trademarked character, but Disney would not have a copyright to this public-domain character. By contrast, Harry Potter is both a copyrighted and trademarked character.

For a tale in the public domain, any person or entity is free to also build upon that concept. *The Wizard of Oz* is an example. The period of copyright has expired on *The Wizard of Oz,* published by L. Frank Baum in 1900. MGM's version of *The Wizard of Oz* was not infringed upon when *The Wiz* or the *Ozard of Wiz* was presented. L. Frank Baum's story exists in the public domain and can be interpreted by anyone with a desire to build upon it. They may interpret it precisely as Baum created and wrote it, or they may modify it and create a derivative work.

If a software program contains elements that have either entered the public domain or contain industry-standard features, such elements or features will not be protected, even if contained in an otherwise original work. Features such as pull-down menus or the opening of multiple windows on a screen are not protected. Software is fixed in a tangible medium of expression when it is placed on magnetic media like a floppy disk or a hard drive.

Computer games are excellent examples of protected software. Their storyline, their user interaction, and their images and music are protected. Piracy of software is common, and can continue for a significant amount of time without the knowledge of the copyright holder. Piracy is an ongoing problem in the gaming industry. The Interactive Digital Software Association estimates that piracy cost gaming companies $3 billion dollars in 2001. For example, a primitive demonstration version of *Doom III* that was shown at the Electronic Entertainment Expo, the trade show of the video gaming industry, leaked out onto the Internet prior to its official distribution date. The version of the game that was leaked required some user coding and created multiple system lockups and was seen as a threat to the final game, which was not to be released for another year. While *Doom III* was being posted for Internet access and the game was being downloaded across the world, an Activision vice president had no idea the game had leaked despite intense security for the game. The company worked hard to protect the secrecy of the screen shots and story details.

MUSICAL WORKS

Clearly musical works are protected by copyright. Patrons who download music from the Internet typically infringe upon copyright. The rights of artists, publishers, and record companies, who are typically the copyright holders, are protected by the Copyright Act.[5] The Act protects "original works of authorship fixed in any tangible medium of expression, currently known or later developed, from which the work can be perceived, reproduced or otherwise communicated, either directly or indirectly, with the aid of a machine or device" just as it would protect any other work.[6] Historically, the front line in copyright protection for musical works has been one artist copying the works of another, although there are fewer than 100 reported cases involving the taking of another's musical work.

The front line today for copyright infringement that involves music (and books on tape to a lesser degree) occurs primarily with downloading of musical works through the use of MP3 compression technology on the Internet. This provides a download of near CD-quality, digitized sound recordings and the ability to store them using minimal disk space. With a 56K modem, it can take as much as half an hour to download a single song.

The Recording Industry of America (RIAA) has taken an active role in limiting music piracy through the Internet. They routinely send cease-and-desist letters to the operators of infringing Web sites. They have filed suit against manufacturers of MP3 players, are considering action against search engines that help find MP3s, and actively lobby Congress for legislation to protect the copyright of musical artists.

The exclusive rights granted to the copyright holder are found in Section 106 of the Copyright Act, and include the following rights:[7]

(1) to reproduce the copyrighted work in copies or phonorecords;

(2) to prepare derivative works based upon the copyrighted work;

(3) to distribute copies or phonorecords of the copyrighted work to the public by sale or other transfer of ownership, or by rental, lease, or lending;

(4) in the case of literary, musical, dramatic, and choreographic works, pantomimes, and motion pictures and other audiovisual works, to perform the copyrighted work publicly;

(5) in the case of literary, musical, dramatic, and choreographic works, pantomimes, and pictorial, graphic, or sculptural works, including the individual images of a motion picture or other audiovisual work, to display the copyrighted work publicly; and

(6) in the case of sound recordings, to perform the copyrighted work publicly by means of a digital audio transmission.

The music publishers and writers derive a portion of their income from licensing performance rights. There are three major organizations that handle the majority of this licensing: the American Society of Composers, Authors, and Publishers (ASCAP), Broadcast Music, Inc. (BMI), and the Society of European Stage Authors and Composers (SESAC). The digital transmission of music is handled by Record Industry Association of America and Sound Exchange.

Although the copyright owners have standing to file any suit, it is more often one of these organizations that monitor the illegal downloading of their clients' music, send the cease-and-desist letters, and file suit, when necessary, on behalf of their clients.

The Federal Anti-Bootlegging Statute

Live musical performances were not protected by federal copyright law until the enactment of the Uruguay Round Agreements Act, enacted December 8, 1994. For the first time, federal law protected the unauthorized fixation and trafficking in sound recordings and music videos of live musical performances. This authority coincides with the authority that resides in the state courts, and in this particular instance, the federal law did not preempt the states' rights. In fact for those concerts bootlegged before 1972, only state law only continues to protect these performances.

This activity has also been criminalized. The Criminal Infringement of a Copyright Act, also introduced in 1994, criminalizes the "unauthorized fixation of and trafficking in sound recordings and music videos of live musical performances"—what music fans have always referred to as "bootlegs." The term originated from the practice of hiding a tape recorder in a boot at a concert, for the purpose of copying and distributing the tape. The statute also authorizes U.S. Customs to seize bootlegs at the border, like any other contraband, to counteract importation from countries with little or no protection for taping of live performances.

Reproductions of performances other than live performances, such as unauthorized reproductions of previously recorded or fixed but unreleased performance such as studio "outtakes," are subject to prosecution under the criminal copyright law.[8]

The No Electronic Theft Act

The No Electronic Theft Act (NET), enacted in December 1997, addressed computer-based piracy by instituting criminal penalties for copyright infringement by electronic means under the Criminal Infringement of a Copyright Act. The criminal statute provides that a trader in illegal MP3s be imprisoned for a maximum of three years for a first offense and six years for a second offense, together with a fine for distributing as little as $1,000 worth of music.

Most significantly to students and minors who post and download copyrighted material, the statute amended the Copyright Act's definition of "financial gain"[9] to include "receipt, or expectation of receipt, of anything of value, including the receipt of other copyrighted works." This places under the Act's ambit the MP3 "ratio sites" that require a user to upload a file before they may download one, as well as trading areas for digitized music. Libraries that provide Internet service access should be sensitive to any downloading of music or software programs that might occur in their library.

THE AUDIO HOME RECORDING ACT OF 1992

The 1992 Audio Home Recording Act (AHRA)[10] clarified the status of home audio copying. This issue was unresolved by the Supreme Court's oft-quoted decision in *Sony Corp. v. Universal City Studios, Inc.*[11] The *Sony* case is recognized as important because it confirmed as a legally accepted practice the act of home-video copying for "time-shifting" purposes; that is, record now, and watch later. That concept is understood by most four-year-olds in our society. Time shifting was defined as an act of taping a broadcast program to watch at a later time, then erasing the copy. It was defined by the court as not building a library of copyrighted works. Under the AHRA, liability does not attach for copyright infringement for making, importing, or distributing a "digital audio recording device, a digital audio recording medium, an analog recording device, or an analog recording medium" or for using any of these devices or media for personal, noncommercial recording.

Libraries that provide audio and video media should notify patrons that the copying of the library-provided materials is an infringement of copyright and not a use consistent with the library's policy. This notice should be posted on the equipment. Some libraries engrave small plastic plates and attach them to the equipment.

Manufacturers and distributors of digital audio recording devices and blank digital tapes pay a percentage-based royalty to the Copyright Office to be pooled and shared among artists, music publishers, and record companies.[12] The AHRA also mandates that any digital audio recording device or digital audio interface device must conform to the Serial Copy Management System (SCMS) or some other approved system that prevents successive generation copying beyond the initial allowable copying.[13]

The new technology of MP3 players allows multiple copying of a recording without degrading the quality. In *Recording Industry Association of America v. Diamond Multimedia Systems, Inc.*[14] RIAA sued the creator of an MP3 player, Rio. Rio is a portable music player that allows a user to store and play downloaded MP3 files. The RIAA contended that the Rio was a digital audio recording device that enabled music piracy. The Ninth Circuit unanimously ruled that the Rio was not a digital audio recording device as defined by the American Home Recording Act, since it is incapable of recording. The court noted the distinction between recording and downloading. VCRs record and MP3 players download files from a computer hard drive. The court stated the American Home Recording Act protected the act of recording and not downloading. Consequently RIAA's claim that MP3 players enable piracy by recording was not an accurate claim.

Because MP3 players were not recording devices and, therefore, not subject to the American Home Recording Act, they were not required to conform to an approved system that prevents successive generation copying beyond the initial allowable copying. This means MP3 players, at least for now, can reproduce copies freely and are not subject to the anti-piracy devices to which VCRs are subject.

However, downloading copyrighted music is still a violation of the U.S. Copyright Act. There are, however, more and more sources providing legal downloading of music, such as Apple and *Listen.com*. AOL and MSN also provide access to music for a fee. This downloading of music from the vendor is accomplished within the confines of the law of copyright.

TECHNOLOGY ENABLES COMPARISONS OF ALLEGED INFRINGEMENT MATERIALS

Technology has not only enabled the tracking of copyright infringement, but it has also enhanced the ability to determine if material has been copied in the production and creation of new material. The Web sites *Plagiarism.org* and *Turnitin.com* are for-profit companies designed to offer educators plagiarism detection. These companies, and others like them, make a digital fingerprint of any submitted document using a specially developed set of algorithms. The document's fingerprint is cross-referenced against the company's database of papers. They also employ automated Web crawlers to search the Internet for possible matches. They take the student's paper and create a custom, color-coded originality report, complete with source links, for each paper.

Copyright infringement cases concerning music have relied on expert witness testimony and extensive charts and graphs. Technology has not only transformed the way music is distributed, but it has transformed the way copyright infringement can be analyzed. Notation software can graphically and audibly demonstrate the similarities or differences between musical works.

During the infringement trial of Barry Gibb of the Bee Gees, the plaintiff's attorney played a recording of a performance of the melody of plaintiff's number "Let It End" for Maurice Gibb, who was under oath. Maurice erroneously identified this music as taken from the Bee Gees's song, and the plaintiff rested their case. The jury found the Bee Gees liable for infringement, although the judge ultimately disregarded their verdict.[15] Juxtaposition and manipulation of the two melodies contained in the digital files of the two songs in comparison suggest the melodies are clearly similar.

DVDs already feature content protection that cannot be disabled without committing a felony.

EUROPEAN RIGHTS

Database rights have become significant with the universal use of technology. In Europe databases were provided protection in 1996. Until 1996 database owners could not claim copyright protection if a database contained only factual data. In 1996, the European Parliament adopted Directive 96/9/EG,[16] which provides for a new intellectual property right on the extraction of data from databases and on the making available of the database itself.

ELECTRONIC TRESPASS

However, there does exist a state right in trespass that can serve to limit access to factual information. The company eBay used these laws in California to prevent a company called Bidder's Edge from spidering its auction Web site and offering eBay auction information on its own site. Even though anyone can freely browse the auctions on eBay's site, this access is subject to certain conditions, so the court regarded the site as private property. This act, while not a specific violation of copyright, was found to be an act of trespass pursuant to California law.[17]

LIBRARIES AND ELECTRONIC RIGHTS OF COPY

It is easy to read through these bills and laws and conclude that they do not apply to the library. That is not the case. The ALA and libraries are involved on the front lines of many of these issues.

When the movie industry sued the online hacker magazine *2600* for posting and linking to DeCSS code that could be used to crack DVD security, alleging copyright violation, librarians filed a brief in favor of *2600,* claiming such a restriction limited free speech. They lost this case and the hacker magazine was not allowed to link to sites showing how to hack anti-piracy DVD code.[18] The DCMA prohibits any software that could possibly be used to circumvent digital copy protections for any reason, including a legitimate "fair use." *2600 Magazine* remains enjoined from distributing the software on its Web site, or even printing the program's source code for study.

A mother sued a library in Livermore, California, demanding filters after her son downloaded reams of porn from its computers. The library stood its ground, refusing to filter. The library won at the trial and at appellate court levels, and does not have to filter.[19]

When a filtering bill was passed by Congress, the Children's Internet Protection Act, which required schools and libraries receiving federal funds to filter material that may be inappropriate for children, the American Library Association sued the U.S. government.[20] It argued that the act restricted free speech by preventing adults from viewing content that is legal for them to see. The ALA won.

Librarians remain involved in all aspect of copyright law because libraries are involved in all aspects of copyright law.

NOTES

1. Eudora is an e-mail program named after the Southern writer Eudora Welty. The program was created by Steve Dorner in 1990 at the University of Illinois in Urbana while working for NCSA (National Center for Supercomputing Applications). The first version of the program, which took about a year to develop, consisted of about 50,000 lines of code. Dorner envisioned widespread use of e-mail, and the use of post offices was a recurring theme in the writings of Eudora Welty. Dorner envisioned e-mail as "Bringing the P.O. to where you live," and used this phrase for the program's motto. I often saw Miss Welty tending her garden. My roommate baked her a cake for her eightieth birthday and took it to her. I only wish I had gone with her.

2. 991 F.2d 511 (9th Cir. 1993).

3. Sony v. Universal Studios, 464 U.S. 417 (1984); Recording Industry Association of Amer. Inc., et al. v. Diamond Multimedia Systems, Inc., 180 F.3d. 1072 (9th Cir. 1999).

4. Random House v. Rosetta Books LLC, 150 F. Supp.2d 613 (S.D.N.Y. 2001).

5. Copyright Act, 17 U.S.C. §§ 101 et. seq.

6. 17 U.S.C. § 102a.

7. 17 U.S.C. § 106.

8. 17 U.S.C. § 506(a) and 18 U.S.C § 2319.

9. 17 U.S.C. § 101.

10. 17 U.S.C. §§1001–1010.

11. 464 U.S. 417 (1984).

12. 17 U.S.C. § 1004.

13. 17 U.S.C. § 1002.

14. 180 F.3d 1072 (9th Cir. 1999).

15. Selle v. Gibb, 741 F.2d 896 (1984).

16. In 1996, the European Union passed Directive 96/9/EC, concerning the legal protection of databases to introduce a new law (a "sui generis" right). The purpose of this Directive was to offer greater protection than the various Member States' national copyright laws provided.

17. *See* eBay Inc. v. Bidder's Edge Inc., 100 F. Supp. 2d 1058 (N.D. Cal. 2000).

18. Universal City Studios v. Reimerdes. III F. Supp. 2d 294 (SDNY Aug. 17, 2000) commonly known as Motion Picture Association of America v. 2600 Magazine.

19. Kathleen R. v. City of Livermore, 87 Cal. App. 684 (2001).

20. United States v. American Library Assn., Inc. 539 U.S. (2003).

7

THE FAIR USE OF COPYRIGHTED MATERIAL

We can keep the past only by having the future, for they are forever tied together.
—Robert Penn Warren, *All the King's Men*

Public libraries often are used by students and faculty. The doctrine of "fair use" of copyright material allows a more liberal use of copyright material and is an exception to the law of copyright. Often the doctrine of fair use is considered to be the exclusive domain of education. That is not correct; the concept of fair use of copyrighted material is not limited exclusively to education. We have the rap group 2 Live Crew to thank for bringing the issue of fair use to the forefront of public and consumer awareness. It was their parody of Roy Orbison's *Pretty Woman* that brought the notion of fair use out of the educational closet. The courts determined that 2 Live Crew's version was a parody and, as such, was not an infringement upon the copyrighted work.[1]

Fair use interpretations are more restrictive for use in commercial endeavors than for educational uses. Factors that determine non-educational fair use are:

1. the purpose and character of the use, including whether the use is of a commercial nature or is for non-profit educational purposes
2. the nature of the copyrighted work
3. the amount and substantiality of the portion used in relation to the copyrighted work
4. the effect of the use on the potential market[2]

Because of the extensive use of libraries by students, this chapter briefly addresses the Educational Fair Use Guidelines. Fair use in American copyright law originated in the nineteenth century as a judicial doctrine that excused certain uses of copyrighted works. It allowed copyrighted material to be used in certain situations. In order to determine whether a use of copyrighted material was a fair use the court examined whether the use of the copyrighted material embraced only a small portion of the original work and whether it was for socially beneficial purposes.

The concept of fair use of copyrighted materials comes from British law and was principally found in three British cases, *Mawman v. Tegg, Wilkins v. Aikin,* and *Roworth v. Wilkes,* that addressed fair abridgement and fair quotation.[3] The United Kingdom and Canada recognize a concept known as "fair dealing." The beginning of fair use under American law is generally traced to the 1841 case of *Folsom v. Marsh.*[4] As early as 1802, Lord Ellenborough wrote of the need, while protecting copyrighted material, to allow others to build upon it. "While I shall think myself bound to secure every man in the enjoyment of his copy-right, one must not put manacles upon science."[5] Forty years later, in *Folsom v. Marsh,* Justice Story added a balancing test for the fair use of copyrighted material and stated that the courts should "look to the nature and objects of the selections made, the quantity and value of the materials used, and the degree in which the use may prejudice the sale, or diminish the profits, or supersede the objects, of the original work."[6]

The fair use of copyrighted materials was not governed by federal statute until the enactment of Section 107 of the 1976 Copyright Act. It was, however, governed by case law. This statute codified an honored and important legal concept. This very short statute, which has a long arm and a very broad sweep, is included below:

Sec. 107.—Limitations on exclusive rights: Fair use

Notwithstanding the provisions of sections 106 and 106A, the fair use of a copyrighted work, including such use by reproduction in copies or phonorecords or by any other means specified by that section, for purposes such as *criticism, comment, news reporting, teaching (including multiple copies for classroom use), scholarship, or research,* is not an infringement of copyright. In determining whether the use made of a work in any particular case is a fair use the factors to be considered shall include—

(1) the purpose and character of the use, including whether such use is of a commercial nature or is for nonprofit educational purposes;

(2) the nature of the copyrighted work;

(3) the amount and substantiality of the portion used in relation to the copyrighted work as a whole; and

(4) the effect of the use upon the potential market for or value of the copyrighted work.

The fact that a work is unpublished shall not itself bar a finding of fair use if such finding is made upon consideration of all the above factors.

This is known as the Purpose, Amount, Nature and Effect analysis (PANE). If this statute were all that were left to guide individual librarians there would be no uniformity in guidance. Each institution would be left to create its own interpretations. For this reason guidelines have been created to aid institutions in their application of Section 107 to their individual situations.

AFFIRMATIVE DEFENSE

Fair use is not a get-out-of-jail-free card. It is a legal defense, an affirmative defense, and as such must be plead and presented to the court for a legal decision based upon the facts of the defense presented. Fair use allows someone other than the copyright owner to use the copyrighted material in a reasonable manner without the owner's prior consent.[7] The most important fact to understand in this simple sentence is that "fair use" is a *defense*. A defense is used by a defendant who is actively involved in a lawsuit. A defense is employed as a legal strategy after suit is brought. That means after you have been served with process, after you have retained an attorney, after you have lost hours and hours of sleep and spent days and days in the kind of emotional turmoil that only being a defendant in a lawsuit can bring. There's a reason people hate lawyers. This is it. Defendants, even innocent defendants, can be hauled into court and forced to prove their innocence. Frivolous and non-frivolous lawsuits are filed for the same price, typically $150.00 charged by the clerk who files the suit.

The doctrine of fair use gives preference to non-profit educational uses of copyrighted material. And this is an excellent point for your attorney to make once you have been sued. It does not, however, by any means give the educational community carte blanche.

The prerequisite necessary to avail oneself of the legal defense of fair use is to have and to demonstrate an understanding of copyright laws. The courts have resolutely stated in the case of *Basic Books v. Kinko's*[8] that simply ignoring copyright laws and having no guidelines by which to evaluate what is a fair use of an author's work is not a basis from which an educator or a librarian may claim the fair use defense.

THE PURPOSES FOR WHICH FAIR USE MAY BE EMPLOYED

The statute notes uses other than teaching and scholarship that allow the fair use of materials subject to the protection of copyright. The statute clearly defines the purposes for which fair use of copyrighted material will not be determined to be an act of infringement as:

- criticism
- comment
- news reporting
- teaching (including multiple copies for classroom use)

- scholarship
- research

If the purpose for which copyright material is used does not fall into one of these categories it most likely will not be determined to be a fair use. However, even when works are being fairly used the notion of purpose, amount, nature, and effect should be respected. Obviously, commenting on a piece does not allow the full reproduction of a piece. As consumers of media, viewers are accustomed to seeing small movie clips displayed in conjunction with a movie review. This portion of the movie is presented as a fair use exception to the restrictions of the law of copyright.

The categories, however, are not all-revealing and have been the subject of litigation. A good example of a use not found in this list is the military use of copyrighted materials. It has been determined that the United States military has a fair use right of copyrighted materials. Numerous Army intelligence activities reproduce copyrighted materials for distribution to military personnel. Intelligence centers reproduce copyrighted text, photographs, and line drawings in classified intelligence documents for internal defense use. Tactical intelligence organizations provide copies of copyrighted photographs, line drawings, and imagery to war fighters for intelligence purposes. These have been deemed also to be fair uses.

NASA images generally are not copyrighted. You may use NASA imagery and video and audio material for educational or informational purposes, including photo collections, textbooks, public exhibits, and Internet Web pages. These can even be used in a "for profit" situation, so long as NASA is not associated with the images as an endorsement of commercial goods or services

The use to which the copyright material has been put will be one factor the court will consider when determining whether there is a fair use of copyrighted material.

FOUR-FACTOR TEST

The doctrine of fair use of material protected by copyright is a legal defense against claims of copyright violation. Those charged with the infringement of a work subject to the protection of the copyright laws offer the fair use doctrine as a defense or justification for the alleged infringement. In order to determine whether an alleged infringement of copyrighted work constitutes a fair use rather than an unlawful one, the courts have applied a four-factor test as mandated by federal law.

There is no congressional guidance in our federal law on how to weigh the four factors of fair use. The courts in interpreting fair used have employed a case-by-case approach to fair use. In a case-by-case approach the court will look at the facts of each individual case and decide whether or not there has been a fair use of the work or an infringement upon the rights of copy. The Supreme Court has stated that the last two factors are the most important in making the determination of copyright infringement.

In no statute and in no case has there been an articulation of a bright line rule to determine what is a fair use of a copyrighted material. The fact is there are no hard and fast rules to follow, no legislatively or judicially approved rules, and no guidelines set in legal stone. The guidelines we have are set in clay and they are not law. As each application of the doctrine of fair use is applied to each unique individual situation it is very difficult to determine what is and what is not a fair use of a work.[9] Application of a case-by-case interpretation means there are "no hard and fast rules." We call them as we see them and that depends on the circumstances of the case and who's doing the calling, or ruling.

The entire panel of the Supreme Court does not agree on a determination of what is and is not a fair use of a copyrighted work, and yet librarians, who are not attorneys, must make these decisions for the benefit of their library.

BURDEN OF PROOF IN INFRINGEMENT OF A COPYRIGHT

The plaintiff has the burden of proof in a case of copyright infringement. The one who claims that an infringement upon their copyright has been made must prove a prima facie case of infringement before the doctrine of the fair use of a copyrighted material is presented for review.[10] Fair use has been called "the last resort of scoundrels." (Usually by plaintiff's attorneys and occasionally by the judiciary. The defense counsel refers to it as a noble defense and your best chance to escape liability.) After the complaining party has proven that the copied work is owned by them, that it has been registered for copyright, and that the defendants have copied their work or infringed upon their work, fair use as an affirmative defense is presented in a trial for copyright infringement. It is the defendant (the claimed infringer) who claims that the portions copied were used fairly and invokes the doctrine of fair use.

The History of Fair Use

Fair use in American copyright law originated in the nineteenth century as a judicial doctrine that excused certain uses of copyrighted works, particularly if those uses embraced only a small portion of the original work which were for socially beneficial purposes.[11] Education is the chief socially beneficial purpose. Fair use remained a judicially created and applied doctrine until 1978 when the Copyright Revision Act of 1976 took effect, which included the first American fair-use statute. This statute can be reviewed at 17 U.S.C, Section 107, entitled "Limitations on Exclusive Rights: Fair Use." Through nearly two decades of earlier debate, every proposed revision bill included at least some acknowledgment of fair use.[12] The bill that Congress finally passed in late 1976 affirmed that fair-use rights existed, especially for teaching, research, scholarship, and news reporting, and it offered four factors for evaluating whether a use was "fair."

The fair use of a copyrighted work, including such use by reproduction in copies or phonorecords or by any other means specified by that section, for purposes such as criticism, comment, news reporting, teaching (including multiple copies for classroom use), scholarship, or research, is not an infringement of copyright. To determine whether the use made of a work in any particular case is a fair use, the following four factors should be considered:

1. the purpose and character of the use, including whether such use is of a commercial nature or is for nonprofit educational purposes

2. the nature of the copyrighted work

3. the amount and substantiality of the portion used in relation to the copyrighted work as a whole

4. the effect of the use upon the potential market for or value of the copyrighted work

Despite congressional intent to consider other factors and to keep fair use flexible for diverse and changing circumstances, most analyses and court rulings have relied extensively—if not exclusively—on the four statutory factors: purpose, nature, amount, and effect; or if you prefer an acronym: the four factors are a PANE—purpose, amount, nature, and effect.

The fair-use formula calls for some balance of these factors, with courts generally assessing the number of factors that militate in favor of each party in an infringement lawsuit. The factors are also not necessarily weighed equally; the effect on the value of the original often receives greatest weight, particularly when a court concludes that the use may have obviated a potential sale of the original work.[13] Providing an income for the creator is an important purpose of the copyright law.

The old adage that "ignorance is no excuse" holds true for copyright. We are all responsible for knowing the rules and abiding by them. Knowing the rules and taking some reasonable steps can go a long way toward avoiding a claim of infringement.

The Rights of Copy or Copyrights

The five exclusive rights of the copyright owner give the owner the exclusive right to copy, adapt, distribute, display, and perform the work. The mnemonic here is: "Don't Copy don't PADD with copyrighted work" or "C-P-A-D-D: Copy—Perform—Adapt—Distribute—Display." Permission from the copyright owner to use the work in the capacity of one of these five rights is required. Fair use is an exception to these rights of the copyright owner.

New works build to one degree or another on the previous works of others. It can be difficult to determine when something new is created or when there is simply an adaptation. Ideas are not subject to copyright. Adaptation of facts and style do not infringe upon a copyright. Ideas, facts, and style are elements of a work that are not protected by copyright and can be reused. They may give life to a new original expression. The line is not always an easy one to draw. Also, works that consist entirely of information that is common property and containing no original authorship cannot be copyrighted. For example, standard calendars, height and weight charts, tape measures and rules, and lists of tables taken from public documents or other common sources cannot be copyrighted.

The Guidelines

A common question is, "do we have to follow *the* Guidelines?" Unfortunately, there is not simply one set of guidelines. Guidelines, such as Educational Classroom Guidelines, which govern the amount of material that may be copied under specific circumstances without infringing upon the copyright of another, are not the law. They are just guidelines. Some of them have been adopted by organizations, others have been refuted by organizations. The important point is that different guidelines have different degrees of acceptance and none of them have the authority of law.

Generally, when people in education refer to "The Guidelines" they are referring to the Classroom Guidelines.[14] These guidelines are not statutory, though the publishing industry has indicated a preference that they should be binding. Many educational institutions in an attempt to avoid litigation treat the Classroom Guidelines as if they were the law.

The law is precisely as found in Title 17 U.S.C. Section 107, and the cases that interpret this statute. It is essential that librarians have guidelines that govern the use of copyrighted material. The Classroom Guidelines are only recommendations. In law they are known as a safe harbor. A safe harbor in law is a place of legal protection to be used to shelter the user from a lawsuit. There can be exceptions, but obviously a library cannot have anyone and everyone in the library making a good faith effort to conform to copyright law. A library can have a designated person who can, on a case-by-case basis, make exceptions to the guidelines. Exceptions are made one at a time, on an individual basis applying the law to the facts.

Based on historical legal precedent, every library should have guidelines for the use of copyrighted material, and the fair-use guidelines for academic institutions will not be identical to the fair-use guidelines for the library. Guidelines are just that, guidelines, and even more importantly, they indicate the minimum amount a party may copy without (probably) being in violation of copyright law. This means that copying may be done that exceeds the amount defined in the guidelines without being in violation of the Fair Use Copyright statute. What is most important to understand is that it is perfectly acceptable to have exceptions to guidelines if these exceptions are made by those who are familiar with the law of copyright, fair use exceptions, and if they have exercised their best judgment.

If guidelines are adopted without exception under any circumstance the library may be shortchanging itself. Wholesale adoption of any set of guidelines is clearly an attempt to insulate the library from litigation. If a library adopts guidelines without putting a librarian or at least a copyright officer in a position to permit exceptions, the library is definitely shortchanging itself. Guidelines have been adopted across the board, which makes the publishing industry quite happy but may not be the best result for libraries.

Before anyone places themselves in the position of making exceptions to the guidelines they should clearly understand the limits of the guidelines and understand the law of copyright. The guidelines are not the law of copyright. The law on the fair use of copyrighted material is based on a four-pronged test that is examined in detail in the following section.

The Four-Factor Test for the Fair Use of Copyright Material

The Purpose and Character of the Use to Be Considered in Fair Use

Where the purpose and character of the use of the copyrighted material is to create or produce a new work or a work that is different from the original work, *the fair use doctrine will be applied when the use is for non-profit educational purpose and not for commercial gain*. This use of material subject to copyright is considered to be transformative. A transformative work changes the work from which it was copied. A transformative use is protected by the fair use doctrine.[15] Quoting a source in a paper is a transformative use, as is any commentary or criticism of the original. A transformation takes a portion of one work, incorporates it into another, and creates a new work.

The Nature of the Copyrighted Work in Fair Use

The fair use doctrine examines the nature of the copyrighted work in relation to its established purpose. The use of factual material is more susceptible to fair use.[16] Historical and geographical data are examples of factual materials that are more likely to be considered within the realm of fair use. Works of fiction, as found in novels, poetry, or short stories, are less likely to be considered the subject of fair use and more likely to be the subject of copyright protection.

Private, unpublished research and creative works are much more likely to be protected than published works. In private and unpublished works the author still retains the right to control the final tangible expressions before publication. For example, the letters of Princess Diana that have been published would violate our American fair use statute. Princess Diana's estate owns the words of the letters, and they alone have the right to publish them. The owner of the letters owns simply that, the letters.

The Amount and Substantiality of the Material Used

The third factor of the fair use doctrine evaluates the quantity of the work in proportion to the total work of the copyrighted material. The court has historically noted the percentage used of the material from which the material is taken and the actual amount used. However, in this analysis the court also looks at the quality of the amount taken. If the nature of the amount taken is such as to take the "heart and soul" of the work, the amount taken can be quite small but will be deemed to be an infringement upon copyright. If the essence of the work taken creates an adverse market impact for the work from which the portion was copied the quality of the amount taken will override the quantity of the amount taken. The overall importance of the portion copied to the work from which it was copied will be analyzed.

The copying of entire works for use in the classroom will not be considered a fair use. This includes out-of-print material. However, it is important to note that a library may make a copy of an out-of-print material for preservation purposes. This is quite different from a publisher producing an out-of-print material for sale. Copying that would not be considered fair use for educational purposes may be acceptable pursuant to Section 108 of the Digital Millennium Copyright Act (DMCA).

The Effect of the Use on the Work's Market Value

The United States Supreme Court has characterized the effect of the use of the work on its market value as the most important element in fair use analysis. The Court has generally held that "fair use . . . is limited to copying by others which does not materially impair the marketability of the work which is copied."[17] The other three factors remain elements of consideration in the doctrine of fair use, notwithstanding the focus of the Court on the fourth factor. A showing of widespread use that would negatively affect the potential market of the copyrighted material would preclude a fair use defense.

Summary of Principles of Fair Use

In summary, the U.S. Copyright Act now codifies broad principles underlying fair use, but ultimately offers few details for understanding its meaning in specific applications.[18] These decisions are made by the court on a case-by-case or an individual specific basis.

Each case must be evaluated independently and decided upon the specific facts presented. It was the intention of Congress that the law governing the fair use of copyrighted materials in an educational, not-for-profit setting be an adaptable law that is flexible and useable, applicable to changing needs and circumstances. The law itself provides no clear and direct answers about the scope of fair use and its meaning in specific situations. These insights are gained by reviewing the various courts' interpretation of the law of Congress. *No court has referred to the guidelines in reaching this case-by-case evaluation of what is and what is not a fair use of a material subject to copyright.* The significance of this important fact is that guidelines are not the law.

Guidelines are clearly not included in any statute, nor has any court ever relied on them for decisions they have reached regarding issues of copyright infringement. In sum, they are neither statutory law nor are they common law. They are no more and no less than they title implies; they are *guidelines.* Their greatest legal significance is the fact that they are included in the House Report on the Copyright Law. They are a part of the legislative history of the 1976 amendments, and as such, can be considered by the court in determining the intent of Congress in amending the Copyright Act in 1976.

Neither Congress nor the courts have made these guidelines the law, although many universities and school systems have adopted them as the inflexible, single rule of the institution with no exceptions allowed.

Four-Factor Test the Only Law That Governs the Fair Use of Copyrighted Material

The four-factor test that guides all decisions with regard to copyright is the only true law and guidance upon copyright infringement. In life balance is important. Librarians must balance their family life with their work. In their work they must balance their duties with their administrative duties. They must balance their expenditures of funds and their expenditure of time. One of the principal obligations of anyone who manages in any area is balance. All of law looks for balance. Certainly, the application of the four factors of fair use in an issue of the fair use of copyrighted material is a matter of balance. If most factors lean in favor of fair use, the activity is allowed; if most lean the opposite direction, the action will not fit the fair-use exception and may require permission from the copyright owner. All four factors must be weighed and balanced.

It is important to note that the principles of fair use are not the guidelines of fair use. Guidelines have evolved from the principles of fair use.

Guidelines for Educational Fair Use Exceptions to the Copyright Laws

Congress and the courts have acted deliberately to not create a lawfully binding standard from these guidelines. It would, however, be disastrous to have nothing to guide individual libraries and librarians in developing policy for copyright protection in their libraries. The guidelines are simply proposed guidance. Many argue that these guidelines destroy the legitimate purpose of copyright exceptions, which is to honor the spirit of the right of copy as balanced with the right of education. However, in the real world, where decisions must be made every day, these seven guidelines created by no legislature and endorsed by no judiciary affect education and library activities in a significant manner. The open question is whether they should be wholly accepted and endorsed in every library as *the* guidelines to govern the library.

CONTU GUIDELINES AND INTERLIBRARY LOAN

No one understands the concept that information has monetary value more than librarians. Information is their stock in trade. The cost of that information for libraries is found in its acquisition, delivery, and in its storage. Whether a library chooses to borrow information from another library or maintain the information within the library is often a decision based in economics. Some of the most expensive information to retain is found in journal articles and some of the most difficult decisions libraries make turn on the decision to subscribe to a journal or to employ interlibrary loan for that journal.

CONTU (The National Commission on New Technological Uses of Copyright Works) published a set of guidelines on acceptable uses of photocopying in 1978.[19] The CONTU guidelines were developed to help librarians and copyright proprietors understand the amount of photocopying for use in interlibrary loan arrangements that is permitted under the copyright law. Section 108(g)(2), shown here, is the pertinent section of the copyright fair use law that governs interlibrary loan.

The rights of reproduction and distribution under this section (Fair Use of Copyright material) extend to the isolated and unrelated reproduction or distribution of a single copy or phonorecord of the same material on separate occasions, *but do not extend to cases where the library or archives, or its employee*—engages in the systematic reproduction or distribution of single or multiple copies or phonorecords of material described in subsection (d): Provided, That nothing in this clause prevents a library or archives from participating in interlibrary arrangements that do not have, as their purpose or effect, that the library or archives receiving such copies or phonorecords for distribution does so in such aggregate quantities as to substitute for a subscription to or purchase of such work.[20]

The CONTU guidelines provide guidance in the application of Section 108 to a library's obtaining copies of articles from relatively recent issues of periodicals (those published within five years prior to the date of the request) from another library. The CONTU guidelines cap the amount of photocopying that the library can request for the community in any calendar year, with what is referred to as "the rule of five." The CONTU guidelines permit a borrowing library to receive in a calendar year five articles from the most recent five years of a specific journal or other periodical.

For a request for an entire book or an entire journal, the requesting library must determine that a copy cannot be obtained at a fair price. When requesting journals, articles from journals, and small portions of a copyrighted work when the request is for the same work, the library must certify that is it complying with the CONTU rule of five. The library is required to retain the records of the request for the library loan for three years. It is important to note that *if the requesting library has in force an order for a subscription to the journal or an order for a book or sound recording, then the request need not count as one of the five.* The library may treat the request as being filled by its own library. The rule of five does not apply to journals or articles from journals that are over five years old.

When patrons request copies that exceed the CONTU allowance, the patron may be asked to pay a royalty or the fee necessary to obtain these copies. These guidelines apply to interlibrary loan of digital documents as well as paper documents.

The guidelines are silent as to other important issues that libraries must themselves regulate, such as the quantity of copies of an article or articles published in a periodical. The guidelines are silent to the issue date of a request for material that is more than five years prior to the date when the request for the copy is made. These issues were left to future interpretation.

The Guidelines prepared by the National Commission on New Technological Uses of Copyrighted Works (CONTU), 1976, are included here for review:

1. As used in the proviso of subsection 108 (g) (2), the words, " . . . such aggregate quantities as to substitute for a subscription to or purchase of such work" shall mean:

   a. With respect to any given periodical (as opposed to any given issue of a periodical), filled requests of a library or archives (a "requesting entity") within any calendar year for a total of six or more copies of an article or articles published in such periodical within five years prior to the date of the request. These guidelines specifically shall not apply, directly or indirectly, to any request of a requesting entity for a copy or copies of an article or articles published in any issue of periodical, the publication date of which is more than five years prior to the date when the request is made. These guidelines do not define the meaning, with respect to such a request, of ". . . such aggregate quantities as to substitute for a subscription to (such periodical)."

   b. With respect to any other material described in subsection 108 (d) (including fiction and poetry), filled request of a requesting entity within any calendar year for a total of six or more copies of phonorecords or from any given work (including a collective work) during the entire period when such material shall be protected by copyright.

2. In the event that a requesting entity

   a. shall have in force or shall have entered an order for a subscription to a periodical, or

   b. has within its collection, or shall have entered an order for, a copy or phonorecord of any other copyrighted work, material from either category of which it desires to obtain by copy from another library or archives (the "supplying entity"), because the material to be copied is not reasonably available for use by the requesting entity itself, then the fulfillment of such request shall be treated as though the requesting entity made such copy from its own collection. A library or archives may request a copy or phonorecord from a supplying entity only under those circumstances where the requesting entity would have been able, under other provisions of section 108, to supply such copy from materials in its own collection.

3. No request for a copy or phonorecord of any material to which these guidelines apply may be fulfilled by the supplying entity unless such request is accompanied by a representation by the requesting entity that the request was made in conformity with these guidelines.

4. The requesting entity shall maintain records of all requests made by it for copies or phonorecords of any materials to which these guidelines apply and shall maintain records of the fulfillment of such request, which records shall be retained until the end of the third complete calendar year after the end of the calendar year in which the respective request shall have been made.

5. As part of the review provided for in subsection 108 (i), these guidelines shall be reviewed not later than five years from the effective date of this bill.

There are many sources for articles once the library's acquisition limits have been reached. Some services provide individual articles on a one-by-one request basis, while others offer subscription pricing to permit sharing to patrons or group members without increasing library costs.

The Guidelines for Classroom Copying are the guidelines that have the greatest impact on K-12 education. However, it would be much too simple to have just one set of guidelines. There are many. The following guidelines can be found online.

Classroom Guidelines are formally known as the *Agreement on Guidelines for Classroom Copying in Not-for-Profit Educational Institutions with Respect to Books and Periodicals,* H.R. Rep. No. 94–1476, at 68–70 (1976).

The Music Guidelines are formally known as *Guidelines for Educational Uses of Music,* H.R. Rep. No. 94–1476, at 70–71 (1976).

The Off-Air Guidelines are formally known as *Guidelines for Off-Air Recordings of Broadcast Programming for Educational Purposes,* H.R. Rep. No. 97–495, at 8–9 (1982). These guidelines first appeared in 127 Cong. Rec. 18, at 24,048–49 (1981).

The Digital Imagining Guidelines are formally known as *The Proposal for Educational Fair Use Guidelines for Digital Images,* in Information Infrastructure Task Force, Working Group on Intellectual Property Rights, Conference on Fair Use: Final Report to the Commissioner on the Conclusion of the Conference on Fair Use, November 1998, and found in the CONFU Final Report 33–41.

The Distance Learning Guidelines are formally known as *The Proposal for Educational Fair Use Guidelines for Distance Learning,* and found in the CONFU Final Report 43–48.

The Multimedia Guidelines are formally known as the *Proposal for Fair Use Guidelines for Educational Multimedia,* in CONFU Final Report 49–59. A slightly different version of the Multimedia Guidelines was the subject of a non-legislative report issued by a congressional subcommittee in December 1996. See the Staff of House Subcomm. on Courts and Intellectual Prop. of the House Comm. on the Judiciary, 104th Cong.

Good Faith Compliance with Guidelines

Guidelines are essential for the working librarian. There must be some articulated principle to which actions and behavior can adhere and on which policies can be based. It is important for the library and its personnel to have some sense of confidence that their policies comply with the law and their compliance with guidelines is an indication of good faith on the part of the library with the understanding that guidelines are flexible. This flexibility should be monitored by a single source and authority within the library rather than modified by every individual employee of the library on a case-by-case basis. This wholesale across-the-board modification could result in a de facto non-application of guidelines.

The guidelines have evolved from the principles codified in the Copyright Act of 1976 and the case law on which this statute was based. This sword cuts both ways; while the guidelines are considered to be the "minimum" intrusions permissible on the rights of copy, there is room for exception and interpretation. However, the farther the action of copy deviates from the guidelines the less likely the actions will be considered to have been taken in good faith. Good faith is an important fact the court considers in its assessment of damages and penalties. Because Congress never enacted the guidelines and no court ever has read them into law in a legal decision, the guidelines are not themselves binding on the public as a rule of law.

Damages for Infringement and the Concept of Good Faith

Damages for infringement upon a copyright come in two forms: statutory, incurred as a result of the act of infringement upon copyright, and actual damages in the form of lost profits. While it is extremely unlikely that damages will be sought from a library, their very existence will serve as a deterrent.

A more likely case scenario is that a cease-and-desist letter will be sent by the owner of the copyright. However, even this course of conduct is extremely undesirable.

Statutory damages are available to copyright owners who successfully prove infringement. While a work need not be registered to collect damages in the form of lost profits, it must be registered to collect the statutory damages,[21] or those damages articulated in the statute itself.[22]

Statutory damages will be preferred by the copyright holder when the actual damages are minimal. Statutory damages allow the court to award up to $30,000 per work infringed.[23] Statutory damages may reach as high as $150,000 if the infringement was "willful."[24] Should the court find that the infringer was "innocent" or acted in good faith, the statute directs:

In a case where the infringer sustains the burden of proving, and the court finds, that such infringer was not aware and had no reason to believe that his or her acts constituted an infringement of copyright, the court in its discretion may reduce the award of statutory damages to a sum of not less than $200. This decision, to impose damages to an amount of $200.00 lies solely within the discretion of the court.

These damages are guaranteed to scare a faculty into compliance and create a situation in which virtually no one wants the duty of deciding when exceptions should be made for the guidelines.

The Court Has the Power to Dismiss a Faculty Member or Librarian Defendant

An "employee or agent" of a nonprofit educational institution, library, or archives may be eliminated as a defendant while the institution remains a defendant. In order for a defendant to be released as a defendant, the infringer must demonstrate that he or she "believed and had reasonable grounds for believing that his or her use of the copyrighted work was a fair use under Section 107 of the Copyright Act."

The decision of a court to eliminate the employee or agent will be determined on the good faith action of the employee. Because what is and is not a fair use of the work of another is vague and often decided on a case-by-case basis Congress has given the courts the discretion to eliminate one of the largest financial consequences of infringement for educators and librarians *who apply fair use in a reasonable manner*. It is of utmost importance to note this is not an automatic immunity for librarians. The provision in no fashion exonerates libraries or librarians. It allows the court to make a determination as to the good faith actions of the librarian and library.

It is extremely likely that the courts will presume that educators understand copyright law and the guidelines and have made their best effort to apply them before any educator is dismissed from a suit. The educator will have to prove to the court that they were "innocent infringer[s]." While this proof is only necessary after the prima facie case of infringement is made, this is clearly the reason strict applications of guidelines are found around this country.

Classroom Guidelines Are a Strict Demarcation Not a Genuine Good Faith Attempt

Many of the guidelines and particularly the Classroom Guidelines demarcate a strict line, measured by counting words and instances of copying, in an effort to define fair use.

Their very existence destroys the Congressional intent of the notion of fair use. Good faith may intrinsically require an understanding and application of the law. Guidelines can be a method for establishing good faith. Guidelines for employees, faculty, or anyone else in a position to make fair-use decisions may demonstrate the good faith of the organization, and the application of the guidelines by the individual can manifest that person's good faith as well.

A set of guidelines may be a valuable tool for establishing good faith. In specific instances the existing guidelines may not be appropriate. In these instances the efforts expended in producing fact-specific guidelines should be documented. For example, discussion with attorneys, law professors, other departments, and any other experts should be footnoted in the guidelines. If the objective of an educator making policy is to avoid litigation, adopting and following the guidelines offers the prospect of discouraging a lawsuit.

Obtaining Permission for the Use of Copyrighted Materials

When a use of photocopied material requires permission, complete and accurate information should be sent to the copyright owner. The American Association of Publishers suggests that the following information be included in a permission request letter in order to expedite the process:

- title, author and/or editor, and edition of materials to be duplicated
- exact material to be used, giving amount, page numbers, chapters and, if possible, a photocopy of the material
- number of copies to be made
- use to be made of duplicated materials
- form of distribution (classroom, newsletter, etc.)
- whether or not the material is to be sold
- type of reprint (ditto, photography, offset, typeset)

1. The request should be sent, together with a self-addressed return envelope, to the permissions department of the publisher in question. If the address of the publisher does not appear at the front of the materials, it may be readily obtained from the library.
2. The process of granting permission requires time for the publisher to check the status of the copyright and to evaluate the nature of the request. It is advisable, therefore, to allow enough lead time to obtain permission before the materials are needed.
3. The Copyright Clearance Center (CCC) also has the right to grant permission and collect fees for photocopying rights for certain publications. Libraries may copy from any journal that is registered with the CCC and report the copying beyond fair use to CCC and pay the set fee.

Unpublished Works May Be Subject to Fair Use

Unpublished works may be subject to more stringent protection, the theory being that the author might still have the opportunity to modify the work. Unpublished work can be registered for copyright protection just as published work.

Copyright Symbol

To copyright your work the correct form for a copyright notice is "Copyright 200? (year of creation) by Your Name." You may also use the C-in-a-circle symbol instead of the word "Copyright." Copyright notices stopped being mandatory in this country in 1989 when the U.S. joined the Berne Convention, but using a notice is still a good idea. That way, you put others on notice that you consider a work to be your property, and that nobody should use it without your permission.

ANTICIRCUMVENTION DEVICES AND THE LIBRARY

Section 1201 of the 1998 Digital Millennium Copyright Act made it illegal to circumvent a technological protection measure employed to restrict access to or distribution of copyrighted material. The DMCA included a provision which allowed for modification and flexibility of exemptions to the Copyright Act under Section 1201(a)(1). The Librarian of Congress may, in consultation with the U.S. Copyright Office, conduct a triennial review of the impact of existing exemptions. The Librarian is allowed to permit further exceptions if, after holding reviews, such exceptions are found to be necessary. The U.S. Copyright Office conducts public hearings and submission of written comments from interested parties.

The most recent ruling indicates that during the period from October 28, 2003, through October 27, 2006, the prohibition against circumvention of technological measures that effectively control access to copyrighted works shall not apply to persons who engage in noninfringing uses of four classes of copyrighted works. Two classes were retained:

The two "classes of works" subject to the exemption from the prohibition on circumvention are:

- compilations consisting of lists of Web sites blocked by filtering software applications
- literary works, including computer programs and databases, protected by access control mechanisms that fail to permit access because of malfunction, damage, or obsolescence

Two classes were added:

- People with vision or print disability are allowed to circumvent technological protection measures in order to access literary works, including eBooks, via a 'screen reader' or text-to-speech or text-to-Braille device
- Circumvention is allowed in the case of computer programs and video games in formats that have become obsolete.

The American Library Association reports that:

Libraries, researchers, technologists and other critics of this section of the law have insisted that the anti-circumvention provision stifles fair use of copyrighted information and chills legitimate research crucial to the advancement of science and technical innovation . . . Because technology is changing rapidly, and waiting the statutory three year period to review the Rule might cause damage to scholarship, the Librarian intends to ask Congress to shorten the review period.

The Librarian will ask Congress to consider "more appropriate" criteria for assessing harm that the anti-circumvention prohibition might bring: "As presently crafted, the statute places considerable burdens on the scholarly, academic and library communities to demonstrate and even to measure the required adverse impacts on users.

There needs to be more "precise guidance regarding the definition of a class of works, as well as the standard of proof for what classes would qualify for the exemption."[25]

CONCLUSION

Whether or not a patron is using copyrighted material fairly will be a decision that the patron generally must make. The library is also a user of copyrighted materials in its day-to-day operation. Most libraries should have a designated copyright officer to whom all questions regarding fair use may be addressed. Often this officer will work with the city attorney or outside counsel in developing a fair use policy for both the library and library patrons. It is not unreasonable for a librarian or librarians to have the authority to make exceptions on a case-by-case basis to the appropriate fair use of copyrighted materials if the decisions are founded upon an understanding of and respect for the law.

While the legislators have given vague legal guidelines concerning "fair use," they have left the interpretations to those on the front lines and in the trenches. It can be the librarian who determines what is and is not an educational fair use of a copyrighted work. Reviewing the statute itself, cases interpreting it and speaking with the city attorney are a good start in understanding the fair use of a copyrighted material for both the library and its patrons.

REFERENCES

17 USC § 107, "Limitations on exclusive rights—Fair use" is available at the Legal Information Institute of Cornell Law School at *http://www4.law.cornell.edu/uscode/17/107.html*.

CONFU—The Conference on Fair Use, Final Report of the United States Patent and Trade Office may be reviewed at *http://www.uspto.gov/web/offices/dcom/olia/confu/*.

At the request of a faculty member, the Library may place on reserve photocopied or electronic excerpts from copyrighted works in its collection in accordance with guidelines similar to those governing formal classroom distribution for face-to-face teaching. In general, the library believes that these guidelines apply to the library reserve shelf because it functions as an extension of classroom readings and provides an individual student's right to photocopy for personal scholastic use under the doctrine of fair use.

1. If the request calls for only *one* paper copy to be placed on reserve for one semester, an entire article or an entire chapter from a book or an entire poem may be photocopied.

2. Requests for *multiple* paper copies on reserve should meet the following guidelines:

   a. The amount of material should be reasonable in relation to the total amount of material assigned for one term of a course taking into account the nature of the course, its subject matter and level (17 U.S.C. Sec 107 (1) and (3));

   b. The number of copies should be reasonable in light of the number of students enrolled, the difficulty and timing of assignments, and the number of other courses which may assign the same material (17 U.S.C. Sec 107 (1) and (3));

   c. The material should contain a notice of copyright (17 U.S.C. Sec 401).

   d. The effect of photocopying the material should not be detrimental to the market for the work. (In general, the library should own at least one copy of the work.) (17 U.S.C. Sec 107 (4)).

3. The uses of photocopied or electronic material in the reserve collection that require advance permission from the owner of the copyright are:

   a. Repetitive copying: The reserve use of photocopied or electronic materials in multiple courses or successive years will normally require advance permission from the owner of the copyright (17 U.S.C. Sec 107 (3)).

   b. Consumable works: The duplication of works that are consumed in the classroom, such as standardized tests, exercises, and workbooks, normally requires permission from the copyright owner (17 U.S.C. Sec 107 (4)).

   c. Creation of anthologies as basic text material for a course (a.k.a. "course packs"): Creation of a collective work or anthology by photocopying a number of copyrighted articles and excerpts to be purchased and used together as the basic text for a course will in most instances require the permission of the copyright owners. Such photocopying is more likely to be considered as a substitute for purchase of a book and thus less likely to be deemed fair use (17 U.S.C. Sec 107 (4)).

If requested staff will request permission to use photocopied or electronic material through the Copyright Clearance Center at the department's expense; however, all material coming with permission or not requiring permission will be processed first. We will put items requiring permission on reserve while permission is being sought but, if permission is denied, the item will be removed.

Copyright owners may grant permission to use an article for a fee. These fees will be the responsibility of the department that requests the item be placed on reserve.

Note that there is a sample letter for requesting permission to use a copyrighted work on our Web page at: http://library.austin.cc.tx.us/services/FacSrvcs/Reserves/sampltr.htm.[26]

NOTES

1. Campbell v. Acuff-Rose Music, 510 U.S. (1994).

2. 17 U.S.C. § 107.

3. Mawman v. Tegg, 38 ER 380 (1826), 2 Russell 383, per Lord Eldon; Wilkins v. Aikin, 17 Ves. 422; Roworth v. Wilkes, 1 Camp 94.

4. 9 F. Cas. 342 (C.C.D. Mass. 1841) (No. 4901). *See, e.g.*, Pierre N. Leval, *Toward a Fair Use Standard*, 103 HARV. L. REV. 1105, 1105–25 (1990).

5. Carey v. Kearsley, 4 Esp.168, 170 Eng. Rep. 679, 681 (KB 1803).

6. 9 F. Cas. 342, 348 (No. 4901) (CCD Mass. 1841).

7. See BLACK'S LAW DICTIONARY 415 (6th ed. 1991).

8. 758 F. Supp. 1522 (S.D.N.Y. 1991). A Federal District Court in New York ruled that Kinko's Graphic Corporation infringed when it photocopied "course-packs" designated by professors that included book chapters. Kinko's then sold the coursepacks to students for classwork at a profit. The court found that most of the fair use factors worked against Kinko's in this case, especially given Kinko's profit motive in making the copies. The court found that the Classroom Guidelines did not apply to Kinko's. The court did not rule that coursepacks could not constitute fair use in other circumstances.

9. The reversals of many leading fair use cases also reflects an incongruity among the various federal courts and evidences a failure of a uniform and cohesive direction in the law with regard to the fair use of copyrighted materials. *See, e.g.,* Harper & Row, Publishers, Inc. v. Nation Enters., 557 F. Supp. 1067 (S.D.N.Y.), *aff'd in part, rev'd in part,* 723 F.2d 195 (2d Cir. 1983), *rev'd,* 471 U.S. 539 (1985) (granting damages award which was reversed by the court of appeals, that was in turn reversed by the Supreme Court); *see also* Salinger v. Random House, Inc., 650 F. Supp. 413 (S.D.N.Y.), *rev'd,* 811 F.2d 90 (2d Cir. 1986) (denying plaintiff's motion to enjoin defendant's publication of biography about the plaintiff; decision reversed by court of appeals based on differing interpretation of fair use standard).

10. To prove prima facie infringement, the author must have a valid copyright, be in compliance with statutory requirements if any exist, show copying, which can be established by showing that the infringer had access to the work, and show that the two works were substantially similar. *See* Narell v. Freeman, 872 F.2d 907, 910 (9th Cir. 1989).

11. The beginning of fair use under American law is generally traced to Folsom v. Marsh, 9 F. Cas. 342 (C.C.D. Mass. 1841) (No. 4901). *See, e.g.,* Pierre N. Leval, *Toward a Fair Use Standard,* 103 HARV. L. REV. 1105, 1105–25 (1990).

12. Copyright Act of 1976, 17 U.S.C. § 107. Since its original enactment in 1976, the fair-use provision has been amended by the Judicial Improvements Act of 1990, Pub. L. No. 101–650, 104 Stat. 5089 (1990), and further amended in 1992 to address the fair use of unpublished works.

13. The principle that the fourth factor is the most important factor was underscored in a decision from the U.S. Supreme Court. *See* Harper & Row, 471 U.S. at 566. At least one district court judge has been highly critical of that principle, asserting that the Supreme Court and lower courts actually have not held that the fourth factor is of greater importance, even though they make such a statement in the decisions. *See* American Geophysical Union v. Texaco Inc., 802 F. Supp. 1, 20–21 (S.D.N.Y. 1992), *aff'd on other grounds,* 60 F.3d 913 (2d Cir. 1995), *cert. dismissed,* 516 U.S. 1005 (1995).

14. These are the guidelines agreed to by the Association of American Publishers and the Author's League of America in their attempt to interpret 17 U.S.C § 107 for classroom use.

15. *See* 17 U.S.C. § 107 (stating the first factor). Princeton Univ. Press v. Michigan Document Servs., Inc., 99 F.3d 1381, 1400 (6th Cir. 1996); Basic Books, Inc. v. Kinko's Graphics Corp., 758 F. Supp. 1522, 1532 (S.D.N.Y. 1991).

16. *See* Kinko's Graphics Corp., 758 F. Supp. at 1532–33 (emphasizing that factual works are given less protection). *See* New Era Publications, Int'l v. Carol Publ'g Group, 904 F.2d 152, 158 (2d Cir. 1990) (holding that use of a small percentage of a published work is fair use). *See also* Michigan Document Servs., Inc., 99 F.3d at 1389 (stating that the greater the volume or signficance of the portion copied, the less likely the copy to be considered fair use).

See Kinko's Graphics Corp., 758 F. Supp. at 1534 (finding infringement occurred where "in almost every case, defendant copied at least an entire chapter of a plaintiff's book" for classroom use).

17. Harper & Row, 471 U.S. 539 at 566–568.

18. 17 U.S.C. § 107 (1994).

19. Contained in the Report of the Conference committee on the New Copyright Law (H.R. No. 1733, 94th Cong., 2d Sess., at 71–73) reprinted in 1976 U.S.C.C.A.N. 5812–14. *See* <http://www.cni.org/docs/info.policies/CONTU. html>.

20. Emphasis added.

21. *See* 17 U.S.C. § 411 (1994 & Supp. IV 1998).

22. *See* 17 U.S.C. § 504(c) (1994 & Supp. IV 1998).

23. 17 U.S.C. § 504(c)(1).

24. 17 U.S.C. § 504(c)(2).

25. Used with permission of the American Library Association. "DMCA Section 1201 Anti-Circumvention Rule Making." Last Update: 29 October 2003. <http:// www.ala.org/Content/NavigationMenu/Our_Association/Offices/ALA_Washington/Issues2/Copyright1/DMCA_The_Digital_Millennium_Copyright_Act/DMCA _Section_1201_-_the_Anti-Circumvention_Rule.htm>.

26. This policy is excerpted from the following article with minor changes and is used by permission: Mary Hutchings, *Model Policy Concerning College and University Photocopying for Classroom, Research and Library Reserve Use*, 43 (4) COLLEGE AND RESEARCH LIBRARIES NEWS, 127–31 (1982).

8

UNPUBLISHED MATERIALS AND
LIBRARY USE

A library is the delivery room for the birth of ideas, a place where history
comes to life.

—Norman Cousins

Libraries often find themselves to be the owners of unpublished materials.
Permitting these materials to be reviewed is a wholly different course of conduct from permitting these materials to be used in published materials. Copyright protects unpublished materials. However, the courts have not been as
liberal with the use of unpublished materials as they have with the fair use of
published materials. The court has allowed for a narrow use of these materials in the context of the fair use statute, which would be for:

* teaching
* research—not for profit
* scholarship
* news reporting
* criticism

The U.S. Supreme Court in the case of *Harper & Row v. Nation Enters*[1] clarified many of the missing parameters governing the fair use of unpublished
works. However, because this 1985 case contained so many extreme issues,
such as a purloined manuscript that usurped the sale of excerpts from the manuscript by Gerald Ford to the *New York Times* in addressing his reasons for the
pardon of former United States President Richard Nixon, it can be difficult to
apply the reasoning to issues that are less clear-cut and more subtle.

The Copyright Act in 1976 included within its realm for the first time historical manuscripts, literary manuscripts, and other unpublished works, including new media such as computer programming. While the Copyright Act was passed in 1976, it was not until 1992 that the statute that specifically allowed the fair use of unpublished materials was clarified by Congress. In 1922, 17 U.S.C. § 106 was amended to specifically include the four-factor test in evaluation of the fair use of copyrighted material.

While Section 106 clearly states that unpublished works are subject to the fair use exception to the law of copyright, in 1985 the Supreme Court had already noted in the case of *Harper & Row v. Nation Enters* that "the scope of fair use is narrower with respect to unpublished works."[2]

Courts have often noted that the copyright owner has an interest in the "first publication" of the work. This notion of first publication protects the rights of the copyright owner to determine how and when this new information will be published, rather than giving that right to a third party.

Three important cases that illustrate the notion of fair use of unpublished works involve well known personalities J. D. Salinger, Marjorie Kinnan Rawlings, and L. Ron Hubbard, the founder of the Church of Scientology. A fourth case, which did in fact allow the use of published works of L. Ron Hubbard, is also discussed here for the purpose of comparing that which is considered fair use of published material with that which is considered fair use of unpublished material.

J. D. SALINGER

Since publishing *Catcher in the Rye,* Mr. Salinger has guarded his privacy and lived a life of reclusiveness in New Hampshire; he has given no interviews and published nothing since 1965, although he continues to write. Salinger sought to prevent Ian Hamilton, critic for *The London Sunday Times,* from quoting or closely paraphrasing unpublished letters that were written by Salinger and available to researchers in archival collections, including the University of Texas, Harvard University, and Princeton University. Most of the letters were written between 1939 and 1961. Most were written to Whit Burnett, Salinger's friend, teacher, and editor at *Story* magazine, and Elizabeth Murray, Salinger's friend. A few were written to Judge Learned Hand, Salinger's friend and neighbor in New Hampshire, Hamish Hamilton and Roger Machell, Salinger's British publishers, and other individuals, including Ernest Hemingway. In total, roughly seventy-nine letters were available and forty-four were used as a foundation for the biography. There were few resources other than the letters available.

While these universities had purchased these letters or received them as donations for their collection, they could not purchase the right of copy with these letters. The ownership of the copyright of the letters was retained by

J. D. Salinger. These letters are deposited in the library archives for anyone to read, but publication of the contents was restricted, not only by the law of copyright, but by agreements Hamilton made with the libraries prior to access to the materials. Hamilton signed form agreements furnished by the libraries, restricting the use he could make of the letters without permission of the library and the owner of the literary property rights. The Harvard form required permission "to publish the contents of the manuscript or any excerpt therefrom." The Princeton form obliged the signer "not to copy, reproduce, circulate or publish" inspected manuscripts without permission. After being contacted by Salinger's attorney, Hamilton revised his book by deleting most of the quotes that he had originally sought to include. Hamilton's final copy quoted only two hundred words and paraphrased the remainder of the letters.

Salinger presented several positions for the purpose of denying the use of his letters. One position was that these letters had value and one estimate placed their value at $500,000. The court found that Mr. Salinger was entitled to control the use of the contents and when and if they would published. The nature of the letters were such that they embodied J. D. Salinger's style of writing. The biographer, and his publisher, Random House, sought to convey the essence of Salinger by including his phrasing and observations.

In 1987, Salinger was successful in enjoining both the quoting and paraphrasing of his unpublished letters.[3] The appellate court noted that the application of fair use to unpublished letters typically did not exist:

Pertinent to our case is the fact that the Court underscored the idea that unpublished letters normally enjoy insulation from fair use copying. . . . We think that the tenor of the Court's entire discussion of unpublished works conveys the idea that such works normally enjoy complete protection against copying any protected expression.

The purpose of the publication was to support a biography of J. D. Salinger, and Random House certainly had a profit motive, but significantly the court did not address that motive. Rather, the court found that "the book may be considered 'criticism,' 'scholarship,' and 'research.'" The court found that the use of the quoted material for this purpose did not entitle Hamilton "to a generous application of the fair use doctrine." The court noted that:

[When Hamilton] is pressed as to why he copied a stylistic device that Salinger had employed in one of the letters. He responds: "I wanted to convey the fact that [Salinger] was adopting an ironic term. . . . " When the cross-examiner asks, "Couldn't you have stated that he had an ironic tone," Hamilton replies, "That would make a pedestrian sentence I didn't wish to put my name to." But when dealing with copyrighted expression, a biographer (or any other copier) may frequently have to content himself with reporting only the fact of what his subject did, even if he thereby pens a "pedestrian," sentence. The copier is not at liberty to avoid "pedestrian" reportage by appropriating his subject's literary devices.

In terms of purpose, the appellate court found the first fair-use factor weighed in Hamilton's favor, but not that the purpose of his use entitled him to any special consideration.

The amount copied was very small, but it revealed much about J. D. Salinger in a form that represented his unique style. The appellate court found that Hamilton took the "heart" of the letters. The court reasoned:

The taking is significant not only from a quantitative standpoint but from a qualitative one as well. The copied passages, if not the "heart of the book," . . . are at least an important ingredient of the book as it now stands. To a large extent, they make the book worth reading. The letters are quoted or paraphrased on approximately 40 percent of the book's 192 pages.

In the court's analysis and balancing test, the amount taken was excessive and weighed in Salinger's favor.

The nature of the material was that it was unpublished. The first observation of the court with regard to the nature of the material was a quote from *Harper & Row*: "The fact that a work is unpublished is a critical element of its 'nature.' " This factor was weighed by the *Harper & Row* standard and the court entertained the idea that the narrower scope of the fair use of unpublished material weighed in Salinger's favor.

The effect of the taking was found to be to be capable of potentially impacting a market for the letters as published materials and would diminish that market. Salinger owned the right to sell the contents of the letters. The court found that the letters "made the book worth reading." The court's review of Hamilton's book concluded "infringing copying from 44 of his letters," whether by direct quotations or close paraphrasing. The court noted the book copied "protected sequences," constituting at least ten percent of forty two letters. The letters were the most significant source of information Hamilton had regarding Salinger. That their content and conclusions regarding that content were a significant focus of the manuscript further persuaded the court against finding fair use. The unpublished nature of the works effectively lowered the standard for an acceptable amount.

The court stated that the single most important element of fair use was the impact that the publishing of these letters would have on a future market for these letters. While the value of the letters was indicated to be $500,000, that value would be diminished with their publication in Hamilton's book. The court found that Salinger was entitled to sell his letters and permitted with their ruling Salinger's right "to protect his opportunity to sell his letters." Here, the library owned the letters, but Salinger owned the words.

L. RON HUBBARD

L. Ron Hubbard, the founder of the Church of Scientology, became the subject of an unflattering biography by Russell Miller entitled *Bare-Faced Messiah*. The biography included quotations from Hubbard's unpublished correspondence and other works. The biography contradicted many assertions of Hubbard's "official" biography. After the book's publication and fortified by the Salinger decision, the licensees of the Church of Scientology sought to enjoin the further distribution of Miller's biography. The court decided strongly to protect the unpublished works of Hubbard: "Where use is made of materials of an 'unpublished nature,' the second fair use factor has yet to be applied in favor of an infringer, and we do not do so here."[4]

In another case, a court allowed an unauthorized biography about Hubbard, which relied on published materials rather than unpublished material, to be published.[5] This book was written by a former member of the Church of Scientology and also presented an unflattering portrait of L. Ron Hubbard. The author joined the Church when he was nineteen and was a member for almost nine years. The author recounted the Church's repressive practices toward dissident members. It was the author's position that the Church was a dangerous cult, and that Hubbard was a vindictive and profoundly disturbed man. The author's purpose in publishing the book was to expose his position on the Church of Scientology addressing what he perceived to be the pernicious nature of the Church and the deceit that is the foundation of its teachings. The book painted an unflattering portrait of Hubbard as a thoroughgoing charlatan who lied relentlessly about his accomplishments. The author described Hubbard as "an arrogant, amoral egomaniac," "a paranoid, power hungry, petty sadist," and—perhaps ironically in light of the claims in this case—"an outright plagiarist."

The book quoted widely from Hubbard's works, using passages from Hubbard's writings both in the body of the text and at the beginning of many chapters. Hubbard published nearly 600 fiction and non-fiction works during his lifetime, 111 of which are in print.

The Church of Scientology licensees claimed that the book copied "substantial portions" of certain of Hubbard's works, in violation of its exclusive copyright rights. It was claimed that 121 passages of the book were drawn from 48 of Hubbard's works.

In its fair-use analysis the court reviewed each element of fair use.

The purpose of the book was found to be the use of the quotations in part to convey the facts contained therein, and not for their expression. The court found that quoted passages used for their expression were intended to convey the author's perception of Hubbard's hypocrisy and pomposity, qualities that may best (or only) be revealed through direct quotation. The author's purpose in the use was found to have a valid purpose, as he juxtaposed the grandiose expression of the Hubbards' quotations with the banal (to the author) material contained in the body of the chapter. The author's purpose of criticism was found to be a valid purpose for the fair use of copyrighted material. The panel in *New Era* observed that:

as long as a book can be classified as a work of criticism, scholarship or research, as can the book here, the factor cuts in favor of the book's publisher, whether the copyrighted matter is taken from a literary lion like J. D. Salinger or a purported prophet like L. Ron Hubbard.[6]

The court examined the nature of the work and found all of the works from which the author quoted had been published, noting, "Whether or not a work is published is critical to its nature under factor two, because the scope of fair use is narrower with respect to unpublished works."[7] The court also noted that the nature of the work was factual, and explained that the scope of fair use is greater with respect to factual than non-factual works. "While there is no bright-line test for distinguishing between these two categories, we have referred to the former as works that are 'essentially factual in nature,'[8] or 'primarily informational rather than creative.' "[9]

The court determined that the materials of L. Ron Hubbard used by the author were published. After that important distinction was made, the four-factor analysis was employed by the court: purpose, nature, amount, and effect. This case underscores the important distinction courts give to unpublished material from published material for the purpose of a copyright infringement analysis.

The court in balancing all of the relevant factors found the book presented a strong set of facts for invoking the fair use defense:

The book is a critical biography, designed to educate the public about Hubbard, a public figure who sought public attention, albeit on his own terms; the book quotes from merely a small portion of Hubbard's works and from only those that have been published; and, it will cause no adverse impact protected by the copyright law on the market for Hubbard's writings. In these circumstances, we conclude that the book's use of passages from Hubbard's work is protected fair use.[10]

It was against a backdrop that seemed to create a strict prohibition against the use of unpublished works that Congress enacted the 1992 amendment of the 1976 Copyright Act. By amending the Act, Congress returned to the courts the duty of applying the four-factor test.

MARJORIE KINNAN RAWLINGS

Marjorie Kinnan Rawlings authored *The Yearling,* which received a Pulitzer Prize in 1939, as well as other books such as *Sojourner* and *Cross Creek.* After she died in 1953, a close friend served as a literary executrix by maintaining her papers and continuing to publish them pursuant to Rawlings's will. In her will, Rawlings designated her husband and the Foundation as co-executors of her estate. She also designated one of her closest friends, Ms. Julia Scribner Bigham, as literary executrix of her estate. Bigham was the daughter of publisher Charles Scribner, whose company, Charles Scribner's Sons, published all of Rawlings's works. Neither Marjorie Rawlings nor those she trusted to oversee her estate could have anticipated the litigation which was to accompany a manuscript unpublished at her death. This case appears to involve people of good will and good intentions who ultimately chose a course of conduct mutually beneficial for all . . . but not until litigation and acrimony had run its course.

In her will, Rawlings bequeathed her manuscripts to the University of Florida Library, with any income from publications to be held by the Florida Foundation. Some documents, however, were not administered by Bigham and remained in the hands of family members. One such document was her first, and so far unpublished, novel, *Blood of My Blood*.

Rawlings's husband was appointed to be the sole executor of Rawlings's estate. With the approval of her husband, Bigham acted in the capacity as literary executrix under the auspices of Baskin, from 1953 until her death on October 24, 1961. Rawlings's will left immediate custody of "all manuscripts, all notes, all correspondence, and all literary property of any kind" to Bigham. Bigham, in her role as literary executrix, had the power to destroy any of the "notes, manuscripts or correspondence" she believed should be destroyed. She also had the power to determine which materials would be published. Bigham could keep the literary works as long as she wanted, then she was to turn them over to the University of Florida Library. Any income from these literary materials was to be held in trust by the Foundation, along with the remainder of Rawlings's property.

Acting in her role as literary executrix, Bigham collected Rawlings's correspondence, papers, manuscripts, and other materials from Rawlings's husband. Bigham also obtained some of Rawlings's materials from Scribner's. During the remainder of her life, she wrote an introduction to and published *The Secret River*, and then directed the original manuscript be sent to the University of Florida Library; she published *The Marjorie Rawlings Reader*, and returned the typescript and original materials to Scribner's; she worked to ensure that any works retained by Scribner's were later sent to the University of Florida Library; and she transferred numerous other documents to the University of Florida Library.

After Bigham's death in 1961, Baskin did not ask anyone else to assume the role of literary executor. Instead, as executor of the estate, he assumed that role. Baskin was not as conscientious as Bigham in performing the duties of literary executor. He admitted that he was aware that Bigham had a significant number of Rawlings's documents at the time of her death, yet he never asked Bigham's family to return any of those documents to the Rawlings estate. He stated that he believed the documents were under consideration for publication by Scribner's but admits that he knew the documents were at Bigham's residence. In any event, he failed to confirm whether or not the documents were part of Rawlings's estate and whether or not they were being considered for publication by Scribner. Four years after Bigham's death, on October 24, 1961, the Florida probate court closed administration of Rawlings's estate with Baskin still having failed to clarify the status of those documents.

The documents remained stored at the residence of Bigham's widower in two boxes labeled "MKR letters and papers." In 1987, Bigham's widower was moving from the residence, so he and his children decided to dispose of the contents of the boxes. Ms. Ann Hutchins, Bigham's daughter, contacted Mr. Glenn Horowitz, a nationally known dealer of rare books and literary and historical manuscripts, to help them sell the material. Horowitz and his staff cataloged the contents of the two boxes as follows:

1. letters written from Rawlings to Bigham from 1939 to 1953

2. correspondence of Bigham in connection with her duties as literary executrix

3. publisher's typescript with editor's blue-penciled emendations of Rawlings's *The Secret River*

4. miscellaneous original typescripts, manuscripts, and story ideas written by Rawlings, including her first novel, *Blood of My Blood*

5. letters written from Bigham to Rawlings from 1940 to 1953

After compiling the catalog of documents, Horowitz contacted Dr. James Meriwether, an officer of Seajay, about the letters. Seajay is a small, non-profit organization dedicated to enhancing public awareness of, and interest in, unduly neglected aspects of South Carolina and Southern culture. After negotiations, Seajay obtained the documents by partial purchase and partial gift from the Bigham estate.

While Seajay purchased the actual manuscript they could not purchase the copyright to the manuscript. *Blood of My Blood* is Rawlings's first novel; it was written in 1928, is 183 pages long, and had never been published. After purchasing the documents, Seajay made one copy of *Blood of My Blood* for Dr. Anne Meriweather. Meriweather, also an officer of Seajay, used the copy in preparing a critical review of *Blood of My Blood*. Seajay made the copy so that Meriweather would not damage the fragile original during her analysis. Seajay also made a partial copy of the manuscript, which it sent to the Rare Books Room at the University of Florida Library. Seajay made this copy both to allow Baskin, or his designee, to view and authenticate it, and to allow the University of Florida Press to view it and determine if it was worthy of publication. Access to the copy was restricted, and photocopying it was prohibited. The University of Florida Library eventually returned its copy to Seajay.

In April of 1988, Meriweather orally presented her critical analysis of *Blood of My Blood* to a symposium of the Marjorie Kinnan Rawlings Society at the University of Florida. Between 150 and 200 members of the Rawlings Society attended the symposium. In the presentation, Meriweather quoted approximately 2,464 words from the text of *Blood of My Blood*, or four to six percent of the total text. Meriweather submitted a hard copy of her paper for publication with the Marjorie Kinnan Rawlings Society Journal. She also hoped to publish an edited version of her presentation as an introduction to *Blood of My Blood*, which the University of Florida Press wanted to publish in its entirety. Meriweather was aware that neither the Society's Symposium nor the University of Florida Press would be able to publish her article, much less *Blood of My Blood*, without first obtaining the permission of the copyright holder. Ultimately *Blood of My Blood* was published by the University of Florida Press in March of 2002, edited by Anne Blythe Meriwether.

In the case of *Sundeman v. The Seajay Society, Inc.*[11] the court opens its opinion with an important and fundamental statement of copyright law: "It is important to note the distinction between the physical ownership of documents, and the ownership of the literary rights in those documents, the later being the copyright. Under 17 U.S.C.A. § 202 (West 1996), the physical document and the copyright are subject to separate transfer."

This is a case of a copyright infringement action brought against two defendants, an author and scholar and the Society to whom the manuscript was transferred. In most circumstances the University foundation might be expected to support a scholarly review of an unpublished novel as a fair use of the novel. Publication of the article that included similar quotations was postponed until the author, Meriwether, could secure permission from the copyright holder. That permission was never forthcoming, and neither Meriweather's article nor Rawlings's book had yet been published.

The court's application of the four factors are a strong endorsement of scholarly study and the use of unpublished manuscripts in the context of critical analysis. With regard to the "purpose" factor, the court resolved that the quotations in Meriweather's manuscript were a "transformative" use that did not replace the purposes of the original work, and that her study "has productive uses as criticism, comment, scholarship, and literary research," all as generally favored under the fair-use statute. In addition, the court held that while Meriweather and Seajay may have been motivated in part by some prospect of royalties or other financial gain from their work, their purpose overall was to expand the scope of knowledge about Rawlings and to serve the public benefit. Moreover, the copies of the manuscript and the quotations in Meriweather's article were also not for any "exploitative motive," because Seajay and Meriweather acknowledged that they could not publish those works without permission from the Foundation.

When analyzing the "nature of the work," however, the court ruled, as in other cases, that the unpublished nature of the work left this factor weighing against a finding of fair use. Through its analysis of the "nature" factor, the court repeatedly noted that the unpublished nature of the work did not prevent a finding of fair use; rather, it only "militates against" fair use.

Noting that the right of first publication should be retained by the author the court closely examined whether the literary criticism took that right from the copyright holder:

> The Foundation is correct in its statement that usurping the copyright holder's privilege to determine whether or not to publish *Blood of My Blood* would favor a finding of unfair use. This argument presupposes, however, that the purpose or effect of the allegedly infringing uses was to supplant the Foundation's right to publish *Blood of My Blood*. As discussed above, we have found that neither the purpose nor the effect of any of the challenged copies amounted to a first publication of *Blood of My Blood*. Thus, we hold that while the unpublished nature of *Blood of My Blood* weighs against a finding of fair use, the allegedly infringing copies have not stripped from the Foundation its right to determine whether or not to publish Rawlings' first work at all.[12]

The purpose for which the literary criticism was to be published was found not to "supplant the copyright holder's commercially valuable right of first publication."

The court examined the "amount" of the work the literary criticism embodied noting that the "amount" factor can be measured both qualitatively and quantitatively. The taking of the copyrighted work of another can be measured most easily in the amount taken. This is typically done as a percentage amount of the work. Deeper analysis is required in measuring the quality of the work taken. Where the quality taken takes the "heart of the work" the taking is not a fair use.

In its analysis of the quantity of material used for a fair-use consideration, the court did not simply rely on a set percentage or overall amount. It noted that for a fair-use analysis "the propriety of the amount quoted and paraphrased by Meriweather must be analyzed in consideration of the purpose and character of the allegedly infringing use." The court noted that this was a literary criticism and examined amounts taken in other cases of literary criticisms. The court found this amount was consistent and appropriate for the fair use of a literary criticism noting that in the other cases the works cited were not unpublished works.

The court examined whether the market for the unpublished manuscript would be diminished by the impact of the literary criticism and the quotes it employed. The court concluded the market was not impacted by the use of the manuscript in the literary criticism. The factual support for this decision was that the University of Florida Press was still interested in publishing the novel. The court examined the nature of the markets for literary criticism and for the work itself were separate and distinct markets. "Blythe's [Meriweather's] paper is not a market substitute for the original work."

The court concluded, "In fact, it is likely that Blythe's [Meriweather's] presentation stimulated interest in *Blood of My Blood* among the Society's members and may actually have increased demand for it."

Three of the four factors of the fair-use test for copyright material were found to weigh in favor of fair use. In this instance, the court found a fair-use allowance in favor of an unpublished work, while noting that the very nature of an unpublished work militates against a fair use.

CONCLUSION

While the courts in some instances allow the use of unpublished materials, they have made the fair use of unpublished materials very difficult. The University of Florida did ultimately publish Rawlings's *Blood of My Blood,* and on their Web page advertising the sale of the book they quote Blythe's critical analysis of the work.

The historical notion that an author of a work should have the right to control and profit from the first publication of that work has found its way into the court's logic and reasoning in the application of the four-factor test. Courts have maintained that the author or the author's designated copyright holder has the right to manage and control their works for as long as a copyright exists.

NOTES

1. 471 U.S. 539 (1985).

2. *Id*. at 564.

3. Salinger v. Random House, Inc., 811 F.2d 90, 92 (2d Cir. 1987).

4. New Era Publications International v. Henry Holt & Co., Inc., 684 F. Supp 808 (S.D.N.Y. 1988), *motion denied*, 69 F. Supp 1493 (S.D.N.Y. 1988) *affirmed on other grounds*, 873 F. 2d 576 (2nd Cir. 1989).

5. New Era Publications Int'l, ApS v. Carol Publishing Group, 904 F.2d 152 (2d Cir. 1990), *cert. denied*, 111 S. Ct. 297 (1990) (action based on quotations from Hubbard's published writings).

6. New Era, 873 F.2d at 583.

7. Harper & Row, 471 U.S. 539 at 564; *see also* New Era, 873 F.2d at 583; Salinger, 811 F.2d at 96.

8. Maxtone-Graham v. Burtchaell, 803 F.2d at 1253, 1260 (2d Cir. 1986).

9. Consumers Union of United States, Inc. v. General Signal Corp., 724 F.2d 1044, 1049 (2d Cir. 1983), *cert. denied*, 469 U.S. 823, 83 L. Ed. 2d 45, 105 S. Ct. 100 (1984).

10. New Era Publications Int'l, 904 F.2d 152.

11. Sundeman v. The Seajay Society, Inc., 142 F.3d 194 (4th Cir. 1998).

12. *Id*. at 197.

9

---·•··•·---

LIBRARY ARCHIVING AND INTERNET SERVICE PROVIDER STATUS

I think there is a world market for maybe five computers.
—Thomas Watson, 1947, Chairman of IBM

It is important to examine any laws that provide libraries with legal immunity for specific actions. The U.S. Copyright Act allows certain legal protections to libraries if specific prerequisites are met by the library. The decision to become an Internet service provider by a library is one that requires legal consultation, advice, and an ongoing vigilance by the library.

Section 108 of the Copyright Act, "Limitations on exclusive rights: Reproduction by libraries and archives," provides an exemption for librarians and archivists. This section allows the library access to a limited group of works within the last twenty years of a work's copyright protection term. However, use of the exemption requires compliance with specific conditions. Without compliance with Section 108(h) requirements, the Act does not protect the activities, resulting in the library not being a qualifying institution; its activities would not therefore be covered by Section 108 protection. Section 108 of the Copyright Act was modified by both the Sonny Bono Copyright Term Extension Act (CTEA) and by the Digital Millennium Copyright Act (DMCA). The DMCA increased the number of archival copies permitted from one to three.

The rights provided to libraries pursuant to Section 108 are greater rights to copy material that has been copyrighted than those rights provided to educators pursuant to Section 107 of the Copyright Act for the fair use of copyrighted materials. These rights are *in addition to* the fair-use rights found in Section 107 for educators. Section 108 does not rely on guidelines. This is a law that provides a determined outcome for libraries and archives under specified circumstances for the actions of copy for the following instances:

- copies made for preservation
- copies made for interlibrary loan
- immunity of the library from liability for the unsupervised use of on-site reproduction equipment

For Section 108 to apply, the following conditions must be met:

(1) the reproduction or distribution is made without any purpose of direct or indirect commercial advantage;

(2) the collections of the library or archives are (i) open to the public, or (ii) available not only to researchers affiliated with the library or archives or with the institution of which it is a part, but also to *other persons* doing research in a specialized field; and

(3) the reproduction or distribution of the work includes a notice of copyright that appears on the copy or phonorecord that is reproduced under the provisions of this section, or includes a legend stating that the work may be protected by copyright if no such notice can be found on the copy or phonorecord that is reproduced under the provisions of this section.[1]

The first question that must be asked is whether or not your library makes its collections or archives available to "other persons doing research in a specialized field." This is the purpose of all public libraries and this question can easily be answered, yes.

Secondly, in order to qualify, all materials upon which the copyright has not expired must reflect notice of copyright on the work. If it is not there automatically, the library should stamp such a notice on the work with a legend that notes that a work may be protected by copyright law. This includes all interlibrary loan materials being forwarded to other libraries. When *archival* material lacks an explicit statement of copyright, a warning that the work may be copyrighted is required to be included on the copies. An example of a notice follows:

The work from which this copy was made did not include a formal copyright notice. This work may be protected by copyright law. Uses may be allowed with permission from the rightsholder, or if the copyright on the work has expired, or if the use is "fair use" or within another exemption. The user of this work is responsible for determining lawful uses.

The benefits of complying with the prerequisites are that it is not deemed to be an infringement of copyright for a library or archives, or any of its employees acting within the scope of their employment, to reproduce more than one copy or phonorecord of a work, except as provided in subsections (b) and (c) of Section 106, or to distribute such copy or phonorecord, under the conditions specified by this section. These copies, however, must be made for archival purposes. Archival copies are not circulating copies; they are made as an insurance policy, and are protection in the event the circulating copies are damaged or lost.

ARCHIVE COPIES

Libraries are no longer limited to making digital copies. Multiple generations of copies in a preservation project may be made. A service copy may be made as an archival copy, as may a camera negative or a printing master. The preservation copies may be in either analog or digital form.

Libraries and archives can now use Section 108 of the Copyright Act to scan or convert to digital format unpublished material for preservation purposes. The digital files, however, can only be made available to the public in digital form within the premises of the library or archives. This means that digital files may not be made available online or on the library's Web site.

Libraries may make copies of digital material in obsolete formats, for example, long-playing record albums. A format is considered obsolete if the machine or device necessary to render perceptible a work stored in that format is no longer manufactured or is no longer reasonably available in the commercial marketplace.

Archive copies, which are not circulating copies, can be made of unpublished materials and published materials. Archive copies are to be used for archival purposes exclusively. This means that the archival copies are not to be loaned to patrons. They are a tool to insure that the library retains all its materials should the original be damaged or lost. For a published work, an archival copy can be made only if the work is out of print (not out of copyright). There is, however, much debate as to the definition of "out of print." The library's purpose for making the archival copy can only be to replace a copy it has or used to have in its collection, but which copy has been damaged, is deteriorating, is lost or stolen, or the format of which has become obsolete.

An example of an unpublished material would be a faculty member's multimedia presentation or a diary or manuscript the library has obtained that has never been published. In order to copy an unpublished work, a library's purpose must be preservation or security, and it must have a copy of the work in its collection. These are all logical, natural instincts for a librarian's sense of survival and self preservation.

Title IV of the DMCA, Section 404, amends Section 108 of the Copyright Act to permit libraries to digitize analog materials without permission for archival purposes.

So we can make just one archival copy? Section 108 has been expanded to permit libraries to make up to three copies. While a digital copy can be made for preservation purposes, a digital copy cannot be made available off the

library premises. It is important to remember that archival copies are not circulating copies.

PATRON COPIES MADE BY THE LIBRARY

Section 108 authorizes libraries to provide patrons with copies. For a
patron the copy may be a photocopy, an electronic copy, or a copy sent by
facsimile machine. In order for the library to make the patron a copy without
liability for copyright infringement:

- The copy must become the property of the patron.
- The library should have no knowledge that the copy will be used for a purpose
  other than private study, scholarship, or research.
- The library should have both a display and order form entitled "Warning of Copyright Violation."

The first requirement is very simple; the copy will belong to the patron.

The second requirement means that if the patron indicates openly to the
library or its staff that the copy will be used for commercial gain, the library
will be deemed to have infringed upon the copyright of the material when the
patron infringes upon the copyright, should infringement of a copyright be
claimed. The library is not required to inquire of the patron their intended
use or demand that the patron acknowledge only legal use of the copy. The
library should deny requests for uses that it believes would violate the law,
should that potential use be made known to the library.

The third requirement refers to a warning sign that should be posted near
all library copy machines,[2] all computer printers, and possibly all computers
with Internet access that indicates the following:

NOTICE: WARNING CONCERNING COPYRIGHT RESTRICTIONS:

The copyright law of the United States (Title 17, United States Code) governs the
making of photocopies or other reproductions of copyrighted material.

Under certain conditions specified in the law, libraries and archives are authorized
to furnish a photocopy or other reproduction. One of these specified conditions is
that the photocopy or reproduction is not to be "used for any purpose other than private study, scholarship, or research." If a user makes a request for, or later uses, a photocopy or reproduction for purposes in excess of "fair use," that user may be liable for
copyright infringement.

This institution reserves the right to refuse to accept a copying order if, in its judgment, fulfillment of the order would involve violation of copyright law.

For fax requests of other requests not made in person, a copy of the
"Copyright Warning" should accompany the transfer of the actual copyright
document.

A different warning is required for the lending of computer software:[3]

NOTICE: WARNING CONCERNING COPYRIGHT RESTRICTIONS:
The copyright law of the United States (Title 17, United States Code) governs the making of photocopies or other reproductions of copyrighted material.

Under certain conditions specified in the law, non-profit libraries are authorized to lend, lease or rent copies of computer programs to patrons on a nonprofit basis and for nonprofit purposes. Any person who makes an unauthorized copy or adaptation of the computer program or redistributes the loan copy, or publicly performs or displays the computer program, except as permitted by title 17 of the United States Code, may be liable for copyright infringement. This institution reserves the right to refuse to fulfill a loan request if, in its judgment, fulfillment of the request would lead to violation of the copyright law.

PATRON COPIES MADE BY THE PATRON

Section 108(f)(1) of the Copyright Act relieves the library of responsibility for unsupervised patron use of copying equipment located in the library so long as the library displays the notice that making copies may be subject to copyright law. This notice should be displayed not only at the photocopying stations of the library but at the locations for printing materials from the Internet.

THE DIGITAL MILLENNIUM COPYRIGHT ACT AND MUSIC DOWNLOADING

The Digital Millennium Copyright Act was enacted by Congress in 1998. The DCMA addressed the issue of downloading of music and World Intellectual Property Organization Treaties. WIPO is a specialized agency of the United Nations, which administers twenty-three treaties in the field of intellectual property.

There is a provision in the Act that makes it illegal for an Internet service provider to link knowingly to infringing material. The DMCA exempts search engines and service providers from liability for linking to pirated material unknowingly. Other significant points for online music are the Act's strong prohibition against devices that circumvent copyright management technology and its provisions for liability of Internet service providers that host infringing material. It has been suggested that the language that limits ISP liability only upon compliance by canceling the user's account after being notified chills protected speech by fostering a "guilty until proven innocent" approach to the canceling of Web sites.

If a library accepts the benefits of being an Internet service provider it should be acutely mindful of the liabilities. It is essential that any library that accepts the benefits of ISP protection pursuant to Section 108 post notices that downloading copyrighted material is expressly prohibited.

COPY THE NEWS?!?

Libraries may copy and retain in their collection audiovisual news programs pursuant to Section 108(f)(3). These are not simply archival copies but can become part of the library's circulation. This law allows not only local news, but regional and national network newscasts, to be copied and retained. Interviews concerning current events are permitted to be retained. This does not include newsmagazines and documentaries.

Not all news shows are eligible for this protection. *Sixty Minutes* and *20/20* are examples of television programs that could not be copied. These are not "straight" news broadcasts. They represent a magazine format and are not considered to be retainable pursuant to Section 108.

LICENSE AGREEMENTS THAT CONFLICT WITH SECTION 108

It is fundamental that parties can enter into any legal contract they so desire. The chapter on licensing points out that often companies and libraries agree to restrictions for the use of the licensed material that are more restrictive than fair use, allowed in Section 107, or Section 108 would allow.

Section 108 is not without ambiguity. The gray area occurs when libraries negotiate with vendors, typically for databases. It is common for the license agreement to place the obligation on the library to prevent patrons from copying images. Generally license agreements state the restriction on copying images will be implemented by requiring the library to post a notice that copying of images from the database is prohibited. This notice typically appears on an opening page to the database. Notice may also be posted in the computer areas.

While the Copyright Act does allow archival copies, that provision can be overridden by a contracted license agreement between the parties. Vendors can circumvent Section 108 with their license agreement by prohibiting the library's creation of an archival or reserve copy of the database.

Are these restrictions binding, and can they in fact eliminate the library's and the patrons' fair use rights and Section 108 rights? Technically, and the law is a technical business, the patron is not a party to the contract. The patron did not enter into any agreements with the vendor. The patron has a privilege pursuant to Sections 107 and 108 of the Copyright Act. Does the library have the right to contract away those statutory rights?

These issues have not been addressed in the context of educational fair use and library copying in a not-for-profit environment.

INTERLIBRARY LOAN AND SECTION 108

Many libraries participate in interlibrary loan agreements. Section 108 covers these agreements. A library has responsibilities as a requester and as a lender under Interlibrary Loan activities. To request a copy of a book, a library must comply with Sections 108(e) and (g), which requires the requesting library to take the following actions before a book is requested:

- Determine that a copy cannot be obtained at a fair price.
- Ensure that the copy becomes the property of the patron.
- Ensure that it has no notice that the copy will be used for a purpose other than private study, scholarship, or research.
- Have both a display and order form with the "Warning of Copyright."
- Ensure that it is not aware or does not have substantial reason to believe it is engaging in related or concerted reproduction or distribution of multiple copies of the same material.
- Make its request for the loan with a representation that it has complied with copyright law, and this is generally included in the standard form of request the library uses.

LENDING A COPY OF A BOOK THROUGH INTERLIBRARY LOAN

The lending library in an interlibrary loan transaction is not the library with the responsibility for compliance with copyright law. That responsibility belongs to the borrowing library. However, it is standard practice for the lending library to require a statement of compliance with copyright law from the requesting library.

The supplying library, in requesting this assurance, is attempting to protect itself from the potential resulting acts of copyright infringement that may occur on the receiving end of the loan. Section 108(g) allows libraries to copy in accordance with the provisions of Section 108, so long as the library has no "awareness" or "substantial reason to believe" that it might be engaging in related or concerted reproduction or distribution of multiple copies of the same material.

Section 108 only applies if the library or archive offers the reproduction service without commercial advantage and is either open to the public or to nonaffiliated researchers. In the past, libraries have had to stamp all materials reproduced for patrons via interlibrary loan or other services with the American Library Association notice stating "Notice this work may be protected by copyright."

Section 108(a)(3) indicates that libraries are now required to include the actual notice of copyright that appears in the front matter or label of the work along with the requested portion. Reproduction of the notice can be by any means, but often it will mean copying the title page of a journal or the verso. This can be done by photocopying or even writing out the information onto the copy. In cases where the work does not include a copyright notice, the library should continue to use the ALA notice.

AMBIGUITIES IN SECTION #108 PRIVILEGES AND RESPONSIBILITIES

As a result of the Sonny Bono Copyright Term Extension Act, Section 108 now contains a limited exemption for libraries and archives that lets them reproduce, distribute, display, and perform certain works in the final twenty years of their extended terms for research and preservation purposes.[4] Now, published and unpublished works are covered under this section and they may be "archived" when the works are not subject to "normal commercial exploitation."

"Normal commercial exploitation" occurs when a copy cannot "be obtained at a reasonable price." However, defining that a work cannot be obtained can be a difficult matter. If a copy is available at a used book store for a reasonable sum, even if it is available only in an obsolete format, it can be "obtained at a reasonable price." Certainly an extensive Internet search of used book stores inventories is a simple matter and would be evidence of a good-faith effort of compliance.

Notice can be filed with the U.S. Copyright Office with the copyright owner advising that the work is available. In December 1998, the Copyright Office issued interim regulations and requested comments on how a copyright owner or its agent may provide notice to libraries and archives that a published work in the final twenty years of its extended term of copyright is subject to normal commercial exploitation or that a copy can be obtained at a reasonable price. However, the Copyright Office has not, more than three years after issuing its notice, acted upon these comments or issued final rules.

Section 108(h) creates difficult and gray areas in its conditions for archiving copyrighted works in the last twenty years of their copyright.

SHOULD YOUR LIBRARY BE AN INTERNET PROVIDER— SECTION 512

If your library provides Internet access it is, in a certain context, already an Internet service provider (ISP). The question for your library to consider is whether your library wants to receive the benefits of being a "designated" ISP and accept the concomitant liabilities.

A library that provides Internet access may qualify as an ISP. Typically, companies like America Online (AOL) are thought of as Internet service providers; however, the library also serves as the ISP for many citizens. This fact has been recognized in many of the access issues in litigation, with the courts noting that the library is often the only access that some people have to the Internet. Section 512 of the 1976 Copyright Act defines a service provider as "a provider of online services or network access, or the operator of facilities therefore." Libraries provide these services for many people and in some instances provide the only Internet access for many. The library may choose to qualify as an online provider of Internet access pursuant to this statute.

What Are the Benefits of Being an Internet Service Provider?

A library will not be held liable for specific Internet functions should it decide to take the steps necessary to qualify as an ISP. Section 512 enumerates four areas in which a library will escape liability for Internet activity of its patrons:

Transmitting, routing, or providing connections for transmitting or routing material through a system controlled by the ISP (Internet service provider), including the intermediate and transient storage of the material as part the transmission routing, or provision of connections if:

- The transmission was initiated by the user of the Internet service and not the ISP.
- The routing is carried out by an automatic technical process not selected by the ISP.
- The ISP does not select the recipients of the materials.
- No copyrighted material made by the ISP is maintained in such a way as to make it available to anyone other than the original user and is not kept longer than is reasonably necessary to transmit the material.

System caching is allowable as long as ISP employees accept industry standards associated with caching.

Linking to sites containing infringing material will not create a liability on behalf of an ISP if:

- The ISP does not have actual knowledge that the material is infringing or of facts that should make the infringement obvious.
- The ISP does not receive a financial benefit directly attributable to the infringement.

In essence this statute gives a library the same immunity for acts of its users that AOL has from the acts of its users. Internet access will not be attributable to any act of the library as long as access and infringement were done without the library's knowledge.

Because the statute indicates that access must be without the ISP's "initiation," access to materials directly through a library-provided bibliography or pathfinder will not be protected. For this reason it is essential that a library periodically review the links it provides to be certain that they have not been "domain-napped" by a provider of pornography.

Internet Service Provider Liability

Title II of the DMCA limits an Internet service provider's liability for copyright infringement. The intent of the act was to protect service providers (such as America Online or a university) from being held liable for infringing acts by users of their networks. More on the "safe harbor" afforded to ISPs by the DMCA can be found at the Association of Research Libraries' Intellectual Property Web page at *http://www.arl.org/info/frn /copy/copytoc.html* and at the Copyright Office's Web site at *http://lcweb. loc.gov/copyright/*.

Internet Service Provider Limitation on Liability for Copyright Infringement

The DCMA added Section 512 for the purpose of limiting liability for certain Internet service provider activity. This section of the Copyright Act recognizes the reality that Internet service providers cannot be responsible for the activities of their patrons. For example, it would be impossible for AOL to know every pornography site that offered contraband pornography. In essence, the responsibility falls upon AOL to act when it has knowledge that illegal activity is occurring, but this section does not place the responsibility on the Internet service provider to seek out all illegal activity occurring on the Internet service that it provides.

Most people and even most librarians do not think of the library as an Internet service provider. However, a library has the potential to be protected from liability just as AOL or any other ISP is if it complies with the statutory prerequisites defined in Section 512. The act broadly defines an ISP as "a provider of online services or network access, or the operator of facilities therefor." Compliance with the prerequisites of Section 512 would offer protection for a library against being held liable for copyright infringements. This protection is statutorily provided, in addition to other copyright defenses and limitations, like fair use. The library is protected against monetary damages for copyright infringement if it complies with the prerequisites of Section 512. Because copyright infringement occurs and liability can result from innocent infringements, this is an important avenue of protection. A copyright owner prevailing in an infringement action may be entitled to receive actual damages and profits of the infringer, or statutory damages plus attorney's fees.

The decision to seek ISP status and protection should be made with the input of an attorney. It could be catastrophic to believe the library had protection when it did not because it had not meticulously complied with all the statutory prerequisites for protection.

Requirements to Be Characterized as an Internet Service Provider

There are four different categories of an Internet service provider as statutorily defined. Each category has a different definition. A library might be an ISP under one category and not another. This is intrinsically confusing and the library must examine each category, the definition provided, and determine whether it qualifies or desires to qualify as an ISP under that category.

The definition of Internet service provider is specific to each category. It is possible to qualify as an ISP in one category while failing to qualify in another category. The four categories for ISPs are:

1. transitory communications
2. system caching
3. storage of information on systems or networks at the direction of users
4. information location tools

Transitory communications occur when the library transmits information. This routinely occurs when patrons access information through the library's Internet system. This act will be protected when the selection of material or recipients was made by the patron of the library and not the library.

For the purpose of the transitory communications limitation, a service provider is defined in Section 512(k)(1)(A) as "an entity offering the transmission, routing, or providing of connections for digital online communications, between or among points specified by a user, of material of the user's choosing, without modification to the content of the material as sent or received." Examples of transitory storage are the temporary retention of Web pages by the library's facilities for use by the patron.

System caching occurs in virtually all Internet transactions. Information that is placed on a system or network at the direction of a user is cached. Directories, indexes, and hypertext links cache information in the system. The ISP then retains the copy so that subsequent requests for the same material can be fulfilled without retrieving the material from the original source on the Internet. Everyone who has cleared their cache understands the importance and function of a cache. Links to cached information must be renewed for speedy access. In Section 512(k)(1)(B), the definition of Internet service provider applies to this activity: "a provider of online services or network access, or the operator of facilities therefore."

The liability of the ISP will be limited if the material is posted by a third party; the storage and access to the material are automatic; the material is unchanged; the material is updated if required by the original site; access to the material is limited based on conditions such as payment or password; and the storage does not interfere with hit information or other technology of the originating site.

It is important for the ISP to remove material or block its access once it is notified that the original site does not have the right to make the material available.

Protection for *storage of information* would rarely apply to a public library. An ISP will not be liable should the patron participate in the storage of information on systems or networks at the direction of users. The ISP qualifies for this limitation if it does not have or should not have actual knowledge that the material is infringing; it does not receive direct financial benefit as a result of the infringement; and it promptly removes or blocks access to the material upon proper notice of infringement. The ISP is also protected from any liability for claims based on the removal of the material unless counter notice is given that the material is not infringing.

The ISP must also have a designated agent registered with the Copyright Office in order to receive such a notice. In Section 512(k)(1)(B), the definition of Internet service provider applies to this activity: "a provider of online services or network access, or the operator of facilities therefore." This is not an action most libraries undertake and is an action undertaken for this purpose. It is a simple process but one which must be accomplished.

ISP users who use information location tools such as hyperlinks, online directories, and search engines that employ the use of copyrighted information will not incur liability on behalf of the library under category 4. However, if library employees perform this activity for the library there is no liability protection. It is important in copyright to examine activities both in terms of patron activities and activities the library undertakes for its ongoing maintenance.

This protection would rarely apply to a public library. Liability is limited for the acts of referring or linking users to a site that contains infringing material through use of information location tools if the ISP does not have or should not have actual knowledge that the material is infringing; the ISP does not receive a direct financial benefit as a result of the infringement; *and the ISP promptly removes or blocks access to the material upon receiving notification of infringement.* In Section 512(k)(1)(B), the definition of Internet service provider applies to this activity: "a provider of online services or network access, or the operator of facilities therefore."

Library Policy Required for Limitation of Liability

In order to be eligible for the liability protections of Section 512, a library must adopt and make reasonable effort to enforce a policy of terminating either Internet access or the patronage of patrons who are repeat infringers. The library/ISP is not required to monitor its Internet service or material accessed by its patrons which violates copyright laws in order to be eligible for any of the liability limitations. However, the library may participate in a monitoring program which does not violate a patron's right to privacy.

With this protection a library will not be responsible for the downloading of musical CDs and movies. As a matter of practice known downloading sites such as KaZaA should be blocked from library access. Web sites, however, that provide music for a fee, such as Apple or Listen.com, do not require blocking.

The statute addresses the issue of privacy of a user's identity on the Internet. Procedures are established by which a complaining copyright owner may obtain the identity of individual subscribers from the ISP and through this request the ISP will be protected from liability under federal or state prohibitions respecting release of information regarding individual subscribers.

For libraries, the initial issue is simple: does the institution qualify as a service provider? The statutory definition is very expansive, encompassing any provider of Internet access or online network services. Broadly interpreted, most library institutions could qualify. However, with qualification comes potential burdens, including creating a Web site agent, registering that individual with the Copyright Office, satisfying the other conditions of the ISP rules, and responding rapidly to notifications of infringement. The burden of compliance may not be worth the benefits of limited liability.

In many cases the decision to become an ISP is one of financial accountability to the entity which sponsors the library. Exposure to financial liability as a result of successful legal claims of copyright infringement by patrons is a real possibility.

Who Is a Patron Under This Act?

Patrons are those persons who access the Internet through the library. This does not include employees of the library. For a non-profit higher education library, the Act provides that graduate students and faculty who teach and research are not considered employees and are considered patrons. This expands the scope of protection a library might have by not categorizing the University educators as employees. This is a logical extension, because in their role as educators they are truly patrons of the library and not employees. In fact, it is not uncommon for this group to be the most active patrons the library has.

What Prerequisites Are Required to Qualify for ISP Protection?

The prerequisites for qualification as an ISP are that the library designate a registered agent with the United States Copyright Office by making available through its service, including on its website in a location accessible to the public, and by providing to the Copyright Office, substantially the following information:

(A) The name, address, phone number, and electronic mail address of the agent.

(B) Other contact information which the Register of Copyrights may deem appropriate. The Register of Copyrights shall maintain a current directory of agents available to the public for inspection, including through the Internet, in both electronic and hard copy formats, and may require payment of a fee by service providers to cover the costs of maintaining the directory.[5]

Once an institution registers as an agent with the Copyright Office, it is obligated to follow the procedures designated in Section 512 for responding to claims. These procedures are not significantly different nor more burdensome than any actions an attorney who represents the library would take.

Before accepting the responsibilities of Section 512, it is important for the library to consult with its attorney and its Internet technology representative to determine that it abides by the limitations on technology imposed by Section 512, such as a policy for termination of persons who are repeated infringers. The library must remove material or disable access to material when a claim for infringement is made. This could conceivably include the responsibility to disable access to servers which provide for the downloading of copyrighted material such as KaZaA. While the infringement status of the "people to people" access is one which is hotly debated, the library would want to block access to these sites certainly after a cease-and-desist letter was received from RIAA or possibly before.

Policies That Support Section 512

Just as a library maintains policies on copyright, employment, safety, conduct, and circulation, a library should address the Section 512 limitations in its policies should it decide to accept the protection and the responsibilities of this section of the Copyright Act.

CONCLUSION

Any library activity that can be undertaken without personal or library liability appears to be a gift. Studies by the Colorado Department of Education show that half the population (or more) depend on their library for Internet access. This is an indication that a library is in essence a major Internet service provider in a literal sense.

Section 108 provides specific immunity to a library for common library activities. Adopting Section 108 privileges is an important consideration for the librarian, and understanding the concomitant responsibilities and liabilities is essential. Recognizing that a library might have certain liabilities for Internet activities is an important duty of library management. With the recognition of potential civil liabilities of the library for actions of its patrons comes the responsibility of evaluation of the benefits of Section 512 and the informed decision as to the adoption of these benefits.

NOTES

1. Copyright Act, 17 U.S.C. § 108(f) (1996).

2. *See* FEDERAL REGISTER (November 16, 1977) for the form that the warning signs to be posted in libraries must take. These must be posted near all library copy machines.

3. FEDERAL REGISTER (February 26, 1991).

4. 17 U.S.C. § 108(h).

5. 17 U.S.C § 512(c)(2)(A) and (B).

10

REGULATION OF ACCESS TO INFORMATION IN A LIBRARY

> We have the power and capability to think with anticipation in a way never before possible. In the past, much of our effort relied on remediation . . . solving existing problems . . . working on solutions after problems occurred . . . Today we can foresee, even predict many of the problems or challenges.
> —Rita Colwell, Director National Science Foundation
> Remarks to Science Writers, 1998

Generally speaking, patrons have the right within a library to access the information they desire through the library, so long as they conduct themselves in accord with both the law and the library policy. This issue has generally not been questioned. There is no question but that the man who set up his electric fry pan and began to fry fish in a corner of a metropolitan library was clearly not conducting himself appropriately in the library, notwithstanding that the library did not have a policy restricting the frying of fish. The Internet, however, presents a whole new kettle (frying pan) of fish.

The freedoms of a patron can be restricted by valid library policy. The key word in that sentence is "valid." An appellate court noted the library's rights to create rules and policies:

The aim of the rules, as correctly identified by the district court, is "to foster a quiet and orderly atmosphere . . . conducive to every patron's exercise of their constitutionally protected interest in receiving and reading written communications." Requiring that its patrons make use of the Library in order to be permitted to remain there is a reasonable means to achieve that end. The Library need not be used as a lounge or a shelter. Clearly the rule is reasonable and perfectly valid.[1]

The library's and the community's right of safety must be balanced with the individual patron's right to access information. If our libraries become unsafe, if parents become unwilling to permit their children to come to the library, then the library's value is severely diminished. The library has both the right and the legal obligation to govern activities that occur within the library through policy and procedure. The librarian must create a policy that serves the library, the safety of the community at large, and individual library patrons.

Legal rights to access information are safeguarded by the U.S. Constitution through First Amendment freedoms. The library, too, has a right to conduct its institution for the good of the public at large and to restrict certain activities that are detrimental to the operation of the library. A library is not a daycare center, a locus for the convening of gang activities, or a homeless shelter. A library has been defined on several occasions by the court. A Maryland Supreme Court's view of a library and its purpose is found in a seventy-five-year-old case, *Johnston v. Baltimore*,[2] which provides a majestic interpretation of the function of a library.

In the recent opinion of *United States et al. v. American Library Association et al.* Justice Rehnquist noted that:

At the present time it is generally recognized and conceded by all thoughtful peoples that such institutions form an integral part of a system of free public education and are among its most efficient and valuable adjuncts. An enlightened and educated public has come to be regarded as the surest safeguard for the maintenance and advancement of the progress of civilized nations. More particularly is this true in republican forms of government, wherein all citizens have a voice. It is also true that education of the people ought not and does not stop upon their leaving school, but must be kept abreast of the time by almost constant reading and study. It would therefore seem that no more important duty or higher purpose is incumbent upon a state or municipality than to provide free public libraries for the benefits of its inhabitants.[3]

To serve the public in its intended purpose and to fulfill its stated mission a library must regulate activities within its perimeter. In evaluating patron rights the librarian must always keep in mind the patron's First Amendment rights. The right of access to legal information is a protected First Amendment right. A library may not restrict a patron's access to legal information based upon the content of that information. In a library,[4] First Amendment rights are greater than they would be in a bookstore, because the library is an arm of the government.

In California, a library was sued for not using filtered computers. In Virginia, a library was sued for using filtered computers. The safe harbor for libraries from liability lies in their policies and the implementation of these policies. There is no safe harbor from law suits. Anyone who can pay a filing fee may file a lawsuit.

IS A LIBRARY A PUBLIC FORUM?

Is a library a public forum, and why does this matter? First Amendment rights are greater in a public forum than in private venues. However, not all public forums are created equal. Some public forums have greater First Amendment freedoms than others. For this reason it is important to determine where libraries fall in this legal continuum that accords greater freedom of speech rights to one forum over another. Historically, libraries have not been venues that accord to their patrons the greatest rights of freedom, such as would be found in public parks or street corners. The greatest freedoms of speech and expression would be found there.

In *United States et al. v. American Library Association et al.*, the Supreme Court once again rejected the notion that a public library is a public forum, and rejected the argument that inviting the Internet into the library makes it a public forum. The Court regarded the duty of the librarian in the selection process employed for the library collection and extended that duty exercised with the print collection to the Internet. The ultimate opinion of the Supreme Court was that: "We have held in two analogous contexts that the government has broad discretion to make content-based judgments in deciding what private speech to make available to the public. . . . Public library staffs necessarily consider content in making collection decisions and enjoy broad discretion in making them." The Court found the Internet to be "no more than a technological extension of the book stack."[5]

The two analogous decisions were the findings by the Supreme Court that held that the Public Television and the National Endowment for the Arts (NEA) were *not* protected public forums.[6] The Court noted the NEA is required to make content-based considerations and the considerations that may be taken into account in the grant-making process are a consequence of the nature of arts funding. It also noted that Public Television exercises editorial judgments regarding the private speech it presents to its viewers. "[B]road rights of access for outside speakers would be antithetical, as a general rule, to the discretion that stations and their editorial staff must exercise to fulfill their journalistic purpose and statutory obligations."[7]

The Court found that analysis and heightened judicial scrutiny are incompatible with the role of public television stations and the role of the NEA; they are also incompatible with the discretion that public libraries must have to fulfill their traditional missions.

Public library staffs necessarily consider content in making collection decisions and enjoy broad discretion in making them. Internet access in public libraries is neither a "traditional" nor a "designated" public forum.[8]

The Court rejected the argument that a public library acquires Internet terminals in order to create a public forum for Web publishers to express themselves. It noted that a library collects books in order to provide a public forum for the authors of books to speak. It provides Internet access, not to "encourage a diversity of views from private speakers,"[9] but for the same reasons it offers other library resources: to facilitate research, learning, and recreational pursuits by furnishing materials of requisite and appropriate quality. The Supreme Court cited the Congressional recognition that "[t]he Internet is simply another method for making information available in a school or library."[10]

In *Brown v. Louisiana*,[11] it was indicated in dictum that a public library is a limited public forum. In *Concerned Women for America, Inc. v. Lafayette County*,[12] a district court's injunction was based on its determination that a public library constituted a public forum. *International Society for Krishna, Consciousness, Inc. v. New Jersey Sports and Exposition Authority*[13] indicated in dictum that a public library is a limited public forum.

In terms of the First Amendment, the existence of a right of access to public property and the standard by which limitations upon such a right must be evaluated differ, depending upon the character of the property or the forum at issue. The First Amendment requires neither equal nor unlimited access to public places. The Supreme Court has identified three categories of government forums to form an evaluation of the First Amendment's mandates. The case *Perry Education Association v. Perry Local Educators' Association*[14] defined the exercise of First Amendment rights for a forum.

The first class of government forums encompasses "places which by long tradition or by government fiat have been devoted to assembly and debate. . . ."[15] This category includes streets and parks and public sidewalks, and other public spaces that "have immemorially been held in trust for the use of the public, and, time out of mind, have been used for purposes of assembly, communicating thoughts between citizens, and discussing public questions."[16] The government's right to limit First Amendment activity in these "quintessential" public forums is "sharply circumscribed." The Court held that content-based government regulations in this context are permissible only where "necessary to serve a compelling state interest and . . . narrowly drawn to achieve that end." Further, content-neutral time, place, or manner restrictions are permissible if they are "narrowly tailored to serve a significant government interest, and leave open ample alternative channels of communication."[17]

The second class of government forums consists of "public property which the state has opened for use by the public as a place for expressive activity."[18] Although the government is not required to open or indefinitely retain the open nature of these forums, once it does so the government is bound by the same limitations as exist in the traditional public forum context. In the Court's words, "[r]easonable time, place and manner regulations are permissible, and a content-based prohibition must be narrowly drawn to effectuate a compelling state interest."[19]

The third category of government property includes "nonpublic" forums that are not "by tradition or designation [forums] for public communication. . . . "[20] The Court reaffirmed that "the State, no less than a private owner of property, has power to preserve the property under its control for the use to which it is lawfully dedicated."[21] In this setting, the government may enact and enforce "time, place, and manner regulations, [to] . . . reserve the forum for its intended purposes, communicative or otherwise, as long as the regulation on speech is reasonable and not an effort to suppress expression because public officials oppose the speaker's view."[22]

In its evaluation, the Court addresses the nature of the library as the "quintessential locus for the exercise of the right to receive information and ideas." Libraries have historically and logically fallen into the second category. Library policy should always address the activity in the context of "[r]easonable time, place and manner regulations," which are permissible. Content-based prohibitions are required to be "narrowly drawn to effectuate a compelling state interest."[23]

Universities were held to be limited public forums. In examining the status of a University, the Supreme Court noted that, "A university's mission is education, and decisions of this Court have never denied a university's authority to impose reasonable regulations compatible with that mission. . . ."[24] First Amendment rights must be construed "in light of the special characteristics of the school environment."

Libraries' policies will be construed in accord with their stated mission. For this reason the questioned activity will be evaluated in accord with its stated mission. The standard by which this evaluation is made will be in terms of reasonable time, place, and manner for the specific activity questioned. The regulation must be drawn so that a reasonable person will understand what is and is not prohibited. In the case of *Kreimer v. Bureau of Police for the Town of Morristown,*[25] the court noted that the library opened its doors for the purposes of: "reading, studying, using the Library materials. The Library has not opened its door for the exercise of all First Amendment activities." It is from this mission that its policies were evaluated.

In determining which uses should be tolerated, the Court noted:

A library is "a place dedicated to quiet, to knowledge, and to beauty." Brown v. Louisiana, 383 U.S. 131, 142, 86 S.Ct. 719, 724, 15 L.Ed.2d 637 (1966). "Its very purpose is to aid in the acquisition of knowledge through reading, writing, and quiet contemplation. Thus, the exercise of other oral and interactive First Amendment activities is antithetical to the nature of the Library. These arguable conflicting characteristics, at least in a First Amendment sense, support our conclusion that the Library constitutes a limited public forum, a sub-category of designated public fora." See Brody v. Spang, at 1118. We thus adopt the reasoning of the United States Court of Appeals for the Second Circuit in *Travis v. Owego-Appalachian School District,* 927 F.2d 688 (2d Cir.1991), where the court held that a limited public forum "is created when government opens a nonpublic forum but limits the expressive activity to certain kinds of speakers or to the discussion of certain subjects. . . . In the case of a limited public forum, constitutional protection is afforded only to expressive activity of a genre similar to those that government has admitted to the limited forum." Hence, as a limited public forum, the Library is obligated only to permit the public to exercise rights that are consistent with the nature of the Library and consistent with the government's intent in designating the Library as a public forum. Other activities need not be tolerated.[26]

Here the importance of the library's mission statement is made most clear in its support of a library's policies and guidelines. If a library's mission is to serve the entire public then its policies will be evaluated in terms of the entire public. If the library's mission is to serve the residents of a specific area then its policies and guidelines will be evaluated within that context. The Supreme Court has found that restrictions on freedoms in a public forum need only be "reasonable and not an effort to suppress expression merely because public officials oppose the speaker's view."[27]

Restrictions can never restrict expression based on the content of the expression. Time, place, or manner regulations that limit permitted First Amendment activities within a designated public forum are constitutional only if they are "narrowly tailored to serve a significant governmental interest, and . . . leave open ample alternative channels for communication of information."[28]

No regulations that purport to restrict First Amendment activities on the basis of content or viewpoint will withstand judicial review. For example, a library could not restrict access to information on witchcraft, nor could it restrict access to information on sex as a prior restraint on a person's right to access. While historically a library may not have included these topics in its print collection, once they are available through the Internet, access cannot be restrained.

WHAT CAN THE LIBRARY REGULATE: RESTRICTING CHILD ACCESS WHILE PERMITTING ADULT FREEDOMS

While making the Internet safe for children is an important concern, the Courts have ruled that safety cannot come at the expense of adults' freedoms. In terms of adult access the library cannot regulate that which the adult is free by law to access through the Internet if Internet service is provided. This concept is known as the "right to access" and is an extension of First Amendment rights. Adults are free to access what they wish to view as long it is legal to access this material. For example, it is not legal to access child pornography. The First Amendment right of access must be balanced with other rights within the library, and it is in that balancing process that free, full, and unfettered access may find limitation.

In *United States et al. v. American Library Association et al.*, the Supreme Court found that the ability of the patron to request that a filter on the library Internet access be removed served to secure the patron's First Amendment right to Internet access, and that the filter was not a prior restraint on the patron's right to access legal Internet material.[29]

A patron, however, has no right to access illegal Internet material. The library is commanded in many states by law to protect children from access to harmful materials. Access to child pornography through the library Internet is as illegal as access to heroin in the library bathroom.

A group of librarians, known as the Minneapolis Twelve, filed a complaint with the Equal Employment Opportunity Commission (EEOC), claiming that they were repeatedly exposed to pornography when library patrons accessed sexually explicit material. The pornographic surfing created a hostile work environment, the librarians said. In 2001, the EEOC issued a preliminary ruling against the Minneapolis Library System, saying the library's unrestricted Internet access policy created a sexually hostile work environment for the workers. The EEOC's preliminary ruling, or determination, is a recommendation. The EEOC suggested that the Minneapolis Library System pay each of the twelve employees $12,000.

Once again, all freedoms must be balanced, and librarians through their valid policies are the ones who must create and enforce this very difficult act of balance. In some states certain materials are deemed by statute to be "harmful to minors." In these states both civil and criminal liability attaches if this material is displayed for minors to view. This material has the potential to be displayed to minors in any library that provides Internet access. In these states the burden is on the library to ensure that no materials that are deemed "harmful to minors" can be displayed for viewing by minors.

Some libraries have interpreted this responsibility as a duty to block and filter Internet access for adults to any material that may be deemed "harmful to minors." Some attorney general's offices have suggested that providing access to material deemed "harmful to minors" without blocking or filtering creates criminal liability on behalf of the library for the act of causing harm to minors. This statute has been successfully challenged on First Amendment and Interstate Commerce grounds. However, in some jurisdictions it remains the law in many states.

First the law with regard to the right to access information will be reviewed. It is only in the understanding of the right of access that restriction placed upon that access and the patrons' right of privacy to that access can be understood.

CAN A LIBRARY REGULATE ACCESS TO PORNOGRAPHY BY ADULTS? FIRST AMENDMENT RIGHT TO RECEIVE INFORMATION

The First Amendment has been found to embody the "right to receive information and ideas."[30] Public libraries play a vital role in promoting the fullest exercise of that right. The First Amendment declares in broad terms

that "Congress shall make no law . . . abridging the freedom of speech. . . ."
As history has confirmed, the "speech" component to this constitutional
right is far-reaching and includes various methods of communication. In
Martin v. City of Struthers,[31] the Supreme Court decided the First Amendment protected not only the right to speak freely, but also the freedom to
receive speech as well.

In *Martin,* the appellant, a Jehovah's Witness, distributed a leaflet to people's homes advertising a meeting of her religious group. Although she "pro-
ceeded in a conventional and orderly fashion," she was convicted and fined
for violating the following ordinance:

It is unlawful for any person distributing handbills, circulars or other advertisements
to ring the door bell, sound the door knocker, or otherwise summon the inmate or
inmates of any residence to the door for the purpose of receiving such handbills, circulars or other advertisements they or any person with them may be distributing.[32]

On appeal she urged that the ordinance as applied to her violated the First
and Fourteenth Amendments guaranteeing the freedom of speech, press, and
religion.

The Supreme Court agreed for three reasons. First, the Court observed
that the framers "knew that novel and unconventional ideas might disturb
the complacent, but they chose to encourage a freedom which they believed
essential if vigorous enlightenment was ever to triumph over slothful ignorance. This freedom embraces the right to distribute literature . . . and necessarily protects the right to receive it."[33]

Second, the Court recognized that there were three potentially conflicting
interests in the case: the appellant's interests in distributing information, the
household dweller's interest in choosing whether to receive that information,
and the interests of the community in protecting all its citizens, including
those who prefer not to receive this information. In the Court's view, the
ordinance improperly "substitutes the judgment of the community for
the judgment of the individual householder," without carefully considering
the interests at stake.

Finally, the Court underscored that the distribution of pamphlets constituted an important means to disseminate ideas "in accordance with the best
tradition of free discussion." The Supreme Court found the freedom to distribute and receive information was "so clearly vital to the preservation of a
free society" it announced that it "must be fully preserved." The Court
declared the ordinance unconstitutional.

In *Griswold v. Connecticut*,[34] the Court, in a plurality opinion, again placed
its imprimatur on the constitutional right to receive information. There, the
appellants, Griswold, the Executive Director of the Planned Parenthood
League of Connecticut, and Buxton, the Medical Director of the League,
gave information and instruction to married persons concerning contracep-

tion. Connecticut prosecuted them for violations of statutes that provided that "[a]ny person who uses any drug, medicinal article or instrument for the purpose of preventing conception shall be fined . . . or imprisoned . . . or be both fined and imprisoned" and "[a]ny person who assists, abets, counsels, causes, hires or commands another to commit any offense may be prosecuted and punished as if he were the principal offender."

The Court struck down each provision as unconstitutional on a variety of grounds, including the First Amendment. The Court reasoned that:

[T]he State may not, consistently with the spirit of the First Amendment, contract the spectrum of available knowledge. The right of freedom of speech and press includes not only the right to utter or print, but the right to distribute, the right to receive, the right to read . . . and freedom of inquiry, freedom of thought, and freedom to teach. . . . Without those peripheral rights the specific rights would be less secure.

The Supreme Court found in this case that the First Amendment, like other constitutional guarantees, encompassed the "penumbral" right to receive information to ensure its fullest exercise.

In *Stanley v. Georgia*,[35] a majority of the Supreme Court agreed that the First Amendment encompasses the right to receive information and ideas. There, the Court reversed the conviction of a defendant prosecuted under a state statute proscribing the private possession of obscene matter. Although the Court agreed that the government has a valid interest in "dealing with the problem of obscenity," this interest did not foreclose an analysis of whether all possession of obscene material, including private possession, could be forbidden.

At the outset of its analysis, the Court observed that "[i]t is now well established that the Constitution protects the right to receive information and ideas," citing *Martin* and *Griswold* as support for that proposition. The Court explained that the "right to receive information and ideas, regardless of their social worth . . . is fundamental to our free society." The Supreme Court determined that, to protect the right to receive information and ideas, as well as the right to "satisfy [one's] intellectual and emotional needs in the privacy of [one's] home," the state was precluded from making private possession of obscene material a crime.

The case of *Board of Education v. Pico*[36] included seven separate opinions. The Board of Education of Island Trees Union Free School District No. 26 ordered that certain books, which it characterized as "anti-American, Anti-Christian, and anti-Sem[i]tic, and just plain filthy, be removed from high school and junior high school libraries within the school district." Students in that district brought suit for declaratory and injunctive relief under the Civil Rights Act, alleging that the school board's actions had unlawfully infringed on their First Amendment right to receive information. The district court granted summary judgment in favor of the Board, but the Court of Appeals for the Second Circuit reversed and remanded, ordering a trial on the merits of the students' allegations. A plurality of the Supreme Court affirmed the court of appeals' judgment, concluding that:

[T]he First Amendment imposes . . . limitations upon the discretion of the School Board to remove library books from the schools and . . . the affidavits and other evidentiary materials before the District Court, construed most favorable to the students, raise a genuine issue of fact whether the School Board might have exceeded those limitations.[37]

The plurality recognized that "local school boards have broad discretion in the management of school affairs." However, the court determined that the discretion "must be exercised in a manner that comports with the transcendent imperatives of the First Amendment."[38] The First Amendment was found to protect not only the right to self-expression, but also the right of self-expression, and as an element of that self-expression guarantee "public access to discussion, debate, and the dissemination of information and ideas."[39]

The Court also found a right to receive information, which is the right of greatest significance to libraries. It stated that that right to receive information:

is an inherent corollary of the rights of free speech and press that are explicitly guaranteed by the Constitution, in two senses. First, the right to receive ideas follows ineluctably from the sender's First Amendment right to send them. . . . More importantly, the right to receive ideas is a necessary predicate to the recipient's meaningful exercise of his own rights of speech, press, and political freedom.

In the plurality's view, this constitutional guarantee carried no less force in the public school library context because "such access prepares students for active and effective participation in the pluralistic, often contentious society in which they will soon be adult members." Indeed, the "special characteristics of the school library make that environment especially appropriate for the recognition of the First Amendment rights of students," for the library, unlike the school classroom, is a place for voluntary inquiry and study. The plurality then identified certain limitations on the school board's discretion to remove books, and affirmed the court of appeals' remand to assess whether those limitations had been exceeded.

The four spirited dissents prompted by *Pico* each focused on the school board's duty to "inculcat[e] fundamental values necessary to the maintenance of a democratic political system," and the broad discretion needed properly to carry out that responsibility. The dissenters believed that the plurality's decision would trigger improper arrogation of the school board's power to the courts. The Court found that discretion for book inclusion in the library of the high school, which in essence was discretion for book removal, would be that "[u]ltimately the federal courts will be the judge of whether the motivation for book removal was 'valid' or 'reasonable.' . . . Discretion must be used, and the appropriate body to exercise that discretion is the local elected school board, not judges."

Justice Rehnquist stated: "The libraries of [elementary and secondary] schools serve as supplements to this inculcative role. Unlike universities or public libraries, elementary and secondary schools are not designed for free-wheeling inquiry; they are tailored, as the public school curriculum is tailored, to the teaching of basic skills and ideas."

Justice Rehnquist also wrote the majority opinion in *United States et al. v. American Library Association et al.* Here the patron's right to receive information was noted. Filtering that could be disabled upon the patron's request was not found to limit the patron's exercise of that First Amendment right. Justice Rehnquist found filtering for public libraries to be appropriate where the patron could request that it be disconnected, finding: "Because public libraries' use of Internet filtering software does not violate their patrons' First Amendment rights, CIPA does not induce libraries to violate the Constitution, and is a valid exercise of Congress' spending power. Nor does CIPA impose an unconstitutional condition on public libraries."[40]

The purpose of filtering was not to limit access by adults to material to which they have a legal and constitutional entitlement but to protect minors. Justice Kennedy noted in his opinion the need to protect minors:

The interest in protecting young library users from material inappropriate for minors is legitimate, and even compelling, as all Members of the Court appear to agree. Given this interest, and the failure to show that the ability of adult library users to have access to the material is burdened in any significant degree . . . [41]

The Supreme Court's decisions confirm that the First Amendment does not prohibit the government from enacting laws that censor information for minors, particularly in school libraries, but the decisions also support and demand the positive right of public access to information and ideas in public libraries in a manner that protects minors from material considered to be harmful.

MAINSTREAM LOUDOUN

Mainstream Loudoun v. Board of Trustees of Loudoun County Library,[42] a Virginia case, was the first case in federal court to address the limitation of Internet access in a public library. In this case the library was found to be a limited public forum. As a limited public forum any content-based restriction or prior restraint access had to be "narrowly drawn to effectuate a compelling state interest." *Mainstream Loudoun* was a precursor to other significant filtering decisions that have been decided in a similar manner.

The Loudoun Public Library adopted a policy that prevented patrons from accessing "certain content-based categories of Internet publications" by installing blocking software on library computers. The Loudoun Library treated adults and children in the same fashion with regard to their access to an unfiltered Internet. The policy of permitting a librarian to unblock a site upon a written request by a patron without guidelines for deciding whether the site should be unblocked was found to violate the First Amendment.

On October 20, 1997, the Loudoun Public Library implemented a policy on Internet sexual harassment. The Internet policy implemented by the board limited three types of speech: obscenity, child pornography, and materials deemed harmful to juveniles. This policy included a provision that allowed for the use of site-blocking software. The Loudoun library used *X-Stop* as its Internet filter.

X-Stop uses forty-three criteria to determine which sites to block, based on guidelines set forth in *Miller v. California*.[43] *X-Stop* also gives the user the ability to block additional sites to the blocked list. The purpose of the software was to block specific sites from minors and to create an atmosphere in the library that would not include potentially offensive material. The purpose of the Board of Trustees for the Loudoun Public Library was to protect children from obscene materials. However, a group of Loudoun County citizens felt that the policy infringed on their First Amendment rights and brought suit under Title VII of the Civil Rights Act of 1964. A group known as Mainstream Loudoun brought suit in district court claiming that the Board's Internet restriction policy violated the First Amendment. The court agreed that the Internet restriction policy was a violation of the First Amendment rights of Mainstream Loudoun.

The court found that a problem was created because the filtering software was not able to distinguish pornography from other types of information.

The court determined that the board could not adopt a content-based restrictive Internet policy unless there was a compelling state interest and a narrowly tailored means. The court stated that "adults are entitled to receive categories of speech, for example 'pervasively vulgar' speech, which may be inappropriate for children."

Of the three types of speech that the Loudoun library sought to prohibit through their policy, two of them, obscenity and child pornography, are not constitutionally protected and can be limited by the government. The court noted that transmitting pornography over the Internet is already illegal, with established laws to contend with those concerns.

This issue was the overly restrictive software used in the Loudoun County library. The software blocked constitutionally protected sites, as well as those the Board sought to filter. The restrictive software not only prevented minors from accessing sites, but it prevented adult access as well. Since the restrictions were overreaching, they did not meet the narrowly tailored means necessary to pass strict scrutiny.

The court noted that the Board did not have to supply Internet access to its patrons, but once Internet access was made available by the library, it could not restrict access in a way that would violate First Amendment rights.

The court found that procedures that Loudoun library patrons had to follow to unblock a site placed an unconstitutional burden on the their right to access speech. To unblock a site, the request had to be in writing and include the patron's name, phone number, and a detailed reason for wanting access to the Web site. Upon this request the library staff would then determine if it was appropriate to allow the patron access to the site. There were no guidelines or policies in place to guide the staff on unblocking a site. The court found the unblocking policy was more egregious than restrictions enacted in previous cases, since it gave control of protected speech to the library staff without any guidelines.

The court concluded that even if minimizing access to illegal pornography and avoiding a sexually hostile environment constituted compelling government interests, the filtering policy was neither reasonably necessary to further compelling state interests nor narrowly tailored to achieve those interests. The court noted several alternatives that were much less restrictive: privacy screens, casual monitoring by the staff, or filtering software for minors only. The court also held that the policy constituted an unconstitutional prior restraint, as the policy neither contained adequate standards for restricting speech nor adequate procedural safeguards for judicial review.

In *Mainstream Loudoun,* the district court concluded that the Board's decision to implement filters was "more appropriately characterized as a removal decision." The court noted the library's policy "involves an active, rather than passive exclusion of certain types of content."[44]

Precedent to guide the *Mainstream Loudoun* court was found in two rulings dealing with print communications and one ruling addressing government regulation of the Internet. The *Mainstream Loudoun* court based its ruling upon three Supreme Court cases in its decision: *Miller v. California,* regarding obscenity, *Board of Education v. Pico,* analyzing restriction of books, and *Reno v. ACLU,* which addressed the regulation of the Internet.

In *Miller,*[45] the Supreme Court ruled that states could define obscenity and restrict it. In *Pico,*[46] the Supreme Court ruled that the community had the right to monitor the curriculum of the students, but that it could not impose its values on the students' voluntary choices of reading material. The Court ruled that the school board could not remove books solely because the ideas or the content of the books were not favored. The court emphasized that the Board could manage decisions that had an impact on the way a school library chooses its books, but not on the content of the individual books.

In *Reno v. ACLU,*[47] the Supreme Court examined the constitutionality of two specific provisions of the Communications Decency Act of 1996. The Communications Decency Act of 1996 (CDA), established under the Telecommunications Act of 1996 to protect minors from viewing obscene material on the Internet, criminalized the transmission of obscene material to minors. The Court found that the means or the tests by which the transmissions were to be judged criminal were unconstitutionally vague because the restrictions violated the First Amendment.

In its decision, the Court found that Sections 223(a) and 223(d) of the CDA regulated speech on the basis of content and could not properly be examined as regulations of the time, place, and manner of speech. Also, there was no basis for qualifying the level of First Amendment scrutiny that should be applied to the Internet since the Internet was more similar to print media than it was to broadcast. The Court found that there were many obscure meanings within Sections 223(a) and 223(d) that made First Amendment analysis difficult.

The Supreme Court case of *United States et al. v. American Library Association et al.* renders many of these decisions moot. However, there are many public libraries that do not receive federal funds. These public libraries are not governed by CIPA and are not required to filter in order to obtain government funds. They are, however, still governed by the U.S. Constitution and patrons' rights to access legal information.

SUIT FOR NOT BLOCKING THE INTERNET

In Livermore, California, a twelve-year-old boy downloaded sexually explicit material from a library. He later printed the material at a relative's home. He took the material to school and shared it with his friends. The library was sued by the boy's mother on the grounds that the library's failure to install filtering software violated her child's constitutional rights. This California case was the first in which a library was sued for not using filters.[48] The court ruled that Congress, under the CDA, intended service providers to be held accountable for published materials, not libraries. Based on that interpretation, the court found that the library was not liable for the actions of its patrons on the Internet. After the decision, the suit was modified with the complaint, stating that the library was a government agency and should be held accountable, since the child was harmed in a way that shocked the conscience.

ACCESSING OBSCENE MATERIAL VIOLATES STATE LAW—BUT WHAT IS OBSCENE?

In four landmark cases, all decided in the twentieth century, the Supreme Court has fashioned an evolving definition of obscenity for the United States that combines both local standards and a national definition of obscenity. Until then, individual states had been left to define obscenity for themselves within the limits imposed by the Supreme Court. Fifty states had fifty definitions all applied on a case-by-case basis to individual incidents.

The purpose of balancing society's will to preserve morality against the inherent dangers of regulating any form of expression is an acceptable goal of a library policy. The Supreme Court has created boundaries for state obscenity regulation that limit such conduct as "That conduct [which] would have to be specifically defined by the applicable state law." The guidelines for those laws and the trier of fact are:

(a) whether the average person, applying contemporary community standards would find that the work, taken as a whole, appeals to the prurient interest; . . .

(b) whether the work depicts or describes, in a patently offensive way, sexual conduct specifically defined by the applicable state law; and

(c) whether the work, taken as a whole, lacks serious literary, artistic, political, or scientific value.[49]

Justice White, writing for the Court, stated that the existence of serious literary, artistic, political, or scientific value *does not vary from community to community*.[50] The significance of this position is that this one single standard of the three enunciated is not one that is subject to an interpretation by the community in which the obscenity occurs, but is subject to a "reasonable man" test and not to the notions of the community. A "reasonable man" lives in no specific community and is guided by no local community guidelines. For guidance in this area of "serious literary, artistic, political or scientific value" a librarian can examine the case precedent of the entire United States.

The test of serious literary, artistic, political or scientific value is not based upon "whether an ordinary member of any given community would find serious literary, artistic, political, or scientific value in allegedly obscene material, but whether a reasonable person would find such value in the material, taken as a whole."[51] Community standards are not to be used for this element of the obscenity test.

The decision of *New York v. Ferber* provided examples of specifically defined prohibited conduct. Those representations or descriptions of ultimate sexual acts, normal or perverted, actual or simulated, could be defined as patently offensive. Specifically defined prohibited conduct could include "patently offensive representations or descriptions of masturbation, excretory functions, and lewd exhibition of the genitals." This would allow guidance for the trier of fact, yet limit a jury's unbridled discretion as to what was patently offensive.

Contemporary community standards are local standards and are not to be based on national standards. Questions of fact, such as what is patently offensive or what appeals to prurient interest, are decided by lay jurors applying the standards of their community with the guidance of the law. The Court indicated that it could only make recommendations, and that it was for the individual states to enact statutes that would regulate obscene conduct.

The CDA also added a section of defenses for employees of businesses promoting or possessing obscene films, and for employees and others associated with schools, museums, or libraries. It is unfair to penalize those persons who may be earning only minimum wage and who are working for the benefit of their employers.

PARENTAL AND STATE RIGHTS TO PROTECT CHILDREN FROM INDECENT MATERIAL

It has long been held that parents have a right to protect children from sexual materials. The state's legitimate interest in protecting, and helping parents to protect, minors from sexually explicit materials is compelling. The Supreme Court has recognized this interest repeatedly in cases that are often referenced and employed for guidance in this area. In *Ginsberg, Sable Communications of California v. FCC,* and *Denver Area Educational Telecommunications Consortium v. FCC,* the Supreme Court found or suggested that the protection of children from harmful materials is a significant and compelling interest that is valid. In *Sable,*[52] the Court noted that this compelling interest "extends to shielding minors from the influence of literature that is not obscene by adult standards." Most recently, in *Reno v. ACLU,*[53] the Supreme Court underscored its historical and consistent position that the protection of children's physical and psychological well-being is a compelling interest worthy of protection by both parents and the state. However, it was found that the means of protecting this interest was not always acceptable in a society that must balance this right and need of protection with the right and need of adults to exercise First Amendment rights.

In *Ginsberg v. New York,* the Court upheld a New York statute prohibiting the sale to minors of material harmful to them, even when the distribution of those materials to adults was protected. The Court identified two interests the state has in limiting the availability of sex materials to minors. First, the Court stated that "the legislature could properly conclude that parents and others, teachers for example, who have [the] primary responsibility for children's well-being are entitled to the support of laws designed to aid discharge of that responsibility."[54]

The Court noted that, while this support would assist parents who wish to limit their children's access to sex material, it would not bar a nonconformist parent from purchasing sex magazines for their children. Second, the Court asserted that "the state also has an independent interest in the well-being of its youth."

The two interests acknowledged by the Court in *Ginsburg* were echoed in its decision in *FCC v. Pacifica Found.*[55] In *Pacifica,* the Court upheld the constitutionality of an FCC finding that the broadcast of George Carlin's "Filthy Words" monologue was indecent and prohibited by statute. In so holding, the Court determined that the broadcast of patently offensive words dealing with sex, although not obscene, may be regulated because of its content. It is important to note that offensive words that clearly were not obscene were subject to prohibition of broadcast.

The Court found that the broadcast was uniquely accessible to children, implicating the government's interest in the "well-being of its youth" as expressed in *Ginsberg*.[56]

Those persons primarily responsible for the well-being of children feel exposure to non-educational, sexually explicit material can have a negative effect on a child's development. The state government has a compelling interest in helping those parents and teachers who wish to avoid the exposure of their children to this material.

Society's interest in shielding children from exposure to indecent material has been reaffirmed in recent cases that address state statutes. The Supreme Court recognized that the government has a compelling interest in protecting children from material that is harmful to them, even if not obscene by adult standards.[57] Regulation is a legitimate means of protecting children.

In three important cases, state statutes prohibiting the use of computers or the Internet to disseminate indecent materials to minors have been found constitutional. In each case, the courts found an indisputably compelling interest in protecting the physical and psychological well-being of minors.[58] The Supreme Court held that portions of the Communications Decency Act[59] violated the First Amendment. The question then remains in the interest of protecting children how much of an adult's access can be regulated.

HOW CAN THE LIBRARY REGULATE PATRON ACTIVITY?

Notice is the most important concept associated with regulation. A library cannot have a regulation that is so vague that only the librarian can interpret it, particularly if the policy will be subject to varying degrees and shades of interpretation. Nor can a library have secret regulations, which it applies without uniformity. Regulations must be understandable so that the potentially offending party will know and understand what is being regulated. Regulations must also be posted so that patrons will understand what is and is not expected of them. These concepts are based in the constitutional protections of due process. A Senator from Virginia cautioned his colleagues to "Put not your faith in the good intentions of men, but to write law tight."[60] This should be the admonishment to all librarians writing library policy; policy should be written tightly so it is understood and covers the acts with detail and specificity.

VOID-FOR-VAGUENESS POLICY

The "void-for-vagueness" doctrine was originally constructed to invalidate penal statutes that do not "define the criminal offense with sufficient definiteness that ordinary people can understand what conduct is prohibited."[61]

Courts have transplanted this due process principle into the First Amendment setting. First Amendment vagueness overlaps with, but is distinct from, an over-breadth challenge. Like the over-breadth doctrine, a meritorious First Amendment vagueness challenge will annul an unclear law that chills protected First Amendment activities. Hence, a vagueness challenge will succeed when a party does not have actual notice of what activity a statute prohibits. Yet the vagueness doctrine, unlike the over-breadth doctrine, additionally seeks to ensure fair and non-discriminatory application of the laws, thus reflecting its roots in the due process clause. Accordingly, it finds repulsive laws that endow officials with undue discretion to determine whether a given activity contravenes the law's mandates.[62]

The concept of a policy being overbroad is a cousin of the void-for-vagueness doctrine.

OVERBROAD POLICY

A law is overbroad if it does not address the specific conduct that is being limited within the allowable area of governmental control. If the policy includes within its ambit other activities that constitute an exercise of protected expression or associational rights, the policy will be deemed to be overbroad. The doctrines of vagueness and over-breadth sometimes overlap since statutes are often overly broad because their language is vague as to what is prohibited.

A statute will be interpreted as overbroad when there is a finding that its "prospective" reach includes constitutionally protected activity. When both conduct and speech are involved, the over-breadth must be both "real and substantial."

The over-breadth doctrine has been used where the statute's purpose regulates the time, place, and manner of expressive or communicative conduct. Courts have ruled inconsistently in their struggle to address issues of protecting minors from material harmful to them while still granting access to adults.

A party may not invoke the over-breadth doctrine unless there is "a realistic danger" that a statute "will significantly compromise recognized First Amendment protections of parties not before the Court."[63] The over-breadth doctrine is an exception to the "traditional rule that 'a person to whom a statute may constitutionally be applied may not challenge that statute on the ground that it may conceivably be applied unconstitutionally to others in situations not before the Court.' "[64] It is "predicated on the sensitive nature of protected expression," and allows "persons to attack an overly broad statute even though [their] conduct is clearly unprotected and could be proscribed by a law drawn with the requisite specificity." Such challenges are "deemed necessary because persons whose expression is constitutionally protected may well refrain from exercising their right for fear of . . . sanctions provided by a statute susceptible of application to protected expression."[65]

Nevertheless, given the "wide-ranging effects of striking down a statute on its face at the request of one whose conduct may be punished despite the First Amendment," the Supreme Court has repeatedly emphasized that "the over breadth doctrine is strong medicine and has employed it with hesitation, and then only as a last resort."[66] This reluctance exists because "there comes a point" where the desire to avoid chilling expression "cannot, with confidence, justify invalidating a statute on its face and so prohibiting a State from enforcing the statute against conduct that is admittedly within its power to proscribe."[67]

The Supreme Court has repeatedly instructed lower courts that, to "succeed in an over breadth challenge," a party "must demonstrate from the text of the statute and from actual fact that a substantial number of instances exist in which the Law cannot be applied constitutionally."[68] The "mere fact" that a challenger "can conceive of some impermissible applications" is not sufficient to render it susceptible to an over breadth challenge.[69]

Policies regulating adult access to content must not be overbroad or attempt to regulate those matters to which an adult has a legal right to access, nor can they be so vague as to leave discretion to the librarian without guidance as to whether the access is acceptable in terms of library policies and standards. Further these policies must be posted and made available to all patrons whether they are Internet patrons or patrons in the physical libraries. Typically, interlibrary loan patrons are deemed to be patrons of the obtaining library and the lending library is not required to provide notice of policies and limitations of First Amendment restraints.

The American Library Association has suggested policies that they believe collectively embody the library profession's understanding of First Amendment constraints on library Internet use. The *Intellectual Freedom Committee* offers the following guidelines to public libraries:

Adopt a comprehensive, written Internet use policy that, among other things should:
Set forth reasonable time, place, and manner restrictions.

Expressly prohibit any use of library equipment to access material that is obscene, child pornography, or "harmful to minors" (consistent with any applicable state or local law); provide for the privacy of users with respect to public terminals; and protect the confidentiality of records, electronic or otherwise, that identify individual users and link them to search strategies, sites accessed, or other specific data about the information they retrieved or sought to retrieve.

Communicate the relevant policies for use of Internet-access computers to all library users, and include the parents of children who may use the library without direct parental supervision. Do so in a clear and conspicuous manner sufficient to alert library users that filtering software is not utilized.

Post notices at all Internet-access computers that use of library equipment to access the illegal materials specified in the Internet use policy is prohibited.

Offer a variety of programs, at convenient times, to educate library users, including parents and children, on the use of the Internet. Publicize them widely.

Offer library users recommended Internet sites. For youth and children, especially, offer them, according to age group, direct links to sites with educational and other types of material best suited to their typical needs and interests (e.g., the American Library Association's *7001 Great Sites for Kids and the Adults Who Care About Them* and its Internet guide for young adults, *TEENHoopla*).[70]

INTERNET POLICY THAT PROHIBITS "OBSCENE" MATERIAL ACCESS

Internet Policy That Prohibits "Offensive" Materials

How can library patrons who object to the viewing of obscene materials be protected? This can be a difficult issue. Policies and guidelines must be specific—neither vague nor overbroad.

Legally, obscene speech is not protected by the First Amendment. However, there is a distinction between that which is "offensive," "indecent," or "vulgar," and that which is obscene. Speech that is offensive, indecent, or vulgar is protected by the First Amendment. A library Internet policy that prohibits "offensive" material from being accessed through the library Internet would not withstand judicial scrutiny. However, many libraries employ just such a policy.

This policy is effectively enforced by the technical failures of the computers. The reality is that pornography often freezes the computer with the associated material also frozen on the screen. Webcasters of pornography have created commands that are counterintuitive to the users' understanding of computer function, for example pressing the back button on the Internet browser commands the pornography program to open another window, rather than to return to the previously accessed Web page. This rapid and continuous opening of windows can freeze a computer terminal. If the librarian is then asked to unfreeze the computer, he or she must decide whether the material accessed is offensive, obscene, or child pornography. Most librarians can identity the user of that terminal through the sign-in sheet, even if the user has fled the premises. It is during this literally frozen moment of access that many decisions must be made that will impact both the patron and the library.

The librarian can generally determine if the material accessed was child pornography, though not always. It is important to note that there are expert witnesses who crisscross this country testifying in child pornography criminal trials as to whether or not the pornography for which a defendant is being prosecuted contains images of a minor or images of an adult. These experts do not agree and it is often left to the determination of twelve jurors to agree, and yet in this instance a librarian must make a decision. In some instances, there is no question but that child pornography has been accessed, and in others there is a legitimate question as to whether the pornography is child pornography or simply pornography. If there is a legitimate question, the best course of conduct is to contact local law enforcement and allow them to decide. While waiting for local law enforcement, the screen should both be covered and observed to ensure that the screen was accessed by only the original accessor and to protect the other patrons from the display of the potentially illegal material.

The Supreme Court cannot always agree what is and is not obscene, and yet the librarian can be called upon to make this judgment. This judgment is based upon local standards, not national standards. Clearly, the Internet is a national and international medium. However, what is transmitted into the individual states will be evaluated using local standards.

The Supreme Court has repeatedly ruled that the definition of what is obscene will be made on a local level and not on a national level. This is known as the "community standard." The standards of the community are to be applied in determining that which is and is not obscene. This community standard may be as small as the community of Hot Coffee, Texas, or as broad as the State of New York. Community standards are defined on a case-by-case basis, which ultimately means that twelve jurors will determine the standard to be applied to obscenity. However, before the case gets to the jury, the librarian must substitute her or his own judgment for that of the community.

DISSEMINATION OF MATERIAL THAT IS "HARMFUL TO MINORS" CRIMINAL IN SOME STATES

Some states have criminalized the display of material that is deemed harmful to minors. This could potentially affect a library. Accessing pornography that is legal for adult access could be a display of materials considered "harmful to minors." What is a librarian to do? On the one hand, a librarian cannot restrict adult access, and on the other hand, a librarian cannot display the material that is "harmful to minors" but which adults are entitled to access. It has been uniformly found that limitations to children that also limit access by adults will unduly burden the access of adults to protected speech although it is nevertheless putatively harmful to minors. The enforcement of the Harmful to Minors Act has been found to restrict the access of both adults and children to material considered "harmful to minors." That is, in efforts to restrict the access of minors to indecent material on the Internet, the Act can create a burden on protected adult speech that is unconstitutional.

Generally "harmful to minors" statutes criminalize the "knowing display in physical space of materials used for a commercial purpose that are harmful to juveniles." States have criminalized any activity which knowingly displays for commercial purpose in a manner whereby juveniles may examine and peruse:

1. Any picture, photography, drawing, sculpture, motion picture film, electronic file or message containing an image, or similar visual representation or image of a person or portion of the human body which depicts sexually explicit nudity, sexual conduct or sadomasochistic abuse and which is harmful to juveniles, or

2. Any book, pamphlet, magazine, printed matter however reproduced, electronic file or message containing words, or sound recording which contains any matter enumerated in subdivision 1 of this subsection, or explicit and detailed verbal

descriptions or narrative accounts of sexual excitement, sexual conduct or sado-masochistic abuse and which, taken as a whole, is harmful to juveniles.[71]

"Harmful to juveniles" is generally that quality of any description or representation, in whatever form, of nudity, sexual conduct, sexual excitement, or sadomasochistic abuse, when it:

(a) Predominantly appeals to the prurient, shameful or morbid interest of juveniles,

(b) is patently offensive to prevailing standards in the adult community as a whole with respect to what is suitable material for juveniles, and

(c) Is, when taken as a whole, lacking in serious literary, artistic, political or scientific value for juveniles.[72]

The criminalization of the dissemination by computer of material that is deemed "harmful to minors" has not withstood judicial scrutiny in several states. It has been found to violate both the First Amendment and the Commerce Clause of the U.S. Constitution. Similar statutes in New York, New Mexico, and Michigan prohibiting the use of the Internet to communicate material deemed "harmful to minors" have already been found unconstitutional.

It has been found that the "harmful to minors" statute is a content-based restriction on expression protected by the First Amendment. Such restrictions are presumptively invalid and can only be upheld if they survive strict scrutiny.[73] To satisfy strict scrutiny, the law in question must be narrowly tailored to promote a compelling government interest. The government has the burden of showing that a content-based regulation of speech "is necessary to serve a compelling state interest."[74] This burden is not insignificant.

Merely asserting that the government has an interest in preventing some harm cannot justify the suppression of free speech if insufficient evidence exists to suggest that such harm is likely to occur in the absence of regulation, that is:

that the Government's asserted interests are important in the abstract does not mean, however, that the [regulation] will in fact advance those interests. When the Government defends a regulation on speech as a means to redress past harms or prevent anticipated harms; it must do more than simply 'posit the existence of the disease sought to be cured.'[75]

In *American Library Assn. v. Pataki,*[76] a New York statute that criminalized electronic transmission to any minor of material deemed "harmful to minors" was challenged. The statute applied to transmissions originating in any jurisdiction. The court struck down the statute as a violation of the Commerce Clause for three reasons: the statute impermissibly projected New York law into other jurisdictions; the burdens it placed on interstate commerce outweighed its local benefits; and it attempted to regulate a medium whose survival required consistent regulation under federal standards. Although the court's resolution of the Commerce Clause issue obviated the need to consider the plaintiffs' First Amendment arguments, the reasoning of *Pataki* would arguably preclude any state-law prosecution even for obscene Internet communication. This concept is being carried forward in other jurisdictions. The *Pataki* decision rested on a finding that the speakers neither knew nor had any feasible way to control where their messages would be received.

Suit was filed in the U.S. District Court for the Western District of Virginia challenging the constitutionality of amendments to the Virginia "harmful to juveniles" law to impose restrictions on Internet content. The issues are similar to those *Pataki*,[77] *ACLU v. Johnson*,[78] and *Cyberspace v. Engler*.[79] The hearing on the preliminary injunction was held on February 15, 2000, and on August 8, 2000, the Court found the statute unconstitutional, granting a preliminary injunction.[80]

Each state's statute must be reviewed. Not only must the current statutes be reviewed, but actions of the state legislature should be watched. Currently, Florida, Ohio, Connecticut, and Michigan have some sort of "harmful to minors" act pending. In some cases these are limited to video games; in other states, however, they are more far reaching. Michigan has, for example, proposed a law that impacts material deemed "harmful to minors." It is proposed that this material should be located in a segregated area or placed behind blinders from the view of children. If the state in which the library is located has a "harmful to minors" statute, the law should be complied with by the library. Under New Mexico and Virginia law, material is considered "harmful to minors/juveniles" only if it has no serious value for "a legitimate minority" of seventeen-year-olds, even if displayed or sold to younger children.

AWARENESS AND APPROVAL PROGRAM FOR MINOR INTERNET PATRONS

An awareness and approval program consists of four elements. The first element consists of a consent form that parents and children sign, in which the library warns parents about Internet material that is accessible and which the parents may find offensive to their children. This material includes not only pornography, but hate speech, biased Web sites purporting to be authoritative, and abusive sites. Through this form it is noted and accepted by the parent that they will be responsible for the access their children have, not the library. The form notes that the library cannot and will not act *in loco parentis;* it notes that the parents must supervise the access of their children and ultimately be responsible for the failure to supervise that access should it be discovered that the child has accessed material deemed undesirable by the parent. The form requires both the child and the parent(s) to sign and to acknowledge that they will all adhere to the library policy.

Secondly, the library staff should conduct an introduction to the Internet for parents and children. This is a mandatory course offered at specific times to which the patrons can agree to attend. The staff offers safety guidelines and rules for using the library's computers. If the library employs a filtering system for children it is essential to educate parents and children on the limitations of filtering programs and the overblocking aspects of the filtering program.

Third, this program is promoted through a public relations plan, which includes locating the children's terminal area in a location that is open and observable by librarians and away from the adult terminal area.

Fourth, if a library perceives a need to filter it can ensure adults' unrestricted Internet access by selectively installing and using a filter. Adult users must be warned that no filter is completely accurate in what it excludes. Hence, if they use a filter, it is impossible to determine what information is not received. Parents also need to know whether their children use filtered terminals. Such terminals often fail to block sites that parents deem inappropriate for their children.

Awareness of the library programs for children's protection and parental involvement are the keys to a successful child protection program. This is one method of an attempt to protect the rights of children while allowing open access to adults.

Some libraries may choose to go one step further and permit parents to agree to the access of non-filtered computers by their children. This can be a difficult proposition for those states with "harmful to minors" statutes. In these instances, if minors are able to access computers used by adults, they may be exposed to the access of other adults or they may have their own access. However, as all librarians know, even with filtered access most twelve-year-olds with only moderate computer skills can bypass the purpose of the filters and access unlimited pornography.

It is essential that a library located in a state with "harmful to minors" statutes make some effort to protect minors from the public display of pornography. Seeking the approval of the attorney general's office for the library's attempt to protect minors from harmful material might be an appropriate course of conduct. In these states it is essential that a library take some action to protect minors and to employ a policy with guidelines for this purpose.

CONCLUSION

A library may restrict obscene material in all states. Defining obscene material, however, is not an easy task and this definition turns on community standards. A library may not restrict access to material based on content, such as sex or religion. In some states, libraries must be certain that minors are in no way exposed to "harmful" materials, and the exposure to minors in some states is a criminal activity for which the library could be responsible. It is in some instances possible to ask the attorney general's office to address the issue of library liability for images that are acceptable for adult review but deemed "harmful to minors." With this opinion from the attorney general's office libraries may find greater comfort in the acceptability of their policies, at least until the law in their state and/or in the nation changes yet again.

NOTES

1. Kreimer v. Bureau of Police for the Town of Morristown, 958 F.2d 1242 (3d Cir. 1992).
2. 158 Md. 93 (1930).
3. United States et al v. American Library Association et al., 123 S. Ct. 2297 (2003).
4. This access does not include private libraries.
5. National Endowment for Arts v. Finley, 524 U.S. 569 (1998) at 574.
6. Arkansas Education Television Commission v. Forbes, 118 S.Ct. 1633 (1998).
7. *Id.*
8. *See* Cornelius v. NAACP Legal Defense & Ed. Fund, Inc., 473 U.S. 788, 802 (1985) (describing types of forums).
9. Rosenberger v. University of Virginia, 515 U.S. 819 (1995).
10. *Id.* at 534.
11. Brown v. Louisiana, 383 U.S. 131(1996).
12. 883 F.2d 32, 34 (5th Cir. 1989).
13. 691 F.2d 155, 160 (3d Cir.1982).
14. 460 U.S. 37, 103 S.Ct. 948, 74 L.Ed.2d 794 (1983).
15. *Id.* 460 U.S. 37 at 45, 103 S.Ct. at 954.
16. *Id.* 103 S.Ct. at 954–55 (quoting Hague v. CIO, 307 U.S. 496, 515, 59 S.Ct. 954, 964, 83 L.Ed. 1423 (1939)).
17. *Id.*
18. *Id.*
19. *Id.,* 460 U.S. 37 at 46, 103 S.Ct. at 955.
20. *Id.*
21. *Id.*
22. *Id.*
23. Kreimer, 958 F.2d 1242.
24. Widmar v. Vincent, 459 U.S. 263, 268 (1981).
25. Kreimer, 958 F.2d 1242.
26. *Id.*
27. United States v. Kokinda, 497 U.S. 720 (1990), *citing* Perry Education Ass'n v. Perry Local Educator's Ass'n, 460 U.S. 37 (1983).
28. Ward v. Rock Against Racism, 491 U.S. 781, 791, 109 S.Ct. 2746, 2753, 105 L.Ed.2d 661 (1989) (quoting Clark v. Community for Creative Non-Violence, 468 U.S. 288, 293, 104 S.Ct. 3065, 3069, 82 L.Ed.2d 221 (1984)). *See also* Brody v. Spang, at 1121.
29. 123 S. Ct. 2297.
30. Kreimer, 958 F.2d 1242.

31. Martin v. Struthers, 319 U.S.141, 63 S.Ct. 862, 87 L.Ed. 1313 (1943).

32. Follett v. McCormick, 321 U.S. 573 (1994).

33. Martin, 319 U.S. 141.

34. 381 U.S. 479, 85 S.Ct. 1678, 14 L.Ed.2d 510 (1965).

35. 394 U.S. 557, 89 S.Ct. 1243, 22 L.Ed.2d 542 (1969).

36. 457 U.S. 853, 102 S.Ct. 2799, 73 L.Ed.2d 435 (1982).

37. *Id.*

38. *See, e.g.*, West Virginia State Board of Education v. Barnette, 319 U.S. 624, 63 S.Ct. 1178, 87 L.Ed. 1628 (1943) (school board cannot compel a student to salute the flag in a public school); Tinker v. Des Moines Independent Community School District, 393 U.S. 503, 89 S.Ct. 733, 21 L.Ed.2d 731 (1969) (suspension of students in a public school for wearing black armbands to protest the Vietnam War violated students' First Amendment rights).

39. Board of Education v. Pico, 457 U.S 853 (1982).

40. United States et al. v. American Library Association et al., 539 U.S. ____ (2003).

41. 539 U.S. ____ (2003).

42. Mainstream Loudoun v. Board of Trustees of the Loudoun County Library, 24 F. Supp. 2d. 552 (ED Va. 1998).

43. Miller v. California, 413 U.S. 15 (1973).

44. Mainstream Loudoun, 24 F. Supp. 2d 522 at 570.

45. Miller, 413 U.S 15.

46. Pico, 457 U.S. 853 (1983).

47. 512 U.S. 844 (1997).

48. Kathleen R. et al. v. City of Livermore, 87 Cal. App. 4th 684 (2001).

49. This is known as the "Miller Test." It is a three-prong constitutional test that applies to actual or simulated sexual materials and lewd genital exhibitors and is found in Miller v. California, 413 U.S. 15, 24–25 (1973). It has been restated in Smith v. United States, 431 U.S. 291, 300–302, 309 (1977); Pope v. Illinois, 481 U.S. 497, 500–501 (1987).

50. New York v. Ferber, 458 U.S. 747 (1982).

51. *Id.*

52. 492 U.S. 115.

53. Reno v. ACLU, 521 U.S. 844 (1977).

54. Ginsburg v. New York, 390 U.S. 629 (1968)

55. 438 U.S. 726 (1978).

56. *Id.* at 749 (quoting Ginsburg, 390 U.S. at 640).

57. ACLU v. Reno, 521 U.S. 844.

58. ACLU v. Johnson, 194 F.3d 1149 (10th Cir. 1999); Cyberspace Communications v. Engler, 55 F. Supp. 2d 737 (E.D. Mich. 1999); American Libraries v. Pataki, 969 F. Supp. 160 (S.D.N.Y. 1997).

59. 47 U.S.C. § 223(a)(1), (d).

60. District Judge James H.MIchael, Jr., July 27, 2001, speaking on the issue of whether government can craft a law narrow enough to shield juveniles from "harmful" Internet sites while still protecting the First Amendment rights of adults engaged in free speech on the Internet.

61. Kolender v. Lawson, 461 U.S. 352, 357, 103 S.Ct. 1855, 1858, 75 L.Ed.2d 903 (1983).

62. *See* Fallon, *Making Sense of Overbreadth*, 100 YALE L.J. 853 (1991). See generally P. Bator, D. Meltzer, P. Mishkin, & D. Shapiro, Hart & Wechsler's THE FEDERAL COURTS AND THE FEDERAL SYSTEM, 184–88 (3d Ed. 1988).

63. Members of City Council of Los Angeles v. Taxpayers for Vincent, 466 U.S. at 801.

64. Los Angeles Police Dep't v. United Reporting Pub. Co., 528 U.S. 32, 38 (1999) (quoting New York v. Ferber, 458 U.S. 747, 767 (1982).

65. *Id.*

66. Ferber, 458 U.S. 769 (citation omitted).

67. Broderick v. Oklahoma, 413 U.S. 601, 615 (1973).

68. New York State Club Assn, Inc. v. City of New York, 487 U.S. 1, 14 (1988); *see also* Regan v. Time, Inc., 468 U.S. 641, 651–52 (1984) (plurality); Members of City Council of Los Angeles v. Taxpayers for Vincent, 466 U.S. 789, 801–02 (1984).

69. Members of City Council of Los Angeles v. Taxpayers for Vincent, 466 U.S. at 800; *see also* United States v. Johnson, 952 F.2d 565, 577 (1st Cir. 1991), *cert. denied*, 506 U.S. 816 (1992).

70. American Library Association Office of Intellectual Freedom Intellectual Freedom Committee, "Libraries and Internet Toolkit—Checklist for Creating an Internet Use Policy" <www.ala.org/Content/NavigationMenu/Our_Association/Offices/ Intellectual_Freedom3/Intellectual_Freedom_Toolkits/Libraries_and_the_ Internet_Toolkit/Checklist_for Creating_an_Internet_Use_Policy.htm>; the American Library Association's Parent's Page 7001 Great Sites for Kids and the Adults Who Care About Them. American Library Association Internet guide for young adults, TEENHoopla, <http://www.ala.org/parentspage/greatsites/amazing.html>; and The Librarians' Guide to Cyberspace for Parents and Kids <www.ala.org/ Content/NavigationMenu/Our_Association/Offices/Public_Information/Available_ PIO_Materials/The Librarians Guide to Cyberspace and Kids.htm>.

71. *Cited from* Virginia Code Ann. § 18.2–391.

72. Standards taken from Ginsberg v. New York and Miller v. California.

73. *See* United States v. Playboy Entertainment Group, Inc., 529 U.S. 803 (2000) (*citing* Sable Communications of Cal., Inc. v. F.C.C., 492 U.S. 115, 126 (1989)). The Supreme Court has emphasized that strict scrutiny applies to content-based regulation of Internet speech. *See* Reno I, 521 U.S. at 870.

74. *See* First Nat'l Bank v. Bellotti, 435 U.S. 765, 786, 788–89 (1978).

75. Turner Broad. Sys. v. F.C.C., 512 U.S. 622, 664 (1994) (quoting Quincy Cable TV, Inc. v. F.C.C., 768 F.2d 1434, 1455 (DC Cir. 1985)).

76. 969 F. Supp. 160 (S.D.N.Y. 1997).

77. 969 F. Supp. 160 (S.D.N.Y. 1997).

78. 194 F.3d 1149 (10th Cir. 1999).

79. 238 F.3d 420 (6th Cir. 2000).

80. American Booksellers v. Webb, Virginia, 882 F.2d 125 (4th Cir. 1989), on remand from the Supreme Court, 488 U.S. 905 (1988), upholding Virginia's HTM display law as construed by the Supreme Court of Virginia in Commonwealth v. American Booksellers, Ass'n, 372 S.E.2d 618 (Va. 1988), which interpreted the law and materials on certified questions from the U.S. Supreme Court, 484 U.S. 383 (1988).

11

LICENSE AGREEMENTS IN THE
LIBRARY

If I buy a book, take care of it, and nobody rips it off, I'll still have it 500
years from now. . . . But if I buy an electronic book and don't keep paying for it, it's gone.
—Jim Neal, Dean of Libraries, Johns Hopkins University

I don't see the doomsday of libraries not existing. But I do see libraries
having a smaller collection. It's going to cost a lot more money than ever
for libraries to be up to date.
—Wayne Overbeck, Professor of Communications,
California State University at Fullerton

License agreements generally represent ongoing expenses to the library, not an
investment in permanent capital. Libraries have historically functioned as the
archive for published history through their capital—their books. Libraries can
archive digital information only as long as they pay a fee that transforms an
investment from capital into an expense. The retention of licensed materials is
typically not indefinite. This approach to information modifies the function of
a library to a limited extent. *Libraries must be prepared to review contracts for the
acquisition of digital works more closely than ever before and bargain for full
access rights.* Licensing limitations on access and use of works are not absolute.
Some equipment that decrypts digitized works may be illegal to acquire or use.
Libraries can negotiate licenses for the following purposes:

- to obtain the right to a hard copy
- to own a copy of the digitized work
- to access the digitized for all reasonably expected purposes, including image reproduction rights for the patrons

It is important for the public library to understand how its patrons are *using its digital works together with the economic and social impacts to the library and its patrons of using digital works that typically do not provide indefinite access.* While weeding is not a legal concept, it can be used in your legal analysis. Ask whether the licensed digitized material would be weeded out if it were a part of the library's print collection. If the work would typically be archived, rather than weeded, the library should negotiate for print support or permanent digitized access to the purchased digitized materials.

A license is a contractual agreement between parties. One party licenses to another the rights to the use of what are generally electronic resources in a library in exchange for a fee. In the case of libraries, the license agreement is for the benefit of its patrons. This is a significant fact in the world of contractual law, because it is virtually impossible for one party to *unilaterally* bind another party to its agreements. *An important concept in contract law is a "meeting of the minds"—an agreement by two parties.* A library may well agree that its patrons will not copy images from the licensed material, but ensuring that patrons do not copy the images is another matter. However, it is important that the final negotiated license terms and conditions that limit a patron's use of the materials are made known to the patrons.

Negotiating a licensed agreement for the use of resources is an important function for each library. Every license is subject to discussion of terms and to negotiation between the parties.

In reaching a licensed agreement, the negotiating parties balance the right to use what is usually electronic material or software with the right of ownership. The keyword here is "balance." This is the process that is used repeatedly in the law. With license agreements the rights of the vendor are balanced with the rights of the user.

The study of license agreements is the study of what is possible in the context of negotiating a license agreement. This art of possibilities is not necessary to commit to memory. However, a familiarity with licensing and with what it can and cannot do is important for all librarians, whether licensing is an element of their job description or not. Like many topics in the law, a familiarity with the topic and a notion of where to find more detailed information is sufficient. This chapter attempts to provide the most useful resources.

A license restricts the freedom a purchaser of the product has to use the purchased product. The freedom that is restricted is the freedom a buyer normally obtains as a result of the purchase of goods. Private entities have the contractual right to regulate the use of their product once it is sold or leased to a library, or to any purchaser for that matter. The library (or the purchaser) has the right to not purchase the product if the licensing agreement is deemed too restrictive. The library also has the right to negotiate more favorable terms for the product or to "negotiate the license." The license serves as a contract between two parties governing the use of an identified product.

The licensee is the purchaser, or to make it easier to remember, the licensee is the purchasee;[1] the licensor is the vendor. A license agreement is a legally binding contract between parties where the content owner allows the use of his or her content for a specified purpose by another party.

FOUR STANDARD LIBRARY LICENSING MODELS

Four standard library licensing models have been developed and can be studied.[2] These examples were sponsored by and developed in close cooperation with four major subscription agents: EBSCO, Harrassowitz, Rowe-Com, and Swets Blackwell, which combined offer subscriptions to 20,000 journals. These models are an important resource for the student and professional. They are based on single academic institutions, academic consortia, public libraries, corporate libraries, and other special libraries. These models represent actual licenses that have been negotiated by these companies, and because these corporations are international, the models contain optional clauses that vary depending on the country, state, or province where the license is to operate. These models are found on the World Wide Web and are updated periodically.

Knowledge of Sections 107 and 108 of the U.S. Copyright Act is essential to understand the rights of libraries and to negotiate a library license for digital materials. Case law will dictate unforeseen consequences that one or both parties may not anticipate in their licensing agreement. The courts' response to protests of unforeseen consequences has been that, "if the owner did not want this result, it could have drafted the *agreement* differently." In some license disputes there may be conflicting case law or no case law. The outcome of license disputes is never certain. Consequently, it is always preferable to initially negotiate a license agreement with specificity.

Unilateral License Agreements (The One Under the Shrinkwrap)

There are three kinds of license agreements. The most common license agreement is one we encounter every day, the unilateral license agreement. The rental of a video tape or the purchase of a CD or a computer game creates a licensed relationship between the purchaser and the licensor. This unilateral licensing agreement occurs as a result of the act of purchase. The complete terms of the license agreement may not be known until the product is purchased and the shrinkwrap is removed, because only part of the agreement is visible through the shrinkwrap.

The purchase of the shrinkwrapped licensed product (with the partially hidden license) offers a take-it-or-leave-it license agreement. Should the library own a product with a shrinkwrap license, its use should be in accord with the licensed agreement. However, the library may wish to use the product in a manner prohibited or not covered by the shrinkwrap agreement. The company may well negotiate terms for use with the library that exceed the shrinkwrap agreement. This negotiation process can be initiated by either a phone call or letter.

End User License Agreements

The second kind of license agreement commonly encountered is the end user license agreement (EULA). This license agreement is typically found on the Web; agreement to this non-negotiable license is entered into by clicking "Agree." This license agreement generally disclaims and excludes any and all implied warranties including fitness for a particular purpose. Jonathan Feldman's comment on end user licensing agreements says it all:

> You'd think that if we didn't agree with a software product's licensing conditions or found them incompatible with our needs, we'd look elsewhere. Instead, we blithely ignore the EULAs and use the stuff anyway. For example, there's emergency management agency dispatch software that uses the JRE (Java Runtime Engine). The JRE's EULA says, "Java technology is not fault tolerant and is not designed, manufactured or intended for use . . . in hazardous environments requiring fail-safe performance . . . in which the failure of Java technology could lead directly to death, personal injury or severe physical or environmental damage." Now that's funny.[3]

We can read end user license agreements completely before acceptance, unlike the shrinkwrapped license agreement. Some publicly funded institutions may be limited in those matters to which they are legally capable of agreement. For example, by state law or institutional policy, some institutions may not agree to the standard EULA, which permits the institution to be sued in a location other than the state in which they are located, while the licensor may require the venue for dispute resolution to be in the state they designate in their license agreement. The vendor may choose a state venue because the law is favorable to them in that state, or merely convenient. At any rate, if your school district, institution, or state law requires that all dispute resolution be handled in your home state, and it is not the same state designated by the vendor, your library cannot agree to this license. Most government agencies have extensive limitations on acceptable terms of agreements.

Companies are also open to negotiation of the terms of this agreement. A library may well negotiate a more appropriate agreement with a EULA.

Bilateral Licensing Agreements

The negotiated two-party license agreement requires some knowledge of the art of the possible and negotiation skills. To negotiate a two-party license agreement librarians should have a basic knowledge of their state's contract law, library custom and usage, and their own bargaining powers. In bilateral licencesing agreements the rights of the user are *in theory* balanced with the rights of the vendor.

Typically, the larger the purchase of the product the greater the bargaining power of the licensee, in this case, the library. Library consortia generally, though not always, have an advantage in the arena of negotiation of a license agreement. The same companies that offer retail shrinkwrap license agreements to the public for the purchase of their product will negotiate a license agreement to large agencies, school districts, or library consortia on a clause-by-clause basis.

There are eighteen standard clauses that typically appear in licensing agreements. These are not vastly complicated and many are straightforward—not the type of clause in which there would be any interest in negotiation. However, nothing in the law is simple and no contract (or license agreement) can cover every foreseeable contingency. There are historical precedents in the interpretation of some of these clauses, and there are no legal precedents in the interpretation of others. Some clauses simply give rise to greater disagreement of consequence, meaning the disagreement translates into dollars. Understanding those licenses that are generally accepted in the library community and in the business community allows the librarian to view his or her own license agreements more objectively, and potentially negotiate for more favorable treatment, or, in the event of a failed negotiation, provide a basis for shopping for other products.

No one knows the needs of a library's users better than the librarian and the library's staff. It is important to meet with the library staff and discuss how the product is actually being used in the library. If the actual use of the product by library patrons is not consistent with the licensed agreement, it is important to negotiate more applicable and favorable terms consistent with patrons' use of the resource during the next licensing period. The actual uses must be reflected in the license agreement.

The eighteen standard license clauses follow:

1. parties to agreement
2. definition of terms used in agreement
3. subject of agreement
4. grant of rights pursuant to license agreement
5. licensor obligation
6. term and termination of license agreement
7. renewal of license agreement
8. fees
9. conditions of use and/or scope of use
10. authorized users

11. limitations of liability

12. governing law of license agreementt

13. alternative dispute resolution

14. complete agreement

15. assignment of license agreement

16. waiver of clauses of license agreement

17. severability of clauses of license agreement

18. audit of use

Parties to Agreement

Identifying the parties sounds simple, and generally it is. Be certain that the party signing the agreement has the authority to bind the party they purport to represent. The licensor may ask you for information regarding your authority to represent the library, and may ask that it be included or attached to the agreement. The librarian also should be certain that the licensor has the authority to bind the licensor. Can a salesman sign for the company or should a corporate representative sign the agreement? If you are uncertain, ask the company, and have their answer in writing. If the response you receive from the company is oral or by e-mail, consider responding with a letter with the following text: "Thank you for indicating that Madame X has the authority to bind XYZ Vendor and Supplier Corporation," *and attach it to the agreement.* If it is not attached, most likely will not matter in the court's construction of the agreement and may not be a part of the evidence of a case.

Definitions of Terms Used in Agreement

This clause defines the terms that will be found in the license agreement. This is an important clause. Be certain the terms are consistent with your library's use of those terms. It is a good idea to have each section of your library approve the terms as defined in this clause of the license agreement. Not all license agreements use the same definitions for the same terms. Your interlibrary loan department may find glaring deficiencies in the definition of interlibrary loan. History may dictate the manner in which the library defines a material breach of the licensing agreement. Clearly, technical interruption of access to all or a percentage of the content is a material breach. The library may define a time period or a percentage for this material breach, or it may include in the clause the inability to contact a representative of the company for repair as a material breach. Library employees should communicate and collectively determine their definition of a "material breach of contract." If this definition is significantly different than the definition offered by the vendor, this could be an area of negotiation. By collaboration with the various departments, their individual needs will be addressed.

Subject of Agreement

The rights the license purports to grant are described in this section of the agreement. Be certain the agreement specifically states that you will receive the full text of articles, if that is your understanding of the product. If you will receive only abstracts, this should be specific in the grant. Define whether the product will have a table of contents, index, or images. If there are images, determine whether the images will be in color or in black and white, and whether there are limitations on the use of the images by the library's patrons.

This section should include an agreement on reimbursement should the agreed-on product be diminished in its content in any way during the contractual period. For example, if you are subscribing to several journals, if one journal ceases publication you may want to devise a formula for reimbursement or credit toward a future license agreement with the vendor.

Grant of Rights Pursuant to License Agreement

The content being granted through the license was described in the previous section, "Subject of Agreement." This section describes the uses your library can make of the content. Do not, under any circumstances, presume that specific rights, such as printing or copying, will be permitted without inclusion and reference in this section. There are standard, permitted uses that can be found in virtually all license agreements that are obtained generally from the vendor's server.

It is important to note whether these standard, permitted uses apply to images, video, and audio. (It is assumed that you have contracted for images, video, and audio in the previous section.) Often the standard, permitted uses apply exclusively to the textual portion of the subject matter. If it has been your experience that your users download images or other non-textual data, attempt to cover this in both your grant of rights section and your subject matter section. If your users download this non-textual data and it is not covered in the "Grant of Rights" section of the license agreement, your library will be in violation of the licensing agreement.

Standard rights in license agreements typically include rights to:

- retrieve
- search
- browse
- display
- view
- download
- print
- forward electronically
- cache

If you will be using portions of the data you retrieve in your library bibliographies, you may want to include that right in your agreement. If your faculty will be printing copies for course packets, this should be included in your license agreement. If your faculty will be designating readings from the server for their classes, this should be included in your licensing agreement. If you will be printing articles to be forwarded pursuant to an interlibrary loan agreement you may have with other schools, this use should be included in your licensing agreement. If articles from the database will be placed on reserve for student use, this use should be noted. If patrons, administration, or students will be allowed to access the database from home, this use should be included.

For university or school use, it is important to determine if faculty are permanently downloading data to use in a classroom. If so, include this use in the agreement. Will some of the information be placed directly on the library or school server? If so, this should be reflected in the agreement.

Vendors prefer to state the uses that are and are not covered in the licensing agreement. This is best for everyone. It is better for the parties to agree than to have the courts determine the acceptable uses at a later date. Often vendors will include the following clause: "all uses not specifically stated herein are excluded from this agreement and are retained by the vendor." This should be a motivation to include all potential uses for the data.

Licensor Obligation

It is natural for the library to presume they will be able to access the content twenty-four hours a day, seven days a week. Technical support is at the heart of licensor obligation. Time is of the essence with regard to technical support. Untimely technical support can be the equivalent of no technical support. If the data is accessed through a CD-ROM, video, or any other in-house digital format, you might consider having back-up copies on location to be used if the current format fails for any reason. If that is not acceptable, you might request overnight mail of replacement format. If there has been a representation that contact will be by a toll-free number, that should be included in this section of the agreement, as should the hours that a representative will be available at that toll-free number. Is there a representative on call twenty-four hours a day, seven days a week, or just nine A.M. to five P.M. Monday through Friday?

If the data is accessed through a vendor's server, you might consider a penalty clause if the server has excessive or extensive periods of inaccessibility. The penalty might be a rebate of fees or a credit toward future use, if you still want future use. Generally, these issues are resolved after a period of time and with improved capacity and technology. You might request that any technical adjustments to servers be conducted when the library is in non-peak use, and that you receive a specified amount of time for notice that technical adjustments are to be made to your server.

Libraries are required to comply with the Americans with Disabilities Act (ADA). Most vendors now supply content that does comply. Often libraries will include a section in the agreement that includes this obligation, which states, "Licensor shall comply with the Americans with Disabilities Act, by supporting assistive software or devices such as large print interfaces, voice-activated input, and alternate keyboard or pointer interfaces in a manner consistent with the Web Accessibility Initiative Web Content Accessibility Guidelines, which may be found at *http://www.w3.org/WAI/GL/#Publica tions.*" It is important that all PDF files are also viewable as HTML files or files that are accessible with readers.

It is a mistake to presume that online content is consistent with print content. The following clause will provide the library with the means of assurance that the content will be similar: "Online content is at least as complete as print versions of the Licensed Materials, represents complete, accurate and timely replications of the corresponding content contained within the print versions of such Materials, and will cooperate with Licensee to identify and correct errors or omissions."

Return on the library's investment can be calculated most effectively and sometimes exclusively with user statistics and data. The following clause assures both the vendor and the publisher that standard statistical data and analysis will be used:

Licensor shall provide to Licensee statistics regarding the usage of the Licensed Materials by Licensee and/or its Authorized Users in conformance with the *Guidelines for the Statistical Measures of Usage of Web-Based Indexed, Abstracted, and Full Text Resources* (November 1998), adopted and approved by the International Consortium of Library Consortia.

However, it is important to contract for privacy and protection of user identity in the compilation of this data.

Term and Termination of License Agreement

There is a beginning and an end to all contracts and all licensing agreements. That is their nature. They cover a specific period of time. This section of the license agreement may address issues regarding "automatic termination." Automatic termination of a licensing agreement occurs under specific circumstances stated in the agreement. Standard contractual termination agreements include bankruptcy, failure to make the license payment, and material breach of the terms of the licensing agreement (who decides this is important if you do not want the courts to define the material breach).

In the event there is no automatic renewal clause or automatic termination clause, the license agreement terminates at the end of the term of the agreement, which typically lasts for one year. All content agreed to be furnished during the term of the license agreement should be furnished for the entire term of the agreement. Should any content become unavailable during the term of the license agreement, a formula should be reached to compensate the library for the reduced content.

Some license agreements permit termination other than the stated license date termination upon notice.

When a library terminates a subscription to a journal the library retains all journals to which there has been a previous subscription. With electronic resources, however, this is more likely to be the exception than the rule. If access is by CD-ROM, continued use of the content past the expiration date should be referred to in this section of the agreement. Backing up online content can be expensive, but if the library chooses that course of action, it should be included in the agreement. In some instances, libraries may choose to print the content and retain it in print format past the license agreement termination. These are all viable options if a mutually agreed upon course of conduct is reached and recorded in the license agreement.

Renewal of License Agreement

A right of renewal typically exists in most license agreements, but there is no guarantee that either the content to be renewed or the price of renewal will be the same as the previous agreement.

If the agreement specifies "automatic renewal," typically the contract will be automatically renewed at the end of the user's year. Automatic renewals vary in application. A two-year contract will typically be renewed for two years, while a one-year contract will typically be renewed for one year. The fee, however, may change. Notice of fee changes prior to renewal can be an element of the renewal clause. A library may request a ninety-day notice of fee increase for budgetary purposes. Likewise, a vendor should have notice if the library intends not to renew. These notice dates should not be concurrent. Once notice or a fee increase is given to a library, a set time for response to the vendor should be allowed.

Publishers do not automatically notify users of termination dates of license agreements. License termination dates should be calendared so that the library may contact the vendor ninety days prior to termination to initiate a new license agreement.

Fees for License Agreements

For new products a trial use of the content may be offered. This trial use may become the basis for the negotiated fee for use. However, initial use may not be indicative of future use as more users become aware of the content's availability.

Essentially, fee arrangements include unlimited use, limited use, and pay-per-use, or any combination of the three use agreements. Some vendors negotiate fees, some offer various packages for which there are no negotiation, and some neither negotiate nor offer packages. Their one and only package may be a take-it-or-leave-it situation.

While subscription fees for unlimited use may allow unlimited use, they may limit the *number* of simultaneous users. If the number of simultaneous users can be negotiated, the chief negotiation tool may be that in non-peak times the library has no users of the content.

Subscription fees for limited use may be based on a sliding scale fee that takes into account the size of the institution, the number of users, or the number of pages downloaded. It may also be based on whether or not there is off-site access. If there is only on-site access the fee may be based on the number of computers with access to the content.

Pay-per-use agreements set a fee for each log-on access, search to the content, or the time of access to the database for both search and access. Downloads may create an additional increment of cost, or they may be included in the search-and-access pay-per-use cost model.

Libraries have an important need to know how their services are being used. A request for monthly or annual statistics for use access should be requested in this section of the agreeement. Some publishers have the ability to provide this data while others cannot. In these instances libraries should secure an agreement to allow them to monitor the use of their patrons so that they will have a basis from which to gauge the importance of the content to their patrons in the future.

Conditions of Use and/or Scope of Use

This section is typically more important for educational institutions as opposed to public libraries. This clause addresses the issue of educational use, as opposed to use for commercial gain. The definition section should address and define educational use and use for commercial gain, as both a direct and indirect product of access to the content. For example, an automotive instructor may be working on a patented engine application and use the faculty access to content for this pursuit. The engine patent may belong solely to the instructor and not to the institution. Under these circumstances it is conceivable that the access to content may be for commercial gain. An access clause for faculty and staff for both educational and commercial gain would allow such an access. Without such access, informing faculty, staff, and students that access is strictly for educational purposes is important.

Educational uses generally include scholarly and scientific research, critical review and analysis, private (not-for-profit) use and research, electronic library reserve, conversion to print library reserve, faculty and staff training, community training, class packages in either electronic or print format, research in the course of the user's business or profession (a for-profit application), and any home school access by off-site students.

Authorized Users

Authorized users can be a simple matter or a complex matter. If the library is a consortia participant, the identity of authorized users becomes more complex. If the library offers off-site use then certainly the matter of authorized users is complex. If the library is a single entity with exclusive on-site access then defining authorized users is generally a simple matter. The key to identifying authorized users is understanding who the users will be and communicating that information to the vendor.

Some exclusive on-site providers permit only registered users, while other on-site providers permit anyone who is on site to access the content. The identity and categorization of users are issues that can be addressed by negotiation. Access from sites outside the library is an important consideration. While the license may currently have user restrictions, it is never too early to begin discussing increased capabilities and the potential impact that may have on future negotiations.

Some libraries define their users in their mission statement and their policy. "Walk-in" users, who are not patrons of the library, may require special consideration if the license agreement refers to patrons. Many librarians limit Internet access to registered patrons and walk-ins do not have the same access as patrons.

This section also addresses the use the patrons make of the content.[4] Yale's Library License addresses these issues. You also may want to address these specifically, as shown in the following list:

Display. Licensee and Authorized Users shall have the right to electronically display the Licensed Materials.

Digitally Copy. Licensee and Authorized Users may download and digitally copy a reasonable portion of the Licensed Materials.

Print Copy. Licensee and Authorized Users may print a reasonable portion of the Licensed Materials.

Recover Copying Costs. Licensee may charge a fee to cover costs of copying or printing portions of Licensed Materials for Authorized Users.

Archival/Backup Copy. Upon request of Licensee, Licensee may receive from Licensor and/or create one (1) copy of the entire set of Licensed Materials to be maintained as a backup or archival copy during the term of this Agreement or as required to exercise Licensee's rights under Section XIII, "Perpetual License," of this Agreement.

Course Packs. Licensee and Authorized Users may use a reasonable portion of the Licensed Materials in the preparation of Course Packs or other educational materials.

Electronic Reserve. Licensee and Authorized Users may use a reasonable portion of the Licensed Materials for use in connection with specific courses of instruction offered by Licensee and/or its parent institution.

Databases. If the Licensed Materials are a database, compilation, or collection of information, Authorized Users shall be permitted to extract or use information contained in the database for educational, scientific, or research purposes, including extraction and manipulation of information for the purpose of illustration, explanation, example, comment, criticism, teaching, research, or analysis.

Electronic Links. Licensee may provide electronic links to the Licensed Materials from Licensee's Web page(s), and is encouraged to do so in ways that will increase the usefulness of the Licensed Materials to Authorized Users. Licensor staff will assist Licensee upon request in creating such links effectively. Licensee may make changes in the appearance of such links and/or in statements accompanying such links as reasonably requested by Licensor.

Caching. Licensee and Authorized Users may make such local digital copies of the Licensed Materials as are necessary to ensure efficient use by Authorized Users by appropriate browser or other software.

Indices. Licensee may use the Licensed Materials in connection with the preparation of or access to integrated indices to the Licensed Materials, including author, article, abstract and keyword indices.

Scholarly Sharing. Authorized Users may transmit to a third party colleague in hard copy or electronically, minimal, insubstantial amounts of the Licensed Materials for personal use or scholarly, educational, or scientific research or professional use but in no case for re-sale. In addition, Authorized Users have the right to use, with appropriate credit, figures, tables and brief excerpts from the Licensed Materials in the Authorized User's own scientific, scholarly and educational works.

Interlibrary Loan. Licensee may fulfill requests from other institutions, a practice commonly called Interlibrary Loan. Licensee agrees to fulfill such requests in compliance with Section 108 of the United States Copyright Law (17 USC 108, "Limitations on exclusive rights: Reproduction by libraries and archives") and clause 3 of the Guidelines for the Proviso of Subsection 108(g)(2) prepared by the National Commission on New Technological Uses of Copyrighted Works.

Typically an electronic reserve clause for educational libraries limits users to students, faculty, and staff of the institution. For all electronic reserve access, notice of copyright limitations to the users should be displayed. Further, electronic reserve cannot be accessed by the entire student body, but only by a specific instructor's class and then only for one semester. If other uses are important to a library they should be addressed in the negotiation.

Limitations of Liability

A warranty is a promise that the licensor (the vendor) makes to the library. Typically a warrantor promises that the information provided is provided free of copyright infringement and the warrantor is authorized to provide the content. In consequence, in the event of liability of the library for the use of material subject to copyright, the warrantor will indemnify the library for all resulting litigation costs and damages. This is good news, but you cannot get blood from a turnip. If the vendor is bordering on insolvency, the library may never be successful in recouping its investment capital. Fortunately, lawsuits are rare and it is more likely that the library will receive a cease-and-desist notice to discontinue use of the material subject to copyright.

Governing Law of License Agreement

Governing laws should be analyzed from two frames of reference. The venue, or the location in which the suit is filed, and the jurisdiction, or the laws of the state or country, in which the suit is filed. This clause is not essential and may be the clause that destroys the agreement for governmental agencies. If the contract is silent as to governing laws, often the first person to the courthouse chooses where the suit will be brought, subject, of course, to a motion to transfer venue, which is not an easy motion to win.

Generally, all libraries that are a part of public institutions require that all governing law clauses be domiciled in the state the institution is located. Contract law (a license is a contract) is governed by state law, and contract law and the resulting damages vary significantly from state to state. A fact-finder's determination of what are good faith and bad faith actions can be governed by extremely different guidelines in different states.

Litigation in a jurisdiction far removed from the library's locale is intrinsically more expensive. Generally, it is always best to have the venue of the suit to be the state and the county where the library is located, and often this is the law that governs the school district.

Alternative Dispute Resolution

With alternative dispute resolution, the courthouse becomes the arbitrator of last resort. Other avenues of dispute resolution must be required to be accessed first. The best of contracts (license agreements) can be ambiguous. One party may understand the contract to mean one thing and therefore be advantageous to their position, while the other party may interpret it completely differently as advantageous to their own position.

Negotiations are carried on by the two parties or their respective attorneys. This requires a good faith effort to meet on middle ground. When negotiations fail, mediation attempts to resolve the disputed issues.

Mediation requires the intervention of a third party. Most states have trained certified mediators who are attorneys. Be sure your mediator has no conflicts or association with any of the parties and is trained in intellectual property agreements. Some mediators will also be board certified by their States in contract law or intellectual property law. Find the most knowledgeable mediator pertaining to this area of the law who is available.

Generally, mediation requires the parties or their attorneys to meet with the mediator at a neutral location. Most mediators are attorneys (and absolutely choose an attorney), and their conference rooms are the sites of the mediation. The parties each have their own separate consulting rooms. The mediator attempts to find the common ground. It is best if the parties begin mediation with position papers that include the contract, the history of the dispute, and the progress made to the date of the mediation on those disputed matters. Position papers are important tools. They should state the party's position as to the status of the law as it applies to the license agreement. The law in intellectual property is not static and not always the same from jurisdiction to jurisdiction. The position paper should also state the facts upon which the parties agree and the facts that are in dispute. Before the law can be applied to the facts a specific set of facts must be determined. Mediators do not determine what the facts are, or whose version of "the truth" is acceptable.

This saves valuable time and gets the ball rolling more quickly. The mediator then goes from room to room in an attempt to represent the concessions each party is willing to make. Often, the formality of the situation causes parties to become more accommodating.

Mediators generally charge by the day or half day. Obviously, a half day is more economical, and if the parties arrive with position papers and a concise list of four or fewer items for resolution, no more than a half day of mediation should be required. If the items are numerous or complex or if the parties have not prepared a position paper, a whole day of mediation (or more) may be necessary. If a half day of mediation is chosen, begin at nine A.M. and break for lunch with one hour of mediation after lunch. A respite and light meal with the knowledge that only one hour remains to resolve the dispute can be advantageous to both parties.

The last point of resolution should mediation fail, prior to hitting the courthouse doors, is arbitration. Arbitrators are members of the American Arbitration Association (see *www.adr.org*). Arbitrators go one step further than mediators. Like mediators, they must understand the basis of the dispute and understand both parties' points of contention. They then apply the facts to the law and render a decision. This clause determines whether this decision is binding or whether the parties may then go to court for resolution.

Some law is red-letter law; the court will interpret the law in the same fashion it has been interpreted by the arbitrator. However, in intellectual property law, there are many areas in which the law is still evolving and being created. The attorneys for the parties are in the best position to advise the parties whether the courts might interpret the law differently than the arbitrator has interpreted it.

An arbitrator renders a position on factual disputes, and this must be done before the law can be applied to the facts. Consequently, there are two areas in which a court may render a finding significantly differently from that of the arbitrator, on the facts and on the law and its application to the facts.

Yet a third factor exists in selection of an arbitrator. The arbitrator will be most familiar with the law of his or her jurisdiction. It is best to select an arbitrator in the jurisdiction in which the suit will be tried. At each stage of the alternative dispute resolution, valuable information is obtained for trial preparation. Each party should arrive at the courthouse door with a complete understanding of the other party's position, and if there are no factual disputes and a set of facts may be agreed upon, the resolution may be submitted by summary judgment, which will require no testimony from the parties, simple written briefs, with sworn attached exhibits, and oral arguments to the court by the attorneys.

Complete Agreement

This clause simply states the license agreement and all appendices and attachments are the complete agreement between the parties. Any agreements made prior to the signing of the license agreement and not included in the license agreement are not binding and are of no force and effect with regard to the license agreement. In fact, prior agreements cannot be introduced into a legal dispute regarding the agreement. This concept arises from the parole evidence rule.

Some of the law that governs license agreements is the same law that governs contractual agreements. It is fundamental in contract law that an oral agreement cannot modify a written agreement. For example, if a vendor submits a contract to a library that indicates that visual images found in the database cannot be subject to educational fair-use exceptions and may be copied by no one, this contract is binding.

Should the salesperson give you a wink and a nod and specifically state as you sign the contract, "this is a small school and there is no one watching, if you get caught using these images our company will take no action," that oral representation is invalid, and of no force and effect. The contractual clause is the binding clause. In fact, because of the "parole evidence" rule should the school be sued the oral representation will not be allowed into evidence.

If the agreement of the parties is not in the license agreement, there is no agreement, and generally most other agreements are not admissible into evidence for the purpose of varying the agreement as signed by the parties.

Assignment of Licence Agreement

Contracts of a personal nature may be assigned. For example, if you contract with a noted artist for your portrait to be painted, that artist cannot assign that duty to another artist. However, contracts of a non-personal nature are often assigned. When you contract with a cleaning service to clean the library the subject of the contract is not personal. Should the business be bought by a large cleaning conglomerate, the original contract continues to be binding upon the purchaser.

If either party to the contract is absorbed by another party, the contract remains binding unless there is a clause to the contrary. If the intention of the parties is to the contrary, the license agreement may simply state that if either party ceases to exist, the contract will also cease to exist. This is not an optimal clause for a library that must provide content and notice of failure to provide content to its patrons. However, the alternative, a transfer of content provision by a new company, can also be fraught with difficulties. Knowing the content provider is of utmost importance. Always know with whom you have chosen to do business.

Waiver of Clauses of License Agreement

The desired clause should state: "The sole method by which a clause of this license agreement can be waived is by written agreement between the parties." Watch out! Do not permit one party's failure to enforce a portion of a contract to create a waiver of that portion of the contract. Portions of a contract can be deemed waived by the conduct of the parties that appear to create a waiver of the clause. The inclusion of this clause that allows a waiver of certain clauses not by conduct but by contract allows a library to lie on surer footing in its contractual agreements.

Severability of Clauses of License Agreement

Severability clauses state that if any part of the agreement becomes invalid or unenforceable, the remaining portions of the agreement survive and remain in full force and effect. This is not always a feasible position, because some clauses are so fundamental to the contract agreement. For this reason some severability clauses often indicate that only clauses that do not alter the entire agreement may be severed, and the entire license will cease to exist should the removal of a specific clause make it unreasonable to continue the license agreement in a reasonable manner.

Audit of Use

It is standard procedure for software companies to include an audit clause, to allow the supplier to review the actual use of its property. It is not unreasonable for the software licensor to periodically verify that you using the software within the scope of the license and the number of copies authorized. You have an obligation to pay the supplier for your actual usage if you are using more software than your license allows.

A reasonable audit clause should indicate the following: "Licensor shall have the right, with reasonable notice to licensee, to audit licensee's use of the software no more than once each calendar year to assure compliance with the terms of the license agreement."

If the licensor desires to charge the library for material overuse, should it also agree to a refund for under use? These are addressable issues. "Material overuse" can be defined in percentage terms.

LICENSING ASSOCIATIONS

To comply with U.S. copyright law, the use of chapters or journal articles generally requires permission, the use of film clips can require permission, and establishments defined by statute[5] that play copyrighted music are required to secure permission to use copyrighted music. A potential user of copyright information can secure licenses or permission from organizations for the legal use of copyrighted material. Obtaining a license or permission from the licensing organization ensures the user is complying with copyright law. Libraries can perform an important service to their users by simply educating them on how to properly acquire permission to use copyright materials. Many, many organizations will allow their materials to be used without charge or with a minimum charge if they are simply contacted.

A new organization, Creative Commons, was designed to help expand the amount of intellectual work, whether owned or free, available for creative re-use. The Licensing Project builds licenses that inform the public that the work is free for copying and other uses. It allows a creator to dedicate the whole work, part of the work, or specfic use of the work to the public domain. See *www.creativecommons.org.*

Licensing Associations exist to permit the use of copyrighted works. Some of the major licensing organizations are listed below:

- *American Society of Composers, Artists, and Publishers* (*ASCAP*) is a membership association of over 140,000 U.S. composers, songwriters, and publishers of music. ASCAP has a board of directors elected by and from the membership. It licenses and distributes royalties for the non-dramatic public performances of their copyrighted works. ASCAP collects royalties for copyright holders and can provide a license to use their music. *www.ascap.com*

- *The Association of American Publishers* (AAP) has 310 members located throughout the United States and is the principal trade association of the book publishing industry. They represent publishers of hardcover and paperback books and publishers of audio and video tapes, computer software, looseleaf services, electronic products and services including online databases, CD-ROMs, and a range of educational materials, including classroom periodicals, maps, globes, filmstrips, and testing materials. *www.publishers.org*

- Broadcast Music Industry (BMI) is an American performing rights organization that represents approximately 300,000 songwriters, composers, and music publishers. This is a non-profit company, founded in 1940, that collects license fees on behalf of those American creators it represents. *www.bmi.com*

- *Cartoonbank.com* is the online home of The Cartoon Bank, a New Yorker Magazine company. It provides a searchable database of cartoon humor. It contains 85,000 records in its central archive, including all the cartoons ever published in *The New Yorker. www.cartoonbank.com*

- *The Copyright Clearance Center* is a non-profit organization that licenses works for both publishers and authors. *www.ccc.com*

- *Ebscohost* offers the complete texts of 1,000 periodicals with one license to clients. *www.ebscohost.com*

- *The Harry Fox Agency* (HFA), established in 1927 by the National Music Publisher's Association, licenses the uses of music in the United States on CDs, digital services, records, tapes, and imported phonorecords. *www.harryfox.com*

- *ILLWeb* is a gateway to electronic and print resources pertaining to all aspects of interlibrary loan (ILL), document delivery, and resource sharing. Designed to be comprehensive and international in scope, ILLWeb features links to resources that will help practitioners locate materials for their clientele, manage the ILL process, and keep up with developments in the profession. *www.illweb.com*

- *The Motion Picture Association and the Motion Picture Association of America* (MPA and MPAA) were formed in 1945 and license the use of films. *www.mpaa.org*

- *The Motion Picture Licensing Corporation* (MPLC) collects and provides licenses on an annual basis for home use videotapes or videodisks of public performances. *www.mplc.com*

- *Movie Licensing USA* is a licensing agent for authorized studios such as Walt Disney Pictures, Touchstone Pictures, Hollywood Pictures, Warner Bros., Columbia Pictures, TriStar Pictures, Paramount Pictures, DreamWorks Pictures, Metro-Goldwyn-Mayer, Universal Pictures, Sony Pictures, and United Artists, and provides Movie Public Performance Site Licensing to schools for the use of entertainment videos. The Movie License licenses the showing of copyrighted movies produced by the studios represented and used by schools for numerous extracurricular activities.

- *The National Writer's Union* is the union for freelance writers working in U.S. markets and can license their work. *www.nwu.org*

- *Online Computer Library Center* (OCLC) is a non-profit, membership, computer library service, and research organization. OCLC provides services to locate, acquire, catalog, lend, and preserve library materials. Interlibrary Loan subscription services are available through OCLC. *www.oclc.com*

- *Plays Online* is an Internet composite representation of plays that are freely available to the public. Links to all the plays known to the Web master that are available in full text versions online for free can be found here. Playwrights are invited to share plays they have made available online. In some circumstances, the Web site hosts texts for playwrights who do not have access to their own Web site. *www.vl-theatre.com/list4.shtml*

- *Reading and Radio Resource* is a non-profit 501(c)(3) volunteer agency, dedicated to providing alternatives to reading for children and adults who are visually or physically disabled and/or learning differenced. They offer over 2,500 titles for distribution to listeners through the *Recorded Books Program. Radio Reading Service, NTRB*, provides a special radio broadcast of over eighteen hours of daily programming for listeners who are print impaired. This organization offers books on tape or CD-ROM and is allowed to provide copyrighted material to their blind patrons. They also offer textbooks on tape and CD-ROM to individuals and school districts for both blind students and students with other infirmities such as ADD or ADHD. *www.readingresource.org*

- *Samuel French, Inc.,* a "Play Publisher's and Author's Representative," was founded in 1830 to provide published scripts to theatrical producing groups throughout the world. Sources of Samuel French's plays range from Broadway and England's West End to publication of unsolicited scripts submitted by unpublished authors. The Samuel French Catalog lists plays, monologues, audition material, classroom guides, classic works, and plays from the professional. *Samuel French's 2003 Catalogue* at *www.samuelfrench.com*

- *The Society of European Stage Authors and Composers* (SESAC) is an American performing rights organization that represents songwriters, composers, and music publishers. This company collects license fees on behalf of those American creators it represents and is located in Nashville. By securing a license from SESAC, for example, music users (television and radio stations, auditoriums, hotels, theme parks, malls, funeral homes, etc.) can legally play any song in the SESAC repertoire. SESAC recently notified all dance schools that they required a license to use music for their students. *www.sesac.com*

- *SoundExchange*™ licenses, collects, and distributes public performance revenue for sound recording copyright holders within digital channels, such as cable, satellite, and webcast transmissions. *www.soundexchange.com*

- *The WATCH File* (Writers, Artists, and Their Copyright Holders) is a database containing primarily the names and addresses of copyright holders or contact persons for authors and artists whose archives are housed, in whole or in part, in libraries and archives in North America and the United Kingdom. The objective in making the database available is to provide information to scholars about whom to contact for permission to publish text and images that still enjoy copyright protection. WATCH is a joint project of the Harry Ransom Humanities Research Center at The University of Texas at Austin and the University of Reading Library, Reading, England. *www.hrc.utexas.edu/home.html*

- *The Recording Industry Association of America* (RIAA) is a trade group that represents the U.S. recording industry. Its members are recording companies. It licenses the use of its members' music for digital distribution. There are two types of performance licenses you'll need for any given song, one for the musical work (the song as it's written on paper) and one for the sound recording (the song as it's recorded). You can get the musical work license from ASCAP, BMI, or SESAC, depending on where the song you want is registered. If you're going to program a noninteractive station (and there are guidelines for what this means) you can get the sound recording license by registering with the Copyright Office. If you want to program an interactive station, you need to get the license directly from the copyright owner. Webcasting is managed by RIAA: they issue licensing and collect royalties for webcasting. *www.riaa.org*

These associations are available on the Web and offer access to most publications and authors.

Authors of dramatic works typically negotiate with the theaters and producers themselves and only entrust a collective management organization for the collection of remuneration. The use of such works takes place in a relatively small range of locations; thus, direct licensing by authors is feasible both practically and economically. Simply obtaining a play from a library does not authorize it to be performed if it is still in copyright.

STREAMING INTERNET RADIO

In September 2002, the Library of Congress, through the Copyright Office, set a standard fee that Webcasters must pay to the copyright owners of songs. A panel heard testimony for 180 days, and the recommendations were incorporated into the decision. Rates for broadcasting a song over the Internet or commercial radio were set to $0.07 per performance per listener, and those rates are applied retroactively from October, 1998. First payments were due October 20, 2002.

Because this standard did not accommodate small Webcasters, and could potentially drive them out of business, on December 4, 2002, the president signed the Small Webcaster Settlement Act of 2002,[6] which allowed the recording industry and small Webcasters to negotiate Webcasting royalty fees lower than those established by the Library of Congress.

SoundExchange, the recording industry's royalty collection clearinghouse, can enter into royalty-rate agreements with small commercial and all noncommercial Webcasters. Rates will be negotiated, and the Act requires that any negotiated agreements must base royalty payments on a percentage of revenue or expenses, or both, and include a minimum fee.

The First Sale Doctrine

The "first sale" doctrine has its roots in contract law where a customer implicitly has a right to enjoy purchased goods without restriction. Unless a licensing agreement provides to the contrary, a patentee (for example, Microsoft) that permits introduction of its patented article (for example, Microsoft Windows) into commerce may lose its rights with respect to the resale of the patented article. If you decide to sell your riding lawn mower because you have won the lottery and no longer intend to mow your lawn, you would assume you could sell the patented Briggs and Stratton engine that powers the mower, and you would be correct.

The first sale doctrine may be limited by license. In general, it applies only to patent claims that "read on" the product sold by the licensee.[7] Sale of a machine does not exhaust the patent rights in method claims covering use of the machine.

As an example, the resale of computers with the Windows 98 operating system has been a difficult proposition. The first sale doctrine allows the sale of the computer, but it does not allow the sale of the operating systems. A licensing restriction on most operating systems will restrict this sale. Microsoft's licensing agreement permits neither the sale nor the gift of its system with the computer. Many organizations that donate computers and their operating systems to needy individuals or organizations have been notified by Microsoft that these types of activities violate the licensing agreement. One solution has been to install open-source operating systems, such as Linux, on these computers.

Microsoft has a licensing agreement that it routinely and uniformly enforces that does not allow the resale or donation of computers with its software. While this restriction could not be enforced at all times, although Microsoft was willing to bring a lawsuit to enforce this right, Microsoft now has a self-enforcing solution by requiring that their software be activated by Microsoft. Users must now activate their products online or experience "reduced functionality mode," or RFM. RFM means Microsoft has the authority to deactivate your software! (See *www.support.microsoft.com/support/kb/articles/Q293/1/51.ASP.*) This newest concept is referred to as license "leasing" and is becoming more popular, at least with vendors.

There are alternatives to Microsoft that do not require a license that a library might consider. There has always been a large contingent of computer engineers who believe that software should be free. Open-sourced Linux software, for example, can be found on the Internet. Open-source support services may be an option rather than the use of a proprietary licensed product. *Red Hat,* which employs a Linux open-source management platform, allows you to pay for support, get free upgrades with source code—and without licenses.

Licensing Photos for Multimedia and PowerPoint Presentations

Two of the most frequently used online resources to create multimedia are Corbis *(www.corbis.com)* and the Alta Vista Photo and Media Finder *(http://image.altavista.com)*. Corbis offers access to over 25 million images, with 1.4 million available online and searchable by keyword. Typically a license to use an image costs three dollars. Alta Vista Photo and Media Finder permits a search of over 17 million images, audio clips, and video files, by keyword and type of media sought. These resources license photos for use in presentations. Some technology companies, such as NetLibrary and Ebrary, hope to balance the desires of all parties.

Ebrary is a digital rights management system for published material. It takes digital publications in PDF format and displays them freely on the Web, through either the Ebrary site or a partner site run by a publisher, library, or research group. Ebrary seeks to be a one-stop shopping center by compiling digital works and allowing people to search across collections. For example, entering a search term into the Ebrary database yields snippets from multiple books on that topic. See *www.ebrary.net*.

Return on Investment Analysis Requires User Data

It is essential that libraries be able to identify users to calculate the true value of the data that has been licensed to the library. Without actual usage information data a library can only anecdotally review the use of the licensed data. The only cost-efficient and accurate assessment of use of licensed content is an electronic assessment that documents the actual use of the licensed content. This is vital to understanding the true return on investment of the subject of the license agreement. Vendors often track this information for themselves but do not share that data with the library. Requesting that it be shared, and including this agreement to share the usage data in the licensing agreement, will help the library determine whether their return on their investment is high or low. When vendors do not have that ability, the library may purchase software to track patron use of the licensed data. It is a good idea to include in the license agreement the fact that the library will use software to track the use of the licensed data.

In analysis of use and users of the content, the concept of patron privacy must be kept in mind. It is a good idea to include the fact that patron identity will not be available should the vendor track the use of the licensed content. No analysis by the provider should in any capacity allow the provider to identify the user. While determining what data is accessed and time of access is acceptable, user identity, including home computer terminal identity, should be protected. The simple fact that the access was off site should be adequate. Tracking and reporting license use is important for both the publisher and the library. This should be done in a mutually beneficial fashion that completely protects the user's identity.

UCITA—UNIFORM COMPUTER INFORMATION TRANSACTION ACT

UCITA (Uniform Computer Information Transactions Act) is a proposed state contract law that will profoundly affect library operations. UCITA will provide the rules that govern licensing of all computer-information products and place limitations on transactions involving computer information. This is a model law intended for passage in all fifty states. UCITA's primary supporters include Microsoft, AOL, and Reed Elsevier, and it is challenged by businesses, technology associations, consumer advocates, educational institutions, law professors, and libraries.

National committees create proposed model laws for states to consider adopting. Some states adopt these proposed model laws precisely as created

by the national committee, while others make modifications to these proposals, or delete whole sections of these model laws. UCITA was adopted as a
proposed uniform law in July 1999, the product of a ten-year effort between
the National Conference of Commissioners on Uniform State Laws and the
American Law Institute to create a new and consistent legal framework for
computer information, transactions, and software.

UCITA's goal is to legitimize a contractual and licensing basis for computer information. On May 30, 2002, the drafting committee revised the
original, proposed model UCITA. The most important change was that
computers donated to schools may retain the software on the computer when
donated. Essentially, however, UCITA remains unchanged. The year 2003
has been targeted as the year to promote UCITA to various legislatures
around the country.

UCITA ignores copyright law. It allows contracts to govern the use of software rather than copyright law. UCITA would validate terms in shrinkwrap
and clickable licenses that restrict uses that are currently permitted under
copyright law, and negate provisions for fair use, first sale, and preservation.
A software vendor or licensor may electronically disable, remove, or prevent
the use of computer information through back doors in the software or hidden shut-down commands activated by phone or other mechanisms.

What Does UCITA Do for Libraries?

An adoption of UCITA in your state would mean that libraries could no
longer assume that they can legally loan software or CD-ROMs to library
users. License provisions could eliminate the right of libraries to lend products, donate library materials, or resell unwanted materials in the annual
library book sale.

License provisions under UCITA could control Section 107 (Fair Use)
and Section 108 (Library Copying) of the Digital Millenium Copyright Act.
These rights of the library and of the patron could be abolished in the licensing agreement by excluding the right to quote from a work, or make a small
portion of the work for personal use, or to use the product in a non-profit,
educational setting. These have historically been subject to negotiation, but
have not been subject to shrinkwrap licensing agreements.

Contact Your State Legislator

State legislators are not aware of UCITA's impact on libraries. An educational effort from the perspective of libraries to the legislators is an important
function of a librarian. Librarians have the obligation to explain the economic
ramifications of UCITA on a library and the importance of full access and use
of information pursuant to the law of copyright to the educational community.

For further information, go to *www.ala.org/washoff/ucita* or *www. affect. ucita.com.*

CONCLUSION

At the time a licensing agreement is drafted, the parties cannot predict the future, and often they cannot weigh the value or relative importance of the licensed content to the library. As users and uses are identified over time the library will understand better the value of the content to the library and the clauses necessary to accurately reflect its use.

While some of the rights enunciated in a license agreement may be inferred from Sections 107, the fair use doctrine, and the privileges found in Section 108 of the Copyright Act, entitled, "Limitations on Exclusive Rights: Reproduction by Libraries and Archives," it is best to include any intended rights in the license agreement. It is possible for libraries to copy whole works for certain reasons, to fill interlibrary loan requests, and to print and distribute copies pursuant to Sections 107 and 108 of the Copyright Act. The more professional course of conduct is to specify the precise uses the library anticipates in the agreement. However, all rights given to a user under the law of copyright may be further restricted by a license agreement, or they may be extended by a license agreement. It is important to remember the law of copyright may be modified by contract or a license agreement between the parties.

INSIGHTFUL WEB SITES

The Liblicense Standard Licensing Agreement of the Yale University Library publishes a Web site on licensing digital information for librarians. The Liblicense Standard Licensing Agreement is an attempt to reach consensus on the basic terms of contracts to license digital information between university libraries and academic publishers. Sponsored by the Council on Library and Information Resources, the Digital Library Federation, and Yale University Library, it represents the contributions of numerous college and university librarians, lawyers, and other university officials responsible for licensing, as well as significant input from representatives of the academic publishing community. The Web site also contains the text of a standard license agreement. This is an important resource for the working librarian and the student. (See *http://www.library.yale.edu/~llicense/index.shtml.*)

The licensing principles found at the International Federal Library Associations can be found at their Web site. (See *http://www.ifla.org/V/ebpb/copy.htm.*)

The University of California Libraries Collection Development Committee, "*Principles for Acquiring and Licensing Information in Digital Formats*" (May 1996). (See *http://sunsite.berkeley.edu/Info/principles.html.*)

The *"Principles for Licensing Electronic Resources"* (July 1997), promulgated jointly by the American Association of Law Libraries, the American Library Association, the Association of Academic Health Sciences Libraries, the Association of Research

Libraries, the Medical Library Association, and the Special Libraries Association. (See *http://www.arl.org/scomm/licensing/principles.html.*)

International Coalition of Library Consortia is made up of roughly sixty-five library consortia and represents over 5,000 libraries world wide. This coalition discusses and updates members on matters of consequence to coalitions. (See *http://www.library.yale.edu/consortia.*)

ASCAP is an organization of U.S and world-wide composers, songwriters, lyricists, and music publishers that licenses and distributes royalties for the non-dramatic public performances of their copyrighted work. (See *www.ascap.com.*)

Association of American Publishers. (See *http://www.publishers.org.*)

BMI is an American performing rights organization that represents songwriters, composers, and music publishers, and collects license fees for "public performance" for copyright holders it represents. (See *http://www.BMI.com.*)

Cartoon Bank is a *New Yorker Magazine* company of single panel cartoons that licenses *New Yorker* cartoons and covers. (See *http://www.CartoonBank.com.*)

Harry Fox Agency licenses musical copyrights. (See *http://www.nmpa.org/hfa.html.*)

Motion Picture Association of America. (See *http://www.mpaa.org/home.htm.*)

Recording Industry of America. (See *http://www.riaa.org.*)

SESAC. (See *sesac.com.*)

NOTES

1. Webster's Unabridged does not contain this word.

2. John Cox Associates and Catchword Ltd. *Model Licenses,* <http://www.licensingmodels.com>, (accessed May 25, 2002).

3. *Licensing Liability,* NETWORK COMPUTING (September 17, 2001) <www.networkcomputing.com/1219/1219colfeldman.com>.

4. The Council of Library Information Resources provides a standard licensing agreement for review. Yale University Library, *Standard License Agreement* <http://www.library.yale.edu/~llicense/standlicagree.html> (accessed May 25, 2002).

5. 17 U.S.C. Appendix VIII; Appendix IX, Additional Provisions of the Small Webcasters Settlement Act of 2002.

6. In 1995, the Musical Licensing Act regarding copyright was introduced in the House and the Senate, and both chambers held hearings. The bill never exited the committee because restaurant and bar owners lobbied Congress for a broader exemption on paying royalties for music broadcast in their establishments. It took three years for the restaurateurs to be successful with their lobbying and win an exemption from the proposed copyright act.

7. Bandag, Inc v. Al Bolser's Tire Stores, Inc., 750 F.2d 903 (Fed Cir. 1984).

12

LIBRARY WEB SITES AND LEGAL CONSTRICTIONS

My, my. A body does get around. Here we ain't been coming from
Alabama but two months, and now it's already Tennessee.
—William Faulkner, *Light in August*

IS YOUR WEB SITE ADA COMPLIANT?

When Thomas Jefferson wrote the following words in 1810 he could not
have envisioned the extent to which the information of the people would be
available to the people through the World Wide Web: "The information of
the people at large can alone make them safe as they are the sole depositary
of our political and religious freedom."[1] Access to electronic and information
technology for people with disabilities is mandated by law and should be supported by library policy. The Americans with Disabilities Act (ADA) administrative complaint can be filed against the library or the city for maintaining
an inaccessible Web site. All sites in their entirety should be accessible by the
blind. Screen readers should be able to audibly read all the library and city
documents in their entirety.

While most libraries are not federal agencies, sensitivity to these issues is
important, and in some instances is governed by state law. In 1998, Congress
amended the Rehabilitation Act to require federal agencies to make their
electronic and information technology accessible to people with disabilities.[2]
Inaccessible technology interferes with an individual's ability to obtain and
use information quickly and easily. Section 508 was enacted to eliminate barriers in information technology, to make available new opportunities for people with disabilities, and to encourage development of technologies that will
help achieve these goals.

The law applies to all federal agencies when they develop, procure, maintain, or use electronic and information technology. Under Section 508,[3] agencies must give disabled employees and members of the public access to information that is comparable to the access available to others. It is recommended that you review the laws and regulations listed below to further your understanding of Section 508 and how you can support implementation. The U.S. Department of Justice states that ADA accessibility requirements apply to Internet Web pages and that the "effective communication" rationale applies to both ADA Title II and III entities.[4]

Basic requirements that allow a minimum accessible Web design standard have been published.[5] They are:

Provide an access instruction page for visitors. This page should publish the contact name and e-mail address of the ADA coordinator responsible for investigating and resolving ADA Title II complaints, as required under the statute, and facilitate the internal resolution of complaints concerning inaccessible Web design.

Provide support for text browsers. Attach "alt" tags to graphic images. This allows screen readers to identify the graphic. Screen readers cannot audibly read out loud the text or links embedded within graphic images. PDF documents are not always accessible by screen readers. Special attention should be paid when PDF files are used.

Hyperlink photographs with descriptive text "D." Accessing the key "D" will take the browser to a description of the photograph. The Center for Accessible Media has a standard by which this can be accomplished, which can be found at *http://www. wgbh.org/wgbh/pages/ncam/accesscam.html#visim.*

Caption all audio and video clips by using "CC" hyperlinks. The Center for Accessible Media has a standard by which this can be accomplished, which can be found at *http://www.wgbh.org/wgbh/pages/ncam/accesscam.html#visim.* It is essential to provide alternative mechanisms for online forms. Online forms that enable keyboard navigation without a mouse are helpful but can be difficult to read by certain text browsers.

Provide a TTY phone number as an alternative means of communication. It is important when building or reviewing your library Web site to avoid access barriers that will limit full access by disabled patrons. Often documents in PDF, table, newspaper, or frame format, require visitors to download software that their computers are incapable of handling. It is important that if a library posts in PDF, the HTML text or ASCII file must also be posted.

Caption Web cast and Video. A person with a hearing disability cannot hear a Web cast or video clip if it is not captioned. A person with visual and learning disabilities cannot navigate a Web page that is not coded to convey Web content to text browsers and screen readers.

Inaccessible Web page design can hide text within images, frames, applets, or animated .gifs or render the text unintelligently in table, columnar, or portable document format (PDF). People who are illiterate can access the

Web because screen readers can audibly read the text out loud from accessible Web pages, electronic textbooks, and Internet kiosks.

Federal Agencies Have a Higher Level of Accountability

While federal agencies are mandated by law to a higher level of accountability than state agencies, all public entities should develop a standard of accountability for the disabled, and the federal model can serve state agencies. All federal agencies must conduct self-evaluations of their electronic and information technology, including Web site design, and report on the extent of accessibility for people with disabilities.[6]

Two important features of the amendment to Section 508 of the Rehabilitation Act of 1973 are first, that federal contracting officers will be held personally liable for violations of the access law in their procurement of products and services, and second, that losing bidders to federal contracts can challenge the award if they believe they can provide a more accessible product or service.

The World Wide Web Consortium (W3C) released the first stable international specification for designing accessible Web sites in May of 1999.[7]

Some states are in the process of requiring all state agencies to adhere to a uniform Web site design. This uniform design is implemented to simplify accessibility by the public to the format and design system. Oregon has developed a "Privacy and Information Disclosure Policy" to inform agencies, Web developers, and Web system administrators, as well as customers, of the limitations of information disclosure. A Uniform Privacy and Information Disclosure notice is used for the Oregon.gov portal; the notice may also be used by agencies if it meets their requirements.

The purpose of the Oregon Navigation and Site Design Policy is to ensure that the Oregon.gov portal and agency Web sites provide content that is accessible to as many customers as possible. It also provides the groundwork for moving to a common look-and-feel for all State of Oregon Web sites, although it does not yet make that requirement mandatory.

Good Web site design is an important element of compliance with the Americans with Disabilities Act. Oregon's policies can be implemented by any library for the purpose of assuring Web access by the disabled.

Access to the Internet

Most libraries provide Internet access. Providing access to handicapped persons is familiar to libraries. Libraries have long been involved in widening their aisles and providing facilities to accommodate the handicapped. However, not all libraries may be familiar with the requirement to provide Internet access to handicapped individuals. The National Institute on Disability and Rehabilitation Research (NIDRR)[8] of the U.S. Department of Education has funded a network of grantees to provide information, training, and technical assistance to businesses, agencies, and schools with responsibilities under the ADA and to people with disabilities who have rights under the ADA.[9]

WEB LINKING IS GENERALLY LEGAL

In the creation of a library bibliography a decision must be made to link to another Web site. This is the wonder of the Internet. However, deciding precisely where to link to that Web site can be a problem. The term "deep linking" has become aversive to many librarians and they believe they can *only* link to a home page. This is simply not always the case.

Deep linking occurs when one Web site links to a Web page in another Web site that is not that site's home page. Web sites do not always have a problem with deep linking. Asking a Webmaster whether you can deep link is a legitimate first step. For example, the Metropolitan Museum of Art of New York City is an extremely large site. Linking directly to the site's section on Egyptian Art may serve the patrons of the library much more efficiently than linking to the museum's home page with a hope and a prayer that the patron can surf through this enormous site to find the chosen page. An e-mail to the Metropolitan Museum of Art can allow deep linking.

Linking technologies are not unique in their function. Some commentators believe an Internet link is no more than an automated footnote or a digitized Dewey decimal reference. There are great sociological benefits associated with linking and the ease of coordination of, and access to, information. The Web solves a critical need for access to dates and information through the use of search engines, indexes, and links associated with such search tools. Essentially, there is a presumptive right to make reference links. Hypertext reference links are allowable in almost all situations. New legal doctrines are emerging that bear directly upon the copying of digital content (such as database protection and anti-circumvention laws).

It is undisputed that some links can be unlawful. Where reference links have the potential to confuse consumers or appropriate business opportunities, issues of infringement arise. When circumstances of the link show a clear abuse that would be actionable in a non-Internet situation, it will also be actionable as a link. The metatag cases that have found infringement are premised on Internet users being confused about the sponsorship of the Web site. Most acceptable cases of linking give credit for the authorship and authority for the Web site. It is always important to disclaim any authorship for or credit for a site to which the library is linking and be clear not to take credit for the site.

Consumer misunderstandings as to the credit for the Web site occur when framing and inlined links are used and the perception is given that the site that is linked to is a part of the original, linking site.

Web publishers have the technological tools to achieve their objectives before they engage in costly and uncertain litigation. Deep linking can be addressed by various means, including requiring password access, blocking requests or links except from certain pre-approved sites, or using frequently changing URLs for subsidiary pages. These are all technological and legal methods to control or restrict deep links, and are more cost efficient than litigation.

Generally the same principles apply to problems of deep linking that apply to other violations of the law of intellectual property. Issues raised by framing or inlining raise much broader and more significant concerns than simple reference hyperlinks. Confusions of association and creation are intrinsic in framing and inline linking. These confusions violate derivative works under copyright and trademark law.

Linking can infringe upon the trademark of a business or violate a copyright. Linking can tarnish a trademark or logo or actually be a misappropriation of the property of another. Linking can create unfair competition. The same violations that can occur with metatag abuse can occur with linking.

The law is silent with regard to the use of framing image links used in Web pages, and few analogies exist to prior technologies. Therefore, it is difficult to predict future court rulings concerning frames, image links, or "stolen" images. These issues are reviewed and analogies are drawn.

1. Hypertext reference (HREF) links permit a viewer to jump from one Web page to another; clicking on the link instructs the viewer's Web browser software to go to the linked location, which is often another Web site and which is specified in the markup written in the HTML language. This form of linking is the most common, and is generally determined to be non-problematic, as long as it does not involve one of the linking methods mentioned below.

2. Framing creates links or associations between Web pages; it is a method, introduced to Internet users in 1996, of arranging and viewing Web pages. Framing allows the operator of a Web site to divide a browser window into multiple, independently scrollable frames with different layouts, and to place separate documents from different Internet sources into each window. Framing is the linking method subject to the greatest abuse. When the HTML instructions called "Frame Tags" allow the Web page designer to display a window within a window, the contents of two or more Web sites, often located on different servers, are displayed on the same Web page. These frames may or may not have visible borders, and the user may reasonably believe that all the information displayed is from the same Web site.

Framing may infringe the derivative rights of copyright holders. A derivative work is a work based upon one or more preexisting works, such as a translation, musical arrangement, dramatization, fictionalization, motion picture version, sound recording, art reproduction, abridgment, condensation, or any other form in which a work may be recast, transformed, or adapted. A work consisting of editorial revisions, annotations, elaborations, or other modifications, that, as a whole, represent an original work of authorship, is a derivative work.

In framing, the copyrighted documents are displayed under circumstances different than those intended by the creator. The frame is often accompanied by work created by the referrer, other works accessed and framed together by the referrer, or a combination thereof. In such cases, the portion accessed and displayed using framing may appear to be an integral portion of the referring page.

Framing could be considered to "recast, transform, or adapt" the referred Web page, thus constituting a derivative work. Framing is performed at the express direction of the Web site author in order to give the appearance that the display appears as one integrated Web site. When A uses framing technology to frame portions of B's Web content on A's Web site, the derivative work issue may arise, although one does not create a derivative work by putting a frame (e.g., a picture frame) around a copyrighted work.

In *International News Service v. Associated Press,*[10] frames were used by one news agency to link to the articles of another news agency. The inference was that the linking news agency actually reported the news to the agency to which it linked. This cause of action essentially prohibits the unauthorized interference by one party with another party's valuable and time-sensitive information. This activity should be specifically prohibited in the library policy and guidelines.

3. Inlined image linking enables graphics to be visible on screen as part of a Web document's main body even though they originate outside the document's HTML code—that is, they come from somewhere else on the Web site publisher's server, or even a different Web site. In image inlining, when A takes B's copyrighted image and places it on A's Web site—perhaps as an integrated element of a composite design such as a collage—A seems to have adapted B's work, and hence violated B's exclusive right to make derivative works.[11] The copyrighted inlined and linked image is displayed under circumstances different than those intended by the creator. When the inlined image link causes a Web image to be displayed and integrated into the referring Web page, this represents an adaptation and could be considered an infringement of the derivative rights of the copyright holder. Image inline linking also infringes upon other rights of copy such as display rights.

4. Deep links take the viewer to portions of a Web site below the home page and its identifying information and advertising. Such interior links, as opposed to surface links that send browsers to another site's homepage, are problematic because they present the site's content out of context. Hence, once the jump is made via the link to the new site, the user sees no frame or further trace of the original site.[12]

Linking is an important function of the Internet. Deep linking can save time for the patron and in some instances is the only method by which the patron can actually find the information they are seeking because some Web sites are so broad and detailed.

Consider the option of providing a link to both the home page and the deep-linked page for the patron's option with an explanation of each link.

Also consider obtaining a written authorization from the Web site for deep linking. A printed e-mail response allowing deep linking should be sufficient.

GETTING SUED FOR NOT LINKING

Public libraries have been sued for not linking to requested sites. In the case of *Putnam Pit, Inc. v. City of Cookeville,*[13] a suit was brought against the city, suggesting that the city violated First Amendment rights when it denied a request to place a hypertext link to the Putnam Pit Web site on the city's Web page. Putnam Pit alleged that the city created a non-public forum by allowing links to other Web sites, and its denial of the plaintiff's request pursuant to its policy may have been based on impermissible viewpoint discrimination.

The significant issue that was appealed was that the policy permitting links on the city's Web site was vague and overbroad and violated First Amendment rights by giving local officials unfettered discretion to deny a link to publications based on their content. The important element in this case, and a lesson for libraries, is that the policy employed by the library must not be overly broad and vague, but specific to a sufficient degree not to give unfettered discretion to deny a link. It is important to have specific detailed guidelines for the evaluation of Web site inclusion for bibliographies. There are several Internet reference sites that provide guides to develop Web site bibliographies.[14]

The Purpose of a Library Bibliography

What is a librarian's purpose in building a Web bibliography? The foremost purpose is to educate patrons about the library and its services. One important function of a library with regard to the Internet is to teach children Internet safety. This should be the mantra of all school and public libraries that provide Internet access to children.

It is important to encourage children and their parents to check the Internet for the children's names. Using all forms of their name, including any activities that might include the student's name, will give the broadest return.

Each student and their parent can evaluate how much information is available on the Web regarding that student. Many children's theaters publish their actors' names. Many Little League baseball teams publish the team's name, players' names, and have a group photo. It is not just Mom and Pop organizations that commit this blunder. Until May of 2002, when the danger was brought to their attention, the Texas Parks and Wildlife Commission published children's Web sites with their full name, age, and hometown. This may not be in the child's best interest. These issues should be discussed.

The Center for Missing and Exploited Children *(www.missingkids.com)* has rules for children in dealing with Internet stranger danger. These can be posted at all computers.

Under no circumstance should the library or the media center in any way publish the identity of students on the Web.

A pedophile's first objective is to identify a child, their age, sex, name, and location. If the pedophnile can simply obtain the child's name and perhaps the name of a sports team or any activity in which he or she is involved the pedophile can secure all other information from that source. Many pedophiles are extremely adept with Internet research. They then befriend the child online. They exploit all information about the child. Suddenly the child's interests become the same interests as the pedophile's. They encourage the child to see the world in which they live as hostile and uncaring. Parents are portrayed as indifferent and unloving, teachers as not caring and incapable of understanding the child's world, and friends as betrayers. The child is left to believe that only the pedophile truly understands and cares for them. Pornography is sent, softening the child to what will ultimately be expected, and then a meeting is set. Pedophiles will even send money or tickets to the child for transportation.

The media center's first objective is to protect the identity of all its students, particularly if they publish on the Web. The second objective is to educate the children as to the potential danger. The third objective is to have the students perform their own name search.

A library might reference the *Three Best Websites for Educating Children on the Safe Use of the Internet.*

Microsoft's "30 Ways to Stay Safe Online" can be found at Stay Safe Online at *http://www.encarta.msn.com/schoolhouse/safety.asp.*

SafeKids.com is an excellent site. SafeKids.Com and SafeTeens.Com are projects of The Online Safety Project (OSP). OSP is operated by Larry Magid, a syndicated columnist, broadcaster, and author of numerous articles about online safety. Magid also operates *www.pcanswer.com,* a Web site that contains his writings about computers and technology. Safesurfin.com is sponsored by America Online.

Criteria for Building Web Bibliographies

What are a librarian's criteria in building Web bibliographies? Generally, these criteria are compatible with a collection development policy, which is presumably in place and already supported by guidelines. While the Web policy follows these existing guidelines, additional Web site guidelines are used to evaluate both the content and the quality of the Web site. A major distinction between a collection development policy and bibliography development policy is investment. In print and electronic resource development, purchase and maintenance costs are relevant. These do not exist in Web bibliography development. Here the major cost is staff time, both to create the bibliography and, later, to determine whether the links are still active and if new sites should be added or old sites replaced. This is not an insignificant investment; the return on investment should be analyzed as an element of the technical facilities offered by the library.

Librarians must periodically determine whether patrons use the bibliography sufficiently to warrant the annual input of time and effort involved in maintaining the site. The bibliography development policy should reflect the patron's needs, which in turn reflect the library collection policy. However, the library may find that certain resources are more accessible on the Web than print, such as genealogy, and emphasize the Web development process of that portion of their collection. Specific subject areas can be prioritized.

Web sites can be selected by the head of each department, or they can be selected by a designated librarian after conference with each department. The policy should indicate how library staff and various departments evaluate the Web sites and the process for handling modifications to the bibliographies, which is ideally done annually.

- A policy based on information categories is an important element of the process. Sites with neutral viewpoints are preferred, and the library's policy may dictate that only viewpoint-neutral sites be included. Government, academic, and cultural resources will generally have neutral viewpoints. Some libraries will want to adopt guidelines defining neutral Web sites.

- The Web site inclusion policy should specifically exclude commercial sites, illegal sites, hate sites, or sites violating school policies.

- The Web bibliography content should be consistent with the library collection development policy. If it varies, the explanation for the variance and guidelines for this variance should be included in the Web selection policy.

- The policy for the Web bibliography form and format should be current, from a recognized authority, organized for easy access and easy use; the design should be inviting; content should be accurate and appropriate; the scope of the chosen Web site should be appropriate for the users.

- ADA Web site accessibility should be evaluated and considered. Software for this evaluation should be adopted, and that software should be evaluated annually.

- The Web selection policy should reflect the mission of the library, the curricula and research interests of the faculty and students, and be relevant to the collection for content and educational value.

- Web selections should be checked periodically, and this period of review should be specified in the policy, as should the updating procedures.

- Extensive guidelines are not necessary and may overregulate choices. However, the greater the number of faculty and staff that are involved in Web bibliographies, the more detailed the guidelines should be. It is important to remember that to create order from chaos excessive links do little to tame the Internet. It is better to have a manageable number of well-chosen links than an excessive number of links that overwhelm the user.

Detailed Criteria for Multiple Web Bibliography Creators

Web links should be reviewed by formal and established link criteria. These criteria join the policy for Web site inclusion with the procedure to be employed by the faculty in the Web site selection. The larger the number of people selecting Web sites the more detailed the criteria should be.

The introduction section of the library Web site selection policy should identify the goal of the bibliography. Web sites should be produced and sponsored by "credible organizations" to be included in your electronic collection management.

The category of Web page is relevant in application guidelines. The purpose of an informational Web page is to present factual information. The URL address frequently ends in .edu or .gov. Informational Web pages are often sponsored by educational institutions or government agencies.

When evaluating the authority of a Web site for bibliography inclusion, consider the following points:

- Is it clear who is responsible for the contents of the page? If it is not clear, the Web site should not be used.

- Is there a link to a page describing the purpose of the sponsoring organization? If this does not exist, the Web site should not be used.

- Is there a way of verifying the legitimacy of the site's sponsor? Is there a contact link readily visible or is the contact information itself readily visible? Contact information should include an address and telephone number. This means a physical address, and not just a post office box. If the legitimacy of the sponsor is in question in any way, the site should not be included. Remember that sites are subject to modification by the sponsor, and if the sponsor is not a reliable authority and the site will not be consistent, it should not be used. Librarians cannot check sites each month to re-evaluate the content.

- The author of the material is often not evident on government and institutional Web sites. However, some Web sites, for example, "Ludwig van Beethoven—The Magnificent Master" at *http://www.geocities.com/raptus/*, do have an author. Review the author's qualifications before accepting the Web site.

- If the material is protected by copyright, is the name of the copyright holder given? This element of the evaluation process can be waived. While it is not essential that the identity of the copyright holder be given, that identity does support the legitimacy of the Web site. Remember, U.S. government information is not subject to copyright.

When evaluating accuracy, consider the following points:

- Are the sources for any factual information clearly listed so they can be verified in another source? This criterion is less important if linking to a major or local newspaper or a government Web site and this point is designed more for the faculty than the librarian. Often faculty will chose a site that is less mainstream and more nontraditional. This is an important basis from which to reject a faculty-chosen Web site.

- Is the information free of grammatical, spelling, and typographical errors? These kinds of errors indicate a lack of quality control and students can be confused by these errors. Such Web sites should never be used.

- Is it clear who has the ultimate responsibility for the accuracy of the content of the material? This authority must be just that, an authority.

- If there are charts or graphs containing statistical data, are they clearly labeled and easy to read? Sometimes increasing the font is all that is needed to make the charts more readable.

When evaluating objectivity consider the following points:

- The first element to consider is also the first point of evaluation. Consider the source. Does the source have a bias or a polarized position, or is the source neutral, giving both sides of the information? Students do not have the world experience necessary to differentiate between biased view points. Advertising on Web sites is inappropriate for a bibliography. However, advertising can be hidden in the content. Consequently, the content should be reviewed for advertising.

- You may want to go one step further, and advise your staff how the library identifies an advocacy Web site and your policy of avoiding all advocacy sites. An advocacy Web site is one sponsored by an organization attempting to influence public opinion. A Web page that tries to commit persons to a point of view is an advocacy Web page. The URL address of an advocacy Web page frequently ends in .org (organization).

When evaluating currency, consider whether there are dates that indicate when the page was last updated and first published.

These detailed criteria will serve as an aid when multiple faculty members are involved in Web site inclusion.

FORMAL POLICY TO PERIODICALLY REVIEW LINKS

Your library should have a policy of periodically reviewing its links. There is a trend in cyberspace of "domain napping," also called "porn-napping." Porn-nappers are operators of X-rated sites who monitor lists of Web addresses for names that are about to expire. If a name becomes available, porn-nappers can acquire the domain for the purpose of redirecting its former traffic to their pornography-based Web site.

Cathcamp.org was a domain name once owned by Michigan's Catholic Campaign for America. Pornographers registered this name when it became available, and Web searchers expecting information on a Catholic camp were redirected to a pornography Web cam. Sites once devoted to the arts, investments, shopping malls, and even a junior chamber of commerce, have been porn-napped.

Ben Edelman began tracing Internet ownership records and found 4,525 Internet domain names funneling unsuspecting visitors to Tina's Free Live

Web cam, an adult entertainment site. Most of the sites are owned by Domain Strategy, a Montreal company that specializes in buying and selling Internet domain names. Edelman published his report on the Web (see *http://cyber.law.harvard.edu/people/edelman/renewals/*). He reported that content on the redirected pages seems to vary between Domain Strategy promotions and the pornographic Web cam. The sites "program their pages so the user's Back button won't work," Edelman said. The images are extremely graphic. Every time a user clicks the Back button on the Internet browser, another pornography site opens. Often, the only way out is to reboot the computer.

CONCLUSION

Library Web sites are an important resource for the library patron. They provide the patron with a review of what the library can offer, and they organize the Internet for patrons' access. However, with the new technology of the Internet comes new potential liability for the librarian. It is important to understand the laws that impact a library's Web site and to respect them. The duties of the librarian have expanded yet again.

NOTES

1. Letter, Thomas Jefferson to William Duane, Monticello, August 12, 1810.
2. Americans with Disabilities Act.
3. 29 U.S.C. § 794(d).
4. *See* 10 NATIONAL *DISABILITY* LAW REPORTER Paragraph 240.
5. World Wide Web Consortium, Web Accessibility Standards Published Web Accessibility Iniative, <www.w3.org/WAI/>.
6. This directive responded to Pub. L. No. 105–220 (Aug. 7, 1998), an amendment to Section 508 of the Rehabilitation Act of 1973. *See* <http://www.usdoj.gov/crt/508/508/home.html>.
7. World Wide Web Consortium, Web Content Accessibility Guidelines 1.0 *See* <http://www.w3org/TR/WAI-WEBCONTENT/>.
8. Contact the Disability and Business Technical Assistance Center with your disability legislation questions. These experts provide technical assistance, resource information, or appropriate referrals. Telephone 800–949–4232 V/TTY, or go to *www.ADATA.org*. Services provided include technical assistance, education and training, materials dissemination, referral networks, and public awareness.
9. The Disability and Business Technical Assistance Centers provide services on all aspects of the ADA and accessible information technology. A newly funded National Center on Accessible Information Technology in Education collaborates with the ten centers to assist schools in assuring that purchase and use of technology is accessible to all users.
10. 248 U.S. 215 (1918).
11. *See* Richard Raysman & Peter Brown, *Dangerous Liaisons: The Legal Risks of Linking Web Sites*, N.Y.L.J. (Apr. 8, 1997), 3.

12. *See* Beverly M. Wolff, *Electronic Media: Recent Litigation Relating to Jurisdiction, Copyright and Other Legal Issues*, SC40 ALI-ABA 549, 567 (1998).

13. 21 F.3d 834 (6th Cir. 2000).

14. See *The Best Free Reference Web Sites* from the American Library Association's Reference and User Services Association (RUSA), Internet Scout Report, and Librarians Index to the Internet. It also lists various resources from which links have, euphemistically, been "borrowed," such as Digital Librarian: Reference Sites, Louisiana State: Ready Reference Sources, and Martindale's—the Reference Desk.

13

—•═•—

TRADEMARKS IN THE LIBRARY

> The practical impact of witholding unrestricted access to the patented
> technology from use by the Web community will be to substantially
> impair the usability of the Web for hundreds of millions of individuals.
> —Tim Berners Lee

Trademarks are an element of our modern-day language. The Golden Arches
are often the first symbol a child understands, and to that extent, this symbol,
a trademark owned by McDonald's Corporation, is a phrase with meaning.
And every parent knows exactly what it means: Happy Meal! Play ground!
Balls! All for $2.99. The Golden Arches are literally worth their weight in
gold.

Trademarks are an element of intellectual property. Intellectual property is
ownable property—it is simply intangible. Just as you can own physical property, you can also own intellectual property. Intellectual property is created
by the mind and experienced by the mind, while physical property exists in
the tactile dimension. Trademarks identify ownership of property; they are
not a new concept and are today found on ancient pottery.

Trademarks are symbols that are owned by an entity. The Nike Swoosh is
a symbol that appeals to teens. Most ladies would recognize the LV emblems
embossed on the leather of Louis Vuitton. Trademarks belong to their owners and cannot be used without the owner's permission. It is obvious that if
Reebok adopted the Nike Swoosh symbol, litigation would result. However,
the Swoosh symbol is not just protected from use by Reebok, it is protected
from use by anyone who desires to adopt that symbol.

Trademarks function to (1) identify one seller's goods and distinguish
them from the goods of others; (2) signify that all goods bearing the trade-

mark come from a single source; (3) signify that all goods bearing the trade-mark share an equal level of quality; and (4) act as primary instruments in advertising and selling the goods. Trademarks also serve as objective symbols of goodwill, representing and reinforcing the consumer satisfaction a business has earned.

A mark must be inherently distinctive or have attained a secondary meaning. McDonald's Golden Arches are a good example of a distinctive trademark. The achievement of a secondary meaning occurs when the mark has become distinctive of the goods in commerce between the states. No one goes to McDonald's for a steak and baked potato. McDonald's represents fast food. To achieve secondary meaning, the public must have come to recognize that the mark refers to products from a unique source. A mark becomes incontestable after five years of use.

TRADEMARKS CANNOT BE USURPED BY LIBRARIES

Libraries cannot usurp trademarked names to describe their reading programs, or borrow trademarked characters to enhance their appeal. They cannot paint pictures of Harry Potter on their walls, nor can they entitle their area of reference CDs "The Bookshelf." Microsoft has trademarked that term for its CD reference materials, and Harry Potter is a character known in every corner of the world. These concepts represent trademark-protected intellectual property.

Copyrighted materials have a life and a period of expiration after which they become public domain. Trademarks, however, can continue in perpetuity or until their owners fail to renew them. As long as Coca-Cola renews its trademarked name it will never come into the public domain. It is also a "famous mark." Trademarks that are famous marks have more extensive protection than do other marks.

Absolutely Arthur the Aardvark

In *Brown v. It's Entertainment, Inc.*, Arthur the Aardvark, a cartoon character, was protected under the federal dilution statute from unauthorized use. Arthur is the subject of over sixty best-selling books and a television series. FAO Schwarz's 1998 holiday catalog featured Arthur, and a balloon replica of Arthur led the 1997 Macy's Thanksgiving Day Parade. Arthur was found by the court to be a sufficiently developed character to be entitled to trademark protection and to prohibit the use of an unlicensed Arthur costume at a toy store opening. The court explained its position of protecting the image and the purity of Arthur: "Should unauthorized Arthur impersonators proliferate . . . the image sought by plaintiffs for Arthur will be difficult to control and might easily become blurred or tarnished, resulting in a loss of credibility, public affection, and consumer interest."

The Federal Trademark Dilution Act of 1995 protects famous fictional characters.[1] Neither a pregnant Minnie Mouse nor a tattooed Mickey Mouse can appear at the behest of some local publisher. They are protected by the Federal Trademark Dilution Act.

The library cannot paint its walls with depictions of these characters unless they are purchased or obtained from a representative licensed to provide these images. However, there is nothing to prevent a library from obtaining promotional materials for a book and placing them in their library. For example, Harry Potter is trademarked by one company and copyrighted by another.

Famous Marks

The Federal Trademark Dilution Act amended the Lanham Act[2] to become "Remedies for Dilution of Famous Marks." This Act protects characters that librarians all know and love. It is under this Act that Bambi, Superman, Casper the Friendly Ghost, Barney, and other characters find protections. Owners of trademarked characters were not satisfied with the requisite duty of proving dilution of their mark in order to protect it. This amendment gave them the national protection they wanted.

In the hearing before the U.S. Congress in 1995 on the extension of trademark protection to famous marks and to characters, Nils Victor Montan, vice president and senior intellectual property counsel for Warner Brothers Film Studio, testified on behalf of Time Warner's affiliated companies, including DC Comics and Warner Brothers Television, producers of such shows as *ER* and *Friends*. "The trademark owner, who has spent the time and investment needed to build up the goodwill in these marks, should be the sole determinant of how the marks are used in a commercial sense,"[3] said Montan. He gave examples of counterfeit T-shirts depicting Bugs Bunny and the Tasmanian Devil smoking marijuana. Without a likelihood of confusion, which was doubtful in a case like this, Montan said character owners needed some additional way to protect their marks.

The pertinent section of the Federal Trademark Dilution Act amending the Lanham Act provides that:

The owner of a famous mark shall be entitled, subject to the principles of equity and upon such terms as the court deems reasonable, to an injunction against another person's commercial use in commerce of a mark or trade name, if such use begins after the mark has become famous and causes dilution of the distinctive quality of the famous mark. . . .[4]

The legislative history of this section reveals that it was intended to prevent such uses as "Buick aspirin," "Dupont shoes," and "Kodak pianos," uses not likely to cause public confusion, but which could, over time, affect the capacity of renowned trademarks to uniquely identify one source. Because its protection is so broad, a "famous mark" must meet an extremely high standard to fall under this protection. There is no requirement that a likelihood of confusion would exist to employ this remedy.

The following eight factors determine the fame of a mark:

(A) the degree of inherent or acquired distinctiveness of the mark;

(B) the duration and extent of use of the mark in connection with the goods or services with which the mark is used;

(C) the duration and extent of advertising and publicity of the mark;

(D) the geographical extent of the trading area in which the mark is used;

(E) the channels of trade for the goods or services with which the mark is used;

(F) the degree of recognition of the mark in the trading areas and channels of trade of the mark's owner and the person against whom the injunction is sought;

(G) the nature and extent of use of the same or similar marks by third parties; and

(H) whether the mark was registered under the Act of March 3, 1881, or the Act of February 20, 1905, or on the principal register.[5]

The statute makes clear that a court may consider these factors, but none is determinative.

INTELLECTUAL PROPERTY OWNERSHIP

Intellectual property is divided into the following four broad categories:

1. *Copyrights.* Original works of authorship or artistic creation that are fixed in a tangible medium of expression may be copyrighted.

2. *Patents.* Novel inventions, such as a machine, formula, or process for making something or an improvement to an existing invention, may be patented.

3. *Trademarks.* Identifiers of source and quality for the products or services they identify.

4. *Trade Secrets.* Confidential business or technical information.

Trademarks are a part of our modern-day society. In ancient caves we find a remnant of a splayed palm representing a symbol of ownership of artwork. Symbols of ownership are everywhere. Coca-Cola®, McDonald's®, and Nike® are familiar symbols. Trademarks have meaning to the public. The letters M-I-C remind baby boomers of the three letters to follow, K-E-Y, representing Mickey Mouse. Children today identify just as strongly with Teletubbies, Kermit, and Barney. These are trademarked characters.

Trademarks can be words, names, symbols, slogans, tag lines, characters, or a design for almost anything. Packaging such as perfume bottles can be trademarked. No one may copy the traditional Chanel No. 5 bottle for their fragrance. Depending on the nature of the trademark, issues such as distinctiveness and secondary meaning may need to be considered to determine registrability and protectibility. Because of the size of the pharmaceutical industry and its extensive use of intellectual property to distinguish one product from another, many of the leading trademark and trade dress infringement cases have involved pharmaceutical products.

The basic legal rules applicable to trademark and trade dress infringement claims are the same for pharmaceutical products as they are for other product types. The name and trade dress of a product may be protected if they serve to identify and distinguish the product as coming from a particular source. The measure for determining whether or not there has been an infringement is whether the name or trade dress of the accused product is likely to cause consumers to be confused as to the product's source.

TRADEMARKED CHARACTERS

On January 16, 1996, when Congress passed the Federal Trademark Dilution Act of 1995, the dilution argument suddenly became a serious option for character protection. The federal dilution protection can be invoked to protect the trademark owner even where consumers are not likely to be confused by the use of the trademark, that is, they are not deceived into believing that Mickey Mouse represents MGM, for example. The Federal Dilution Act creates a limited property right for a trademark owner in his or her trademarked character.

Technically, a number of different legal theories of law are available for the protection of fictional characters under intellectual property law. Copyright is perhaps the most familiar in the world of libraries, but trademark and unfair competition or some combination thereof also protect characters.

Despite the rule that upon expiration of a copyright a character enters the public domain, courts have historically found legal precedent for permitting ongoing trademark rights to continue past the term of copyright. This employment of trademark rights prevents others from using some characters once the character has become the subject of public domain.

Copyright law offers more limited character protection than does the law of trademark. The characters of William Faulkner will never receive the protection afforded Bugs Bunny, simply because of the medium in which he was shared. Judge Learned Hand explained:

If *Twelfth Night* were copyrighted, it is quite possible that a second comer might so closely imitate Sir Toby Belch or Malvolio as to infringe, but it would not be enough that for one of his characters he cast a riotous knight who kept wassail to the discomfort of the household, or a vain and foppish steward who became amorous of his mistress. These would be no more than Shakespeare's "ideas" in the play, as little capable of monopoly as Einstein's Doctrine of Relativity, or Darwin's theory of the Origin of

Species. It follows that the less developed the characters, the less they can be copyrighted; that is the penalty an author must bear for marking them too indistinctly.[6]

Here, Judge Learned Hand addressed the concept of copyright protection of characters by examining what may be copied or used as a source of inspiration in a new work. However, he did not address the notion of trademarked characters that are fully developed and marketed, such as Ronald McDonald, Spider Man, or the Teenage Mutant Ninja Turtles.

TRADEMARKED WORDS

Unique words are created or coined to identify a product. These are typically trademarked words. Good examples would be Xerox or Exxon. These words were not part of our language until they were created to represent their products.

In some instances, ordinary words can also be trademarked. Microsoft Corporation owns the rights to use the word "Bookshelf" as applied to any CD-ROM product. Microsoft trademarked the term to represent its collection of reference books identified as Microsoft Bookshelf. A small company, Scanrom, marketed a CD-ROM disc they called "The First Electronic Jewish Bookshelf." Here the generic term was trademarked for a limited use outside the scope of its standard use. Its limited trademarked use by Microsoft is for CD-ROM reference material.

The word "apple" cannot be trademarked within the produce industry, because it must be employed to describe the fundamental nature of the produce. However, the term can be trademarked to represent a line of computers. The computer industry is well able to function without the term "apple." However, Apple Computers could not trademark the terms "computer screen" or "printer," while the produce industry could develop and trademark an apple named "Computer Screen."

The display of a ™ symbol or ® symbol also indicates that a word is considered a trademark.

The Case of Delta

Delta Air Lines is trademarked, as is Delta Faucets. The Trademark Office examines the relationship of the goods or services in which the mark is used. Delta represents an identical mark that is registrable because the marks are used in connection with sufficiently different goods or services. The simultaneous use of these marks for different services will not confuse a consumer. Delta is not a unique name. However, the name Xerox is unique. Xerox could not be used by a cookie manufacturer for the creation of Xerox Cookies due to the uniqueness of its name.

As Xerox and Exxon are coined names and have no dictionary meaning, they reside at one end of the spectrum. At the other end of the spectrum are generic or common names, such as Microsoft's Bookshelf. The scope of protection for a coined term will be broader than the scope of protection for a generic term such as Microsoft's Bookshelf. While Microsoft may be able to protect CD reference volumes with that name, it could not protect it from use by a library for its *New York Times* Bestseller program, entitled "Bookshelf." However, a library could not entitle its children's collection "Xerox" unless, of course, Xerox Corporation sponsored the collection and supported the use of its name for the "Xerox Children's Collection."

Trademarks are classified as suggestive, descriptive, or generic.

Suggestive trademarks are those that "suggest," rather than "describe" qualities of the underlying goods or services. Examples of suggestive marks include Q-Tips for cotton-tipped swabs and Hamburger Helper for meat enhancement. The law finds that suggestive names go beyond "mere description." A trademark exists because it requires imagination, thought, and perception to determine the nature of goods or services in question. As a name for a convenience store, "Quick Stop" has not risen to the imaginative level required for protection. It is meant to connote speedy service, and such a mark would be classified as a descriptive mark rather than a suggestive mark.

Descriptive trademarks describe the ingredients, qualities, features, purpose, or characteristics of a product or service. These marks are not inherently distinctive, and thus do not receive trademark protection unless they acquire distinctiveness through secondary meaning. Even if they do qualify for trademark protection, descriptive marks are the weakest marks possible and do not receive as broad a legal protection as suggestive, arbitrary, and fanciful marks. Examples of descriptive marks include World Book for encyclopedias.

Generic trademarks occur when a trademark starts out as distinctive or descriptive but then become generic through use. This occurs when the mark becomes part of the common descriptive name of a category or genus of products. Genericide, as it is called, is more likely to happen to marks that are used improperly as nouns instead of adjectives, whether such usage is by the trademark owner or by others.

COMMON LAW RIGHTS OF TRADEMARK PROTECTION

Without a federal trademark registration, a trademark right may only cover the geographic area in which the trademark is being used. A problem may occur when the territories of two common-law trademark owners with similar trademarks on similar goods overlap. This occurred with bar-be-cue in Texas, which is also sold in New Mexico and Louisiana and is considered to be a regional mark. The owner that first used the trademark in the contested market will prevail and the other owner will be prevented from expanding into the overlapping territory. However, in these special instances attorneys must be consulted.

Common-law trademark rights support state trademark registration in multiple states. These state registrations are a public record and serve to inform the public of common-law trademark rights within that state. State registrations are important as a less expensive alternative to federal registration and serve as a deterrent to third parties who may be searching the state databases in an effort to clear a mark for use or registration.

FEDERAL TRADEMARK PROTECTION

Federal trademark registration ensures nationwide protection to registered marks, regardless of the areas in which the mark is actually being used, enables you to use the registration notice ®, and notifies others of your trademark rights. This safeguards future opportunities for nationwide expansion and these marks can be litigated in federal courts as opposed to state courts. The federal statutory protection provides larger damages for infringement than do state common-law remedies.

No formal filing is necessary to use a ™ mark. It can be used at any time to inform the public that trademark rights are being claimed by the owner. The ® mark, on the other hand, can only be used if the trademark is federally registered.

INTERNATIONAL TRADEMARK LAWS

Every country has its own trademark laws. There are over 200 countries with individual trademark laws. While trademark rights are territorial, and many of the basic concepts found in U.S. trademark law hold true in other countries, there are also many differences, including the establishment of trademark rights. Consultation with an attorney is recommended.

ASSAULTS ON A TRADEMARK

The Lanham Act protects assaults on trademarks. The principal forms of assault are infringement and dilution.

Infringement

Infringement occurs when the marks used on two respective goods are likely to cause confusion, mistake, or deception with regard to source, affiliation, or sponsorship. Actual confusion is not necessary to claim infringement, just the likelihood of confusion. An infringement can occur as a result of a similarity between trademarks in appearance, sound, or meaning (for example, Raid versus Raze for insecticide, or Easy Spray versus EZ Spray for window spray, or Hurricane versus Cyclone for fencing).

Dilution

There is the possibility of a dilution action either under federal law or the laws of several states, as defined by Section 45 of the Lanham Act, when "lessening of the capacity of a famous mark to identify and distinguish goods or services occurs, regardless of the presence or absence of (1) competition between the owner of the famous mark and other parties, or, (2) likelihood of confusion, mistake or deception."[7] Determining whether dilution exists is a very complex aspect of trademark law, requiring the expertise of a trademark attorney.

CIRCUMVENTING TRADEMARK LAW WITH DOMAIN NAMES

While generic names have never been trademarked names, their status has been elevated with the introduction of the Internet and laws that pertain to the cyberworld. A trademark can be a domain name and a domain name a trademark. The URL *www.coke.com* takes you to Coca-Cola's Web site.

The legal coexistence of trademarks and domain names is finding a place in the law. A domain name used as a trademark—to promote source identification—will be treated as a trademark. It will be required to meet the same criteria as other trademarks, including non-genericism in the context in which it is used, to find protection in the law. To establish infringement of a domain name, a plaintiff has to show that the offending domain name was being used as a trademark. The use of *Roses.com* by 1–800–Flowers would be an infringement upon the Katy, Texas, florist's right to market her domain name of *Roses.com*. This florist has historically successfully protected assaults on her domain name. While the name is not capable of trademark protection because the name represents the sale of roses, the florist is capable of defending its right to its domain name because it does in fact sell roses. When challenged by Roses Department Store for trademark infringement, it was able to protect its domain name because it had a legitimate florist business that marketed roses to the public.

"Drugs" is an example of a generic name that could not be trademarked in the print world. However, as a domain name, the term has new legal status. Common English words have great value when registered as domain names. Drugs.com is a domain name that has value, although it cannot be trademarked.

Generic domain names appeal to proprietors because of their ease of recall by the public, and because savvy Web surfers may look first to generic names as they search for *Banks.com*, *Toys.com*, *Gifts.com*, or *Flowers.com*. The URL *flowers.com* takes you to *1–800-flowers.com*. *Roses.com* will take you to a florist in Katy, Texas, with a 1–800 number and a wonderfully graphic Web site. These generic Web sites have commercial value.

The term "Roses" cannot be trademarked. However, it can be given intellectual property status as a domain name. There can be no exclusive use in connection with the term roses, however; only one florist may own the .com name. All florists need, and have the right, to use the word "roses" to refer to their product.

A generic term, unlike a descriptive one, cannot acquire secondary meaning and thereby become a trademark. The reason for denying protection to generic terms is that these terms are needed by everyone in the business of providing that type of product; permitting one manufacturer to appropriate a generic term for its exclusive use would impede competition.

The passage of the Anticybersquatting Consumer Protection Act[8] and the establishment by Internet Corporation for Assigned Names and Numbers (ICANN) of the Uniform Domain Name Dispute Resolution Policy and Rules has provided remedies for trademark holders against real cybersquatters.[9]

KEYWORDS

Search engines use keywords to retrieve articles. Commercially, advertisers pay for lists of words they select, and the search engines key specific banner ads for these Web browsers based on the keywords searched.

Playboy Enterprises, Inc. brought a cause of action against both Netscape Communications and Excite, Inc., whose search engines were using the words "playboy" and "playmate" as keywords, so that a user searching for one of those terms was presented with an advertisement for an adult-oriented competitor of Playboy Enterprises along with the search results. They were generating an income by using these terms to send specific advertising to searchers who had used these terms for searching. Playboy Enterprises believed they were capitalizing upon their trademarked protected name.

The district court's opinion stated that "A trademark is not an omnibus property right or a monopoly on the use of the words in the trademark." The district court explained that the "[d]efendants' use of the words 'playboy' and 'playmate' in their search engines does not equate to commercial exploitation of plaintiff's trademarks."[10] The search engines were using these English words as a common representation of an idea or topic. Playboy and playmate are not coined words and may be found in the dictionary. Because the uses were non-trademark uses, the court found neither the trademark infringement claims nor the dilution claims made by Playboy Enterprises to be persuasive.

Clearly, no publisher may publish a magazine named *Playboy* or *Playmate*. However, the use of these terms may be employed in other endeavors; the terms were not removed from the public lexicon by their adoption by Playboy Enterprises.

The U.S. Patent and Trademark Office (USPTO) has explicitly recognized that a domain name can serve two functions. It may be both an address and a trademark. In examining a trademark application, the Patent and Trademark Office looks for specimens of use that present the mark "in a manner that will be perceived by potential purchasers as indicating source and not merely an informational indication of the domain name address used to access a Web site."[11]

U.S. TRADEMARK PROCEDURES FOR SEARCHING TRADEMARKS

The United States Patent and Trademark Office provides an online search for trademarked names at its Web site. This, however, does not reveal the state registrations that must be performed in each individual state. Since common-law protection does apply to trademarks, searching telephone books and trade directories is an important component of a trademark name search.

There are private firms and law firms that will conduct a full trademark name search. If conflicting marks are found, consult with an attorney to evaluate the strength of the trademark and the likelihood of confusion with similar names.

A U.S. Federal Trademark Application may be filed after a due diligence search determines that the name has not been taken by another entity. There are two types of applications: use-based and intent-to-use (ITU).

A use-based application is filed when actual use of the trademark began before the application was filed, and the mark is being used in commerce in direct association with a product or service.

An intent-to-use application is filed before the trademark is used. The application can be filed on the basis of good-faith intent to use the mark in commerce. Eventual use of the mark in commerce is required before issuance of a registration. Currently, the fee for registration is $325 per class. ITUs incur additional fees as they progress to registration.

Examining attorneys and paralegals at the Trademark Office examine both the use-based and ITU applications for technical and substantive problems. The attorneys determine factors such as whether any conflicts exist on the register, if the trademark is merely descriptive, and if the description of goods and the classification are properly set forth. Like the Copyright Office, the examiners in the Trademark Office evaluate the registerability of a trademark, that is, if it falls within their guidelines for registration. They are not concerned with infringements or potential civil actions that may result by the use of the trademark.

Printed materials such as the *Official Gazette* inform the public of applications for trademark registration with the USPTO and offer third parties an opportunity to stop registration of a published trademark by filing a notice of opposition. This review of trademark application publications is called policing. Trademark watching services will, for a fee, police *Official Gazettes* and other publications throughout the world. In the United States, there is a thirty-day deadline beyond the publication date to file an opposition or obtain an extension of time to file the opposition.

Upon the filing of a trademark, the trademark notice changes from a ™ mark to ® mark. Trademarks must be renewed. Trademark rights are contingent upon continued use of the trademark and the filing of a Section 8 Affidavit between the fifth and sixth year of the trademark's life. Renewals require a verified statement attesting to the continued use of a mark. A Section 8 Affidavit must also be filed ten years from the initial registration date, as well as all subsequent ten-year periods throughout the life of the registration. Failure to file the Section 8 Affidavit results in cancellation of the federal registration.

Section 9 is also a request for renewal, filed every ten years from the registration date. Section 8 is filed, and is a prerequisite to the filing of a Section 9 "Request for Renewal" at the ten-year mark. The filing fee is currently $400 per class. If trademarks are not renewed they are cancelled.

Any time after the mark has been used continuously for a five-year period, the registrant has the option to file an affidavit of incontestability—referred to as the Section 15 Affidavit. With the Section 15 Affidavit, the validity of the registration becomes incontestable, making it immune from most challenges. The filing fee is currently $200 per class.

A trademark can be sold through an assignment. This grants the buyer all rights to the trademark, including the good will associated with the trademark. Through a license, a trademark can be "rented" exclusively or non-exclusively to others. If the transaction is an assignment involving applications or registrations (that is, not common-law rights), such a transaction should be made a matter of record in the Trademark Office to avoid complications when subsequent filings with the Trademark Office are made.

Misuse of a trademark diminishes its strength. Loss of distinctiveness can result in marks becoming public domain. The term "genericide" means that a trademark has become the generic term for the goods or services. Trademarks are adjectives—not nouns or verbs. A trademark is not a thing or a kind of thing. It is a brand for a thing.

CONCLUSION

Libraries are not completely prohibited from using all registered trademarks or characters. However, a library should be on notice that when it desires to "borrow" a trademark or a character belonging to another, it should obtain permission. Trademark protection of marks and characters exists, in addition to copyright protection. Libraries must be sensitive to the existence of both.

The Federal Dilution Act can be construed to undermine the public policy of the copyright law, which is to ultimately return work to the public domain.

Trademark protection, unlike copyright protection, has the potential to be permanent if the trademark is renewed. This creates a perpetual life for trademarked characters that they could never obtain with the law of copyright. Courts have historically found that trademark and copyright forms of protection may safely coexist.[12]

The Federal Trademark Dilution Act extends existing trademark protection to an elite category of marks, including characters that Congress found to be deserving of special protection. They have given the owners of the mark the perpetual right to preserve the integrity of the characters and to preserve the right to perpetual income from these characters. Fictions in the law allow perpetual life to corporations and now to nationally recognized marks and characters.

NOTES

1. 15 U.S.C. § 1125.

2. 15 U.S.C. §§ 1051-1127.

3. United States House of Representatives Committee on the Judiciary Subcommittee on Courts, the Internet and Intellectual Property, "Oversight Hearing in the Unied States Patent and Trademark Office," March 9, 2000.

4. 15 U.S.C. § 1125(c)(1).

5. 15 U.S.C. §§ 1125(c)(2), 1117(a)(b), 1118.

6. Nichols v. Universal Pictures, 45 F.2d 119 (2d Cir. 1930). *But see* Warner Bros. Pictures, Inc. v. Columbia Broadcasting Sys., Inc., 216 F.2d 945, 950 (9th Cir. 1954), which suggests that no character is protectible unless it "really constitutes the story being told" and is not just a "chess man in the game of telling the story." This view has since been limited to word portraits, as distinguished from cartoon and other graphic representations.

7. 15 U.S.C. § 1125(c)(1) and (2).

8. Anticybersquatting Consumer Protection Act of 1999, §§ 3001 et seq.

9. ICANN, Uniform Domanin Name Dispute Resolution Policy, <http://www.ican/org/udrp.htm>.

10. Playboy Enterprises, Inc. v. Weller, U.S District Court, SDCA (1998).

11. U.S. Patent and Trademark Office, <http://www.uspto.gov/web/offices/tac/notices/guide299.htm>.

12. *See* Frederick Warne & Co. v. Book Sales, Inc., 481 F. Supp. 1191, 1196–97 (S.D.N.Y. 1979) ("the fact that a copyrightable character or design has fallen into the public domain should not preclude protection under the trademark laws so long as it is shown to have acquired independent trademark significance, identifying in some way the source or sponsorship of the goods"); *see also* Harvey Cartoons v. Columbia Pictures Indus., 645 F. Supp. 1564, 1570–73 (S.D.N.Y. 1986) (deciding issue of trademark infringement even though copyright had expired, thus indicating trademark rights endured despite expiration of copyright).

14

DISABILITIES AND PUBLIC LIBRARIES

> The more folks that are actively engaged in the policy discussion, the
> more inclusive those decisions can become, and the end result can be the
> people's perspective getting a better hearing.
> —Phillip A. Hamilton, House of Delegates, Virginia

A public entity may not refuse to provide a disabled individual with an equal
opportunity to participate in or benefit from its program simply because the
person has a disability. It is discriminatory to deny a person with a disability
the right to participate in or benefit from the aid, benefit, or service provided
by the public entity. This is governed by the Code of Federal Regulations,
Chapter 35, Section 130. As a civil rights law, the Americans with Disabilities
Act (ADA) is subjugated only to the U.S. Constitution. It is the supreme law
of the land. The ADA is intended to protect not only library patrons, but
library employees.

Title II of the ADA's prime directive is a prohibition against public entities
from engaging in discrimination. Any state or local government is a public
entity. Public libraries, whether they receive federal funds or not, are public
entities.

The Americans with Disability Act of 1990 mandates that "no qualified
individual . . . with a disability shall by reason of such disability be excluded
from participation in or be denied the benefits of the services, programs or
activities of a pubic entity or be subjected to discrimination by any such
entity." Access must be made available to those with the disability. The ADA
provides comprehensive civil rights protections for individuals with disabilities. The ADA does not provide a definitive list of qualifying disabilities. It
does, however, outline factors to be considered in looking at each of the

three tests of a disability. Consequently, disability is generally a broad and inclusive term. Title I, II, and III share the broad and non-specific definition of disability as:

- a physical or mental impairment that substantially limits one or more of the major life activities of such individual
- a record of such an impairment
- being regarded as having such impairment

A major life activity is defined by the ADA as one that impedes a person's ability to care for themselves or perform manual tasks, such as walking, seeing, hearing, speaking, breathing, learning, and working. The ADA covers not only people who use wheelchairs, but also people with limited sensory, dexterity, cognitive, or perceptual abilities. Examples of these impairments include not only physical impairments, but mental impairments as well, such as hearing, visual, and speech impairments. Diseases that render the person impaired include cerebral palsy, epilepsy, muscular dystrophy, multiple sclerosis, cancer, heart disease, diabetes, mental retardation, emotional illness, learning disabilities as specified, tuberculosis, alcoholism, and drug addiction. Homosexuality and bisexuality are not physical or mental impairments under the ADA.

TITLE II—ACCESSIBILITY OF SERVICES, PROGRAMS, AND ACTIVITIES

Title II regulations require that public entities make their services, programs, or activities readily accessible to and usable by individuals with disabilities. This applies to state and local governments and their agencies and instrumentalities, which would include public libraries. Excluded from this title are federal agencies covered by the Architectural Barriers Act (ABA) of 1968 and the remainder of the federal government. It should be noted, however, that the ABA, which does apply to the federal government, contains almost identical limitations as those of the ADA. Title II applies to programs and services provided by state or local governmental entities with more than fifty employees.

Program accessibility is distinct from facilities accessibility. Programs and services are made available in a different format than facilities. Creating an accessible facility is one way of making programs and services accessible. Having an accessible facility does not always mean that the programs and services are accessible.

To evaluate whether a program is accessible it must be viewed in its entirety. Some facilities may remain inaccessible as long as the programs and services are accessible in some reasonable location. For example, if some buildings do not have ingress and egress routes, the program could simply be held in another location. A public entity need not take any action that it can demonstrate would result in a fundamental alteration of the nature of the service, program, or activity, or result in undue financial and administrative burdens. It is important not to confuse the obligation for facility access with the obligation for program or service access. In summary, Title II requires a public entity to make its programs accessible in all cases, except where to do so would result in a fundamental alteration in the nature of the program or in undue financial and administrative burden. Congress intended the "undue burden" standard in Title II for programs and services to be significantly higher than the "readily achievable" standard in Title III. Title II may not require the removal of barriers where removal would be required under Title III. The end result is that in most instances Title II serves to provide access to most programs and services.

If there is a genuine belief that an undue burden would result in providing programs or services to persons with disabilities, the head of the public entity or his or her designee must issue a written statement of the reasons for concluding that an undue burden would result.

There are many methods of compliance, including:

- redesign of equipment
- re-assignment of services to accessible buildings
- assignment of aides for assistance
- home visits
- delivery of services to alternate accessible sites
- alteration of existing facilities
- construction of new facilities
- any other method that provides access as required on a case-by-case basis

There are special treatments available to alter historic facilities so the historic nature of the property may be preserved.

By 1993, all public entities were required to have completed "self evaluations" to determine what steps were required to achieve accessibility compliance. Each current service, policy, and practice must be evaluated to determine whether they complied with Title II regulations. In some instances, courts have held the original evaluation to not have been compliant with Title II requirements.

Any new services added since 1993 must also be evaluated. Programs and functions that have changed should be reevaluated. Some programs implemented for Title II compliance have been dropped or modified since their inception. This evaluation process requires public input and comment, including comment by individuals with disabilities. The self-evaluation process has historically been an element of Section 504 implementation and serves as an important method for accessing information.

Vigilance and documentation is required to specifically address each new program and service of the library to determine whether it is disability accessible. It is essential to obtain input and comment in this ongoing process from individuals with disabilities. At least twice a year, each department should evaluate all its programs and services that have been added or modified to determine whether they are accessible by persons with disabilities.

TITLE III—ACCESSIBILITY OF FACILITIES BY THOSE WITH DISABILITIES

Title III of the Americans with Disabilities Act requires places of public accommodation to be accessible to persons with disabilities. This is the visible element of the ADA, and the one with which we are most familiar. This portion of the Act has provided wheelchair ramps and other accommodations that we have all enjoyed. The statute defines "public accommodation" as an entity whose operations affect commerce and whose function falls into one of twelve categories, one of which lumps together a museum, library, gallery, or other place of public display or collection.

It is important to note that Title III does address accessibility for persons with physical disabilities, but it also addresses the need of accessibility for persons with mental and cognitive disabilities, including but not limited to mental retardation. Groups of individuals who have difficulty reading, writing, and processing information will be the beneficiaries of these considerations. Our country contains many non-English speakers and people with low literacy or no literacy, and as our society ages we must address the needs of older adults who may have difficulty with speed of transactions, reading, and mobility.

There are four methods of accommodation for disabled citizens for public facilities:

1. changing the architecture
2. changing the equipment
3. changing the nature of the activity
4. providing direct personal assistance from another person

To accommodate the handicapped, physical facilities must be modified when the following occasions arise:

1. New construction is initiated.
2. Renovations or alterations are made to existing facilities.
3. Modifications to existing facilities would be readily achievable to eliminate architectural barriers faced by the public using the facility.

The U.S. Department of Justice has adopted a set of guidelines for compliant construction, known as the ADA Accessibility Guidelines (ADAAG).

These must be followed for new construction and alteration. Otherwise they are a goal when making readily achievable modifications. Under the readily achievable scenario, the construction of an element for handicapped access to the lesser standard requires that the accommodation must be safe for use. It is important to note that the ADA Accessibility Guidelines are the minimum criteria.

The ADAAG was developed by the United States Architectural and Transportation Barriers Compliance Board (ATBCB), as mandated by Congress. These standards are based on a private-sector standard known as ANSI a117.1, which is the standard for making buildings and facilities accessible and useable. These guidelines provide the scoping and technical requirements for accessibility to buildings and facilities by individuals with disabilities under the Americans with Disabilities Act.[1] These requirements are to be applied during the design, construction, and alteration of buildings and facilities covered by Titles II and III of the ADA to the extent required by regulations issued by federal agencies, including the Department of Justice and the Department of Transportation, under the ADA. While the guidelines are based upon adult dimensions and anthropometrics they also contain alternate specifications based on children's dimensions.

Libraries

Identifying What Needs To Be Done—Ongoing Project For Modification Should Be Done Annually By Committee

Ongoing Evaluation

It is important to study and survey on an ongoing basis any barriers, both programmatic and physical, that discriminate against anyone who is disabled. An ongoing focus to identify barriers to programs and an examination of the alternatives to these barriers is an important function of a library. Social barriers that result from alternative access should also be examined on an ongoing basis.

Priorities should be assigned to address these barriers with the goal being the ultimate removal of barriers in all programs and facilities. Tracking budgets and schedules for use of available funding in barrier removal is an essential element of this consideration, which should be done on an annual basis.

The established Americans with Disability Act system prioritizes access to goods and services as follows:

- Getting to the site
- Getting into the building
- Getting to the goods and service within the building
- Getting to everything else (restrooms, drinking fountains, etc.)

The second priority system is the Barrier Free Environments, Inc. (BFE) chronological order for accessing goods and service. The priorities include:

- Access to the site and site entry
- Information gathering regarding the site and access to the building
- Access to functional spaces and services
- Access to support facilities.

The third method for prioritizing the structural modifications is based on the program and the impact the modification will have on that program. The priorities in conjunction with the on-going work, budget and the schedule can serve as a benchmark and starting point to allow assignment of priorities to required structural modifications both now and in the future.

The priority system used on the proposed structural modifications in the facility survey reflects the following time frames and level of impact:

- Action immediately required (1 year)
- Budget for installation (1–4 years)
- Complete as budget and schedule permit (1–7 years)
- Done as art of the ongoing modifications effort (1–10 years)

The intent of the ADA is to promote response and implementation within a five-year time frame established by the Department of Justice. The completion of the required structural modifications is determined by a variety of factors that would extend the timeline in response to these influences. This includes the self-evaluation and implementation plan, along with the budget and schedules of the library to determine the order and extent of structural modification projects. The law requires that the programs be evaluated and process and procedure revised to remove any barriers that may exist. Structural modifications are only required if the program revisions do not remove barriers and provide access through accommodation. If the library decides to use the structure modification in lieu of the program revisions, the priority of the modification significantly increases. It is not the intent of the law to require immediate structural modification if program alternatives are available.

Priorities should establish time frames based on the severity of structural barriers and impact on the program. Many facilities serve several programs, while others are singular to spaces for individual programs. Relocation of programs is possible in many cases, but when the program requirements for space are specific to that program, there may be no alternative to structural modification if the program requirements do not allow program alternatives.

Case-by-case solutions to the needs of patrons can be an option. Ongoing evaluation should be flexible as the library continues to provide access to the programs on an individual basis. The purpose of the ongoing analysis is to provide the base-level information and projected time frames that must be part of the analysis that the library uses to establish its facility barrier removal for new construction and renovations.

Access Board

The Access Board[2] is an independent federal agency devoted to accessibility for people with disabilities. It operates with about thirty staff and a governing board of representatives from federal departments and public members appointed by the president. Key responsibilities of the Access Board include:

- developing and maintaining accessibility requirements for the built environment, transit vehicles, telecommunications equipment, and for electronic and information technology
- providing technical assistance and training on these guidelines and standards
- enforcing accessibility standards for federally funded facilities

The Access Board provides training on its accessibility guidelines and standards to various organizations and groups. Most training sessions focus on the ADA Accessibility Guidelines, which cover the built environment and transportation vehicles. ADAAG training also addresses new or upcoming sections, such as those covering children's environments, play areas, state and local government facilities, and recreation facilities. In addition to ADAAG, training is available on design requirements for federal facilities, telecommunications equipment, and electronic and information technology.

The Access Board tailors its training to the particular needs and interests of each audience. Board training is of particular interest to design professionals and architects, facility operators and managers, the transportation industry, the disability community, and members of other professions and groups that work with any of the Board's guidelines and standards. Board staff often reserve time for question-and-answer sessions at training events. This kind of interaction is particularly helpful in gauging the information needs of the Board's various audiences.

Most training sessions are held at the request of, or in partnership with, organizations or groups holding conferences and seminars that include accessibility or the ADA on the agenda. Due to budget constraints, the Board usually requests reimbursement of travel costs for its participation. Board policy requires that the events it participates in be conducted in accessible facilities and be communicated, upon request, in accessible formats. The Board likes to arrange additional training opportunities once it is scheduled to be in a particular area.

CONCLUSION

It is important for a library to evaluate accessibility on an ongoing basis and to provide training to its staff. Staff often are the first to notice barriers and suggest resolutions for access. Keeping accessibility in the forefront of all staff and encouraging them to be proactive in reporting difficulties and find-ing solutions are important elements of creating a compliant and accessible library.

NOTES

1. ADA Accessibility Guidelines for Buildings and Facilities (ADAAG), <http://www.access-board.gov/> (accessed January 1, 2003).

2. Access Board, <http://www.access-board.gov/indexes/technicalindex.htm> (accessed January 3, 2003).

15

POLICIES AND PROCEDURES—A
DIFFERENCE WITH SIGNIFICANCE

The most effectual means of preventing [the perversion of power into tyranny is] to illuminate, as far as practicable, the minds of the people at large, and more especially to give them knowledge of those facts which history exhibits, that possessed thereby of the experience of other ages and countries, they may be enabled to know ambition under all its shapes, and prompt to exert their natural powers to defeat its purposes.
—Thomas Jefferson, Diffusion of Knowledge Bill

Understanding the distinction between policies and procedures is fundamental and is often taken very lightly. However, the true art of creating policies and their supporting procedures is found in this important distinction. Policies represent the mission of the library and balance the rights of the library community as a whole with the individual's rights to access and use the library. To this end, policies in their purpose mirror laws. Well-crafted policies should not require the manipulation and change that the underlying guidelines may require. While the policies represent the mission of the library, the guidelines represent the methods by which the library will implement the policies. These should be open to a review with input from those responsible for their enforcement and those who enforcement affects. A good policy is to review your policies and guidelines annually.

Policies must be drafted to comply with laws that govern policies. While policies are used to apply the law to the library and its many uses, the format of the policies themselves must comply with the law by being clear and specific. The logic is simple; policies that are vague and non-specific cannot be understood by those enforcing them, nor can they be understood by those to whom they apply.

Public institutions' policies will be scrutinized by the courts more closely than policies of private entities. Libraries, as predominantly publicly supported institutions, must be governed by policies that can withstand judicial scrutiny, and as public governmental institutions they submit to higher legal standards than are applied to public institutions.

Library policies for all but private libraries come from a combination of sources. The ALA has a large resource of recommendations, such as the ALA Bill of Rights or the Right to Read Program. Other libraries also are tremendous resources for policies. The ultimate source for the creation or a refinement of library policies is the staff of the library adopting the policies. While the skeleton of a library's policy can be obtained outside the library, only the library in which the policies will be implemented can narrow and tailor the policies to conform to the needs of the community the library serves.

Libraries are inextricably tied to the funding of government, and as such, are governed by the public sector. Local taxes provide more than eighty-five percent of the support for public libraries. Academic and research libraries are supported from public taxation, student tuition, grants and subsidies, or tax-free donations. School libraries are totally dependent on local and state taxes. Private libraries exist primarily in law firms and large business enterprises.

A POLICY SHOULD REFLECT A LIBRARY'S MISSION

In creating a policy for your library it is important to evaluate or re-evaluate your library's mission. A library policy emanates from its defined mission. Today many, many libraries place their mission statement on the World Wide Web. These range from the largest institutions, such as the Library of Congress, to the smallest libraries that serve communities of fewer than 10,000 people.

Some libraries choose a broad mission, such as:

The mission of the library, through its excellent service, is to provide materials, information, programs, and facilities to improve the quality of life for all people in our community.

This mission statement emphasizes service to "all" people with service, materials, information, programs, and facilities. Other libraries are more specific in their mission.

The Chicago Public Library offers a beautiful and elegant mission statement:

We welcome and support all people in their enjoyment of reading and pursuit of life-long learning. Working together we strive to provide equal access to information ideas and knowledge through books, programs and other resources. We believe in the freedom to read, learn and discover.

The Library of Congress states:

The Library's mission is to make its resources available and useful to the Congress and the American people and to sustain and preserve a universal collection of knowledge and creativity for future generations.

The New York Public Library states:

The New York Public Library is one of the cornerstones of the American tradition of equal opportunity. It provides free and open access to the accumulated wisdom of the world, without distinction as to income, religion, nationality, or other human condition. It is everyone's university; the scholar's and author's haven; the statesman's, scientist's, and businessman's essential resource; the nation's memory. It guarantees freedom of information and independence of thought. It enables each individual to pursue learning at his/her own personal level of interest, preparation, ability, and desire. It helps ensure the free trade in ideas and the right of dissent.

The mission of The New York Public Library is to use its available resources in a balanced program of collecting, cataloging, and conserving books and other materials, and providing ready access directly to individual library users and to users elsewhere through cooperating libraries and library networks. The New York Public Library's responsibility is to serve as a great storehouse of knowledge at the heart of one of the world's information centers, and to function as an integral part of a fabric of information and learning that stretches across the nation and the world.

The Detroit Public Library states:

The mission of the Detroit Public Library is to support and enhance the quality of life in the city of Detroit and the state of Michigan, by providing library and information services that meet the cultural, professional, educational and recreational needs of our customers

The Mobile, Alabama, Public Library states:

The Mobile Public Library is a public service agency. Our mission is to provide the resources and services needed to open doors to life-long learning, to fulfill citizens' information needs and, to offer and support cultural and recreational activities.

In Truth or Consequences, New Mexico:

The mission of the Truth or Consequences Public Library is to provide accurate information in a timely manner to those who need it, and to provide appropriate recreational reading, listening, and viewing materials to persons of all ages and educational levels.

If your library offers community-service programs, reflect that specifically in your mission. If your library offers cultural and recreational activities, that too should be reflected in your mission. Truly examine the services your library offers, or would like to offer, and let your mission statement reflect those provisions. Library policies have their foundation in the stated mission of the library.

POLICIES MUST HAVE A LEGITIMATE PURPOSE

Library policies protect the resources of the library used to fulfill its mission. The rights of the individual in employing the library resources must be matched with the need to allocate resources equitably for all users, and to this end library policies often restrict the unbridled freedom an individual can have with regard to library resources.

For example, while a library may not impose restrictions on the nature of the content a patron may review through the library, which now includes the Internet, it may impose restrictions on the size of the files the patron can download, as large files may use excessive resources. Due to the limited resources available for provision of public access to the Internet, the library may set limits, for example, on use of large files of still or moving images or sound, or on downloading files in any medium. It may set limits on the time a user may access the Internet, or it may set limits on functions for which a user may access the Internet, such as the use of chat rooms.

Public libraries that accept federal funds must filter Internet access. It is important that the library policy provide a release of the filter for access to all legally available Internet information.

In reviewing a library policy, the court will look at the actual purpose of a policy, and not be bound simply by the stated purpose. If the actual purpose of the policy is to maximize the library's ability to provide Internet resources to the public, then this policy will be valid and enforceable. If the actual purpose is to impose a prior restraint on a person's freedom of access to materials, then the policy is likely to be held unenforceable.

Policies Must Be Applied Uniformly

Policies must be nondiscriminatory in their application. In 1789, Thomas Jefferson noted, "The execution of the laws is more important than the making of them."[1] This same premise applies to the execution of the library's policies. They must be executed uniformly and fairly. For example, a policy that prohibits solicitation in the library must apply to all solicitors. The library may have historically allowed Girl Scouts to solicit the sale of cookies from faculty and staff. However, once a "no solicitation" policy is adopted, the Girl Scouts are excluded as solicitors as are all solicitors. The act of not applying the policy uniformly and across the board would be an act of discrimination. A policy that allows no sleeping in the library cannot be addressed simply to the homeless who sleep in the library but must be applied to all who sleep in the library.

Policies Must Be Specific

Policies must be specific. A policy that requires appropriate dress is too vague to be enforced. Patrons cannot infer from the policy what is and is not appropriate dress, nor can the library staff enforce a policy of appropriate dress when the appropriateness is left to the discretion of the individual staff member. A policy that requires shoes and shirts and does not allow bathing suits would be a valid and enforceable policy. It is clear and concise. Whether a patron is wearing a shirt or shoes is clear and obvious to both the patron and the librarian who must enforce the policy, and generally bathing suits are easily identifiable as swim wear. This policy is clear to all.

Policies that do not meet these tests, that are vague and unclear to either the patron to whom the policy applies or to the librarian charged with enforcement of the policy, could be ruled invalid if challenged in court.

VOID FOR VAGUENESS

The due process doctrine of vagueness—applicable to both criminal and non-criminal regulations—incorporates two basic principles. First, the regulation must "give the person of ordinary intelligence a reasonable opportunity to know what is prohibited, so that she or he may act accordingly."[2] Second, the regulation must provide explicit standards for those charged with its enforcement to prevent discriminatory application. These interests are served by regulations that contain terms "susceptible of objective measurement."

Generally a policy is tested for vagueness with a two-prong test. Under the first element of the vagueness doctrine, a person of ordinary intelligence must be provided with adequate notice of the type of conduct the policy attempts to proscribe.

The second and more important prong of the vagueness doctrine is the requirement that the law will not encourage arbitrary and discriminatory enforcement. The discriminatory standard has the potential to permit a standardless application based on personal predilections. The grant of authority to determine whether a given individual is acting in a criminal manner encourages the enforcement of the policy arbitrarily and according to personal biases.

A standardless policy has the potential of removing undesirable persons (who usually are minorities) from the library before they have the opportunity to engage in criminal activity.

The library policy should describe the unlawful conduct with sufficient particularity so that a person of reasonable intelligence could understand what conduct was prohibited, and it should establish the minimal guidelines for enforcement. A policy to challenge all "suspicious" persons would not be a valid and enforceable policy.

A library policy that prohibits the access of all "objectionable" material through the Internet is a vague policy. There are no standards by which to judge what is objectionable, thus it is "standardless." Neither can the user understand what is objectionable nor can the librarian be guided by what is objectionable. However, many libraries have just such a policy.

OVERBROAD POLICY

A policy is unconstitutionally overbroad if it:

- prohibits activity that is protected by the First Amendment to the United States Constitution
- allows arbitrary enforcement against those considered "undesirable" by the staff
- leaves sole discretion regarding the determination of violation of the policy in the hands of the staff

Although ordinances are normally presumed constitutional, ordinances and policies restricting First Amendment rights are not so presumed. Freedom of movement and association is protected by the First Amendment, as is the freedom of access of material over the Internet if the library provides an Internet.

If a filtering policy employed by a library is not a prior restraint on an adult's freedom to access material over the Internet, a court may still strike it down as being overbroad. The over-breadth doctrine provides that a statute is overbroad if, in addition to proscribing activities that may be constitutionally forbidden, it also sweeps within its coverage speech that is protected by the First Amendment. In other words, "[a] governmental purpose to control or prevent activities constitutionally subject to state regulation may not be achieved by means which sweep unnecessarily broadly and thereby invade the area of protected freedoms."[3]

If a library Internet policy forbids the viewing or downloading of child pornography (which may constitutionally be forbidden), but also forbids the viewing or downloading of hateful speech, the policy is overbroad, and may be found to be unenforceable. Hateful speech is constitutionally protected, as is the access to hateful speech.

The over-breadth of the policy must be "substantial" before a court can invalidate the law on its face. Where a statute or policy is capable of a narrow construction, it will not be found to be overbroad.

Because a library filtering policy may not necessarily be "substantially" overbroad, and because most filtering software allows librarians to reduce the different types of site-blocking criteria, the over-breadth doctrine, by itself, may not provide patrons any relief. The overbreadth doctrine was not discussed in Judge Brinkman's *Mainstream Loudoun* decision.[4] The government has the burden of proving that the law is not overbroad.

A policy is overbroad if it does not contain a provision defining what conduct is required for a breach. By not defining the conduct, an arbitrary enforcement against those considered undesirable may be the outcome of enforcement, regardless of the individual's conduct.

A defendant, claiming that a statute is unconstitutionally overbroad, may challenge the statute on its face. An overbroad ordinance may be subjected to a review on its face and invalidation, even though the application in a particular case may be constitutionally unobjectionable. A statute or ordinance can be constitutionally overbroad if it extends to constitutionally protected speech or other expressive conduct and the over-breadth is both real and substantial. A court must invalidate a law if there is a realistic danger that the statute itself will significantly compromise recognized First Amendment protections of parties not before the court.

A statute that invites arbitrary and discriminatory application and enforcement is overbroad. Inherent First Amendment rights cannot be regulated in an arbitrary non-uniform manner, specifically the inherent right to think freely.

A policy may, however, be both overbroad and vague. The library policy that prohibits access to objectionable material is both overbroad, in that it prohibits access to material that adults, and in some instances children, have a constitutional right to access, and it is vague, in that neither the patron nor the librarian are provided with standards by which to determine whether the material is "objectionable."

IS THE POLICY COMMUNICATED AND APPROPRIATE?

The library policy should be communicated to patrons, staff, and volunteers. It impossible to fairly enforce a policy if it is not communicated. Fair application and enforcement is essential. The library should be cognizant of the reasons for the policy. There are some policies that outlive their usefulness, and the retention of these policies cast the library in an unflattering light. The image of the library is reflected in its policy, and this image and mission should be reflected through the library's specific and quantifiable policy.

Library employees should be trained periodically on library policies and the procedures used to enforce these policies. This can be an excellent opportunity to obtain staff feedback on policies and guidelines. Staff can also provide excellent insight into the communication of library policies and procedures to patrons. Library volunteers typically are not involved in enforcing procedures, but they, too, should be made aware of policies and procedures as they pertain to their functions.

THE DISTINCTION BETWEEN POLICY AND PROCEDURE

Technically, there is a significant distinction between policies and procedures. Policies explain why the library has chosen a certain approach. Policies are general in tone and guide the library and the librarians toward an ideal for the library. Policy statements are public documents and state the library's goals and its purpose; they establish the direction of the library. The library's policy should have the capacity to resolve conflict. Policies are flexible statements and should not be changed routinely.

Procedures are grounded in the library's policies. Procedures are the methods by which the policies are implemented. While policies are flexible statements that are changed infrequently, procedures are less flexible, but should be reviewed for changes on a regular basis. While policies are public, procedures are private. They are the internal guidelines for the library.

It is important to include the community in drafting policies for the library. Community input gives a point of view often lost by those whose lives revolve around the library as intensely as the library staff's. Often the communication process between the staff and the community helps both to recognize and address the needs of various groups. An annual meeting of community and staff in policy review is a large undertaking but can ultimately be beneficial.

LIBRARY GOALS REFLECTED IN POLICY

When developing a library policy, the goals of the institution itself should be paramount. The goals of the library should parallel those same policies. Some issues seem so fundamental that they are often forgotten in the development of policies and their supporting procedures. Procedure-supporting policies should establish which staff position is responsible for each duty. For example, the position responsible for employment interviews should be established. The position responsible to receive subpoenas or to make collection decisions should be established.

The policy for the collection development program will never be more important than when angry parents address the library regarding specific materials they find objectionable. If you have specific policies governing your collection, and these policies are consistent with the institution's policies, it should be the policies that prevail, and not emotions of fear and anger. It is a good idea to incorporate your institution's policies directly into your own policies.

Your policy should require evaluation of the policies periodically and specify the parties to participate in this evaluation. Your policy should also provide for an orderly means of addressing complaints. If your policy requires all concerns regarding the library to be first addressed to the library, this will allow for the simplest and most immediate solutions. Create a library committee to address these issues, and only when they cannot be resolved at the library level should they be addressed at a higher level.

Involving community members in library committees is important to the sense of community in a library. Their input in material selection is crucial.

Involving student representatives in library policies is of equal importance. They bring fresh insight and often are more current on technology than the adults. Involving their parents adds yet another dimension—the reality factor.

However, it is important to understand and implement the distinction between policies and procedures. Broad input and support in policy development is crucial to the success of the library. The more people that have a stake in the library, the more people will support the library. Procedures, the method for implementing the policies, belong to the library alone. Thoughtfully and artfully draft your policies while omitting procedure. Standard procedures are crucial to the functioning of a library, but they must be the domain of the librarian. The Houston Public Library has prepared an outstanding strategic master plan entitled "Standards for Excellence."[5]

Suddenly, librarians face the very real threat of child pornography coming into their library. This is contraband as illegal as heroin and it is only a mouse-click away. The FBI may decide to track a library's computer activities because of a patron's actions. Tracking a computer with the FBI's program *Magic Lantern* may not identify the patron using the computer. For that information, the library's records might need to be accessed, or the library may require surveillance by law enforcement. Suddenly, how a library retains records of patrons using specific computers becomes relevant.

Free speech has always been a flashpoint issue in the library. Filters do inhibit free speech and free access, but our society has determined that we do in fact have a "compelling interest" in protecting our students from pornography.

Libraries are at the center of copyright issues. Library policies should mirror the law of copyright, specifically notice of copyright limitations at both copiers and computer printers. At times it is difficult to distinguish policy from procedure. The best criterion is to simply ask yourself whether this is a matter that should be decided by the librarian, because it impacts the day-to-day functioning of the library, or is this a direction in which the library should be moving?

Never before have so many legal issues focused squarely on the library. It is naïve to think that any library will be the library that escapes critical scrutiny. Therefore, it is important to be prepared for public, critical scrutiny of every action a library takes or doesn't take. Be prepared to defend acts of commission and acts of omission with the library policy as the first line of defense.

CONCLUSION

Clear, specific library policy is the best defense to challenges. It is possible to take each chapter and topic found in this text and decide whether your library should have a formal policy on this issue or whether it should be handled informally. It is fundamental that all libraries should have a policy that respects all state and federal laws. The devil here will be in the details of each policy and the library's attention to the need to narrowly tailor a policy that addresses a legitimate issue of library concern with specific guidelines.

Your policies, procedures, and guidelines should make your day-to-day life simpler and be your greatest ally in times of conflict—which will inevitably come. No difficult job is ever accomplished without conflict. The key is to handle the issue fairly, openly, and with the ability to examine the intrinsic fairness and legality of your chosen position.

NOTES

1. Letter, Thomas Jefferson to Abbé Arnoux, July 19, 1789.
2. Sewell v. Georgia, 435 U.S. 982, 986 (1978).
3. Griswold v. Connecticult, 381 U.S 479 (1965).
4. Mainstream Loudoun v. Board of Trustees of the Loudoun County Library, 2 F. Supp. 2d 783 (ED Va. 1998).
5. Houston Public Library, *Strategic Master Plan—Standards for Excellence* <http://www.hpl.lib.tx.us> (accessed October 15, 2002).

INDEX

About the Author

LEE ANN TORRANS is a Texas-based attorney with a Masters degree in Library Science. She has written several articles on copyright and choreography and frequently lectures on that topic.